1001
QUESTIONS
ABOUT CANADA

1001 QUESTIONS ABOUT CANADA

JOHN ROBERT COLOMBO

1986
Doubleday Canada Limited, Toronto, Canada
Doubleday & Company, Inc., Garden City, New York

ISBN 0-385-25034-7
Library of Congress

Copyright © 1986 by J. R. Colombo
All Rights Reserved.
First ed.

Cover design by Don Fernley
Interior design by Irene Carefoot
Typeset by Compeer Typographic Services Limited

Printed and bound in Canada by John Deyell Company

Canadian Cataloguing in Publication Data

Colombo, John Robert, 1936–
1001 questions about Canada

ISBN 0-385-25034-7 (bound) — ISBN 0-385-25040-1 (pbk.)

1. Canada — Miscellany. I. Title.

FC61.C64 1986   971'.002   C86-093432-2
F1008.3.C64 1986

Library of Congress Cataloging-in-Publication Data

Colombo, John Robert, 1936–
1001 questions about Canada.

1. Canada — Miscellanea. 2. Questions and answers.
I. Title. II. Title: One thousand one questions about
Canada.

F1008.3.C65 1986   971   86-4528
ISBN 0-385-25034-7

This book is dedicated to my children,
Jonathan, Catherine, Theodore,
so they may know more about their country.

CONTENTS

PREFACE

What is *1001 Questions about Canada*?

This book is a work of popular reference about Canada. It is a storehouse of information about the world's second-largest country. The information is arranged in a manner that the author hopes the reader will find engaging. The question-and-answer format permits the author to ask the reader important or interesting questions about the country and its people and to answer them at some length.

The length of the answers is what distinguishes this book, which is a question-and-answer book, from a quiz book. In a quiz book, the questions are longer than the answers. With a question-and-answer book, like the present one, the answers are longer than the questions. There is room to explain the answers and place them in a context that makes them interesting in their own right.

The 1001 questions and answers are arranged by subject. There are ten categories of subjects, as follows: Land, History, Places, Government, Business, Technology, Society, People, Culture, and Canadianisms. In addition, there are a short Preface and a 2,200-entry Index.

The present book was conceived, researched, written, and published for a purpose, a two-part purpose. The author obviously felt it important to make information about Canada accessible to the general reader in a novel and engaging manner. But he also felt it important to deepen that knowledge by raising the reader's "Canadiana consciousness" in a general effort to increase self-awareness and well-being. Conscious Canadianism is superior to unconscious Canadianism. Nationalism has its place. As Harold

Adams Innis once said, "The road to internationalism lies through nationalism."

This compendium of information could be called a primer of basic Canadiana. Questions are raised and answered about subjects of national interest, but an attempt has been made to answer frequently asked questions that admit of no easy formulation or expression. The reader is asked to name the country's highest mountain. No difficulty there. But the reader is also asked whether Riel should be pardoned. Some difficulty there. Most of the questions are mainstream questions in that they deal with events in the past and present that could hardly be overlooked. But there are also a goodly number of tributary or offbeat questions that are frequently asked but seldom answered. How many words do the Eskimos have for snow? Is it true that a thirty-year-old Canadian is as fit as a sixty-year-old Swede? These are a couple of unusual questions found in the book that should really test the reader's knowledge.

Neither the number of questions devoted to a subject nor the length of the answers should be taken as a gauge of the importance of a subject. Invariably it requires more words to explain minor references than it does major ones. Not all subjects could be included. After all, there are *only* 1,001 entries in this book. General interest has been taken to be the guide in the selection of subjects — the general interest of the author as well as that of the reader.

Some subjects lend themselves to the question-and-answer format more readily than others. There are some facts and figures in the book, and some rosters of information, but statistics and lists have generally been avoided. Tabular matter and figures-down-to-the-decimal-point have a fascination all their own, but such material quickly becomes dated and must be sourced — a highly desirable practice but one ruled out by the format of the present book.

Care has been taken to arrange the entries in their proper categories. Yet at times the questions and answers follow one another in an order that is more associative than logical. To give an instance, the section on "Government" has a subsection devoted to the

Crown. That subsection introduces an entry on a royal visit. Now, strictly speaking, royal visits are of no constitutional consequence. What interest they have is social, so the entry on the royal visit could appear in some other section, perhaps "Society" or "People." Yet the reader would normally expect to find a question about a royal visit in a group with questions about the Crown, the Queen, the monarchy, etc. After all, what they have in common is the royal family. This expectation will be met. Conversely, it was not always possible to bring similar entries into a single group. The Canadian Pacific Railway, to give an instance, is represented not only in "History" but also in "Technology." Armed with the Index, though, the reader should encounter no difficulty in tracking down the entries that interest him or her.

The present book was designed to meet the needs of the general reader and not the specialist user. The reader who starts on the first page and reads through to the final page will be carried on a voyage of discovery by a cataract of information. The reader who wishes to use the book more selectively should be able to locate a subject area quickly enough through the arrangement of the ten categories and the name and key-word Index. So that the contents of the ten categories will be apparent at a glance, here is a bird's-eye view of the contents of each chapter in turn.

1. "Land" covers geography, demography, geology, fauna, flora, and primary industries. In more detail, it deals with geographical locale, extremities, zones, age, climate, censuses, population density and distribution, coastlines, rivers, lakes, landforms, islands, mountains, minerals and their extraction, animals, birds, agriculture, wheat, vegetables, forestry, flowers, fishing, and the North and North Magnetic Poles. (Questions 1 to 93)

2. "History" consists of a chronological arrangement of entries on important aspects of Canada's past. They are, more specifically, early discoveries, Norsemen, explorers, New France, Huronia, Hudson's Bay Company, Loyalists, Captain Cook, Northwest Passage, conquest of Quebec, British North America, Red

River, War of 1812, Rebellions of 1837, Responsible Government, Underground Railroad, Fenians, British North America Act, Fathers of Confederation, Riel rebellions, Canadian Pacific Railway, National Policy, immigration, World War I, Prohibition, Balfour Report, Depression, Empire and Commonwealth, World War II, Cold War, Newfoundland, Quiet Revolution, October Crisis, and the Canadian Caper. (Questions 94 to 198)

3. "Places" takes the reader from the East Coast, across the country to the West Coast, then north across the territories, from interesting place to interesting place, accenting lore and travel information. It begins with a few national matters, like place-name lore. Ottawa is treated in some detail. This category ends with national and international matters, including lists of natural and manmade wonders. (Questions 199 to 313)

4. "Government" combines constitutional, governmental, and political matters. There are questions about the following subjects: authority, the Crown, Governors General, Prime Ministers, administrations, premiers, political parties, terminology, constitutions, charters, Parliament, House of Commons, Senate, governments, statutes, Privy Council, courts, disputes, decisions, deputy ministers, Crown corporations, royal commissions, social security programs, capital punishment, internationalism, official languages, Quebec Referendum, bilingualism, and some definitions. (Questions 314 to 399)

5. "Business" deals with commerce and finance, the economy and corporations, labour and unions. Some subjects treated are banks, credit unions, stock exchanges, manufacturing, energy, food and merchandising, Argus Corporation, oil, Inco, minerals, exports, assets, newspapers, magazines, strikes, leading industrial corporations, and multinationality. (Questions 400 to 463)

6. "Technology" embraces inventions, transportation, communications, research and development, and science. Among the topics considered are aurora borealis, dinosaurs, time, disasters, vessels and ships, Northwest Passage, railways, CPR, VIA, Niagara Falls, St. Lawrence Seaway, bridges, hydro power, automobiles, highways, Ski-doo, CN Tower, Yonge Street, telephone, wireless, radioactivity, nuclear physics, photography, cinematography, reactors, radio broadcasting, television, cable, acid rain, medical technology, L'Arche, aviation, metric, Kanata, Telidon, astronomy, satellites, Canadarm, astronauts, technological immortality. (Questions 464 to 582)

7. "Society" runs the gamut from citizenship through education and awards to religion and military matters. Specifically, some subjects are immigration, ethnic breakdown, Doukhobors, Japanese, refugees, private and separate schools, community colleges, universities, societies, Order of Canada, Nobel Prizes, libraries and museums, conferences, movements, religious denominations, saints, papal visit, clubs, exhibitions, Expo 67, Expo 86, holidays, Canadian Army, RCAF, Legion, memorials, "In Flanders Fields," "High Flight," conscription, Camp X, alliances, unification, Canadian Armed Forces, enlistment, peacekeeping, RCMP, CSIS, superheroes, Pugwash, Greenpeace, peace parks and gardens. (Questions 583 to 695)

8. "People" has much information on native peoples, women, sports, and eminent Canadians. The subjects treated include Inuit, language, "snow," igloos, co-ops, carvings, Indians, Great Peace, Reserves, "firsts," totem poles, art, words, dwellings, legendary beings, Ogopogo, Sasquatch, French folklore, Trivial Pursuit, criminals, outlaws, Ambrose Small, Harry Oakes, Sir John A. Macdonald, Sir Wilfrid Laurier, Dionne Quintuplets, Northrop Frye, Marshall McLuhan, performers, singers, Terry Fox, Mount Everest, Charlie Grant, World War II, suffrage, women's "firsts," Olympics, 1988 Games, lacrosse, inventions of games, hockey, Foster Hewitt, Wayne Gretzky, Peter Puck, NHL, Stanley Cup, football, Grey Cup, basketball, various sports and games, Lou

Marsh Trophy, domed stadiums, Sports Hall of Fame. (Questions 696 to 838)

9. "Culture" treats its topics generally chronologically within artistic disciplines. Literature goes from first books through the principal authors and their works to magazines. Art moves from Goya and Krieghoff to caricature and cartooning. Some radio personalities are discussed, then theatre companies and productions are highlighted. Film looks at the NFB and some features, and music moves from the earliest opera through some popular performers to symphony orchestras, ballet, musicians, and singers, concluding with the Canadian contribution to Broadway and Hollywood. (Questions 839 to 925)

10. "Canadianisms" examines some national specifics. Among subjects included are the meaning of "Canada" and "Dominion," coat of arms, colours, mottoes, beaver, National Flag, provincial mottoes, emblems, "O Canada," "God Save the Queen," "The Maple Leaf For Ever," the Huron Carol, other songs, quips, stamps, coins, paper money, cuisine, specialties, leading brands, wines, whisky, language, toast, French, Newfie jokes, melting pot, mosaic, and multiculturalism. (Questions 926 to 1001)

Acknowledgements

Let me express my gratitude to a group of people who graciously assisted me in my work on this book. Philip Singer, of the North York Public Library, was of signal assistance with this publication as he has been with previous books. Michael Richardson, of that library system's Bathurst Heights Area Branch, assisted in a number of ways. Calls for help with specific queries were answered with alacrity by Kamala Bhatia, Joel Bonn, John Brooks, Arthur Bousfield, Orestes Madarash, John Parkyn, James A. Pendergest, Alan Rayburn, Joseph B. Reid, and Lawrence Solomon. I am indebted to Bruce A. Powe, H. W. Tracey, Robert J. Sawyer, and Bill Sherk, who handled entries expertly. Frank Crescia lent a hand with the fact-checking. The Index was completed with the assistance of Philip Singer and Robert J. Sawyer with Brian Clink.

The concept of the book owes much to the series initiated by the publishing house Dodd Mead & Co. Inc. and to the "You Asked Us" magazine feature researched by Prue Hemelrijk. Enthusiasm for the present book was shown by J. G. McClelland; Patrick Crean directed me to Denise Schon and John Neale of Doubleday Canada Limited, who added this title to their list. The editing was done by Dean Cooke. In passing, it is interesting to note that Doubleday Canada Limited is one part of the world's largest trade publishing corporation, co-founded many years ago by a Canadian from Toronto.

A great many reference sources, ranging from encyclopedias to scholarly articles, were consulted in the preparation of the present book. In addition, much information was secured or confirmed orally, so it would obviously be impossible to list the sources of information. Let me add, nonetheless, that any errors are of the author's making and if brought to his attention will be rectified in future editions.

1001 Questions about Canada is dedicated to my three children, Jonathan, Catherine, and Theodore, for the reason stated on the dedication page. It is also dedicated to them because they have always asked more questions than I could answer. The book could as well have been dedicated to my wife, Ruth, who makes so many things, including books, possible.

1. LAND

1. *Where is Canada?*

Canada is a large country on the planet Earth. It occupies much of the northern half of the North American continent in the Western Hemisphere.

2. *How large is Canada?*

Canada is the largest country in the Western Hemisphere. Exceeded in size by the Soviet Union, it is the second-largest country in the world. The third-largest country is China. In area, Canada occupies 9,976,139 square kilometres, or 3,851,809 square miles. As for relative size, Canada is more than forty times the size of Britain, or eighteen times the size of France.

3. *What are Canada's geographical extremities?*

Canada's northernmost point is Cape Columbia, Ellesmere Island, N.W.T. Its southernmost point is Middle Island, Lake Erie, Ont. The distance between these two points is 4,634 km, or 2,879 miles.

Canada's easternmost point is Cape Spear, Nfld. Its westernmost point is Mount St. Elias, Y.T. The distance between these two points is 5,514 km, or 3,426 miles.

4. *Where is Canada's geographical centre?*

The geographical centre, or the point of balance of a map of

Canada cut from a large globe, is Eskimo Point, N.W.T. The small community is on the west coast of Hudson Bay.

5. *What are the country's major climatic zones?*
The climate varies greatly from region to region in Canada. There are five major climatic zones. The Arctic zone comprises most of the Yukon Territory and the Northwest Territories. The Northern zone consists of the northern portion of the prairie provinces and most of Ontario, Quebec, and the Atlantic provinces. The Prairie zone covers the main grain-growing areas of the Prairie Provinces. The Cordilleran zone is the Rocky Mountain region. And the Pacific zone embraces the coastal part of British Columbia and its offshore islands.

6. *What are the seventeen geological provinces?*
Geologists divide Canada into seventeen geological provinces or landform regions and arrange them in four groups. The Shelves group consists of the Arctic, Atlantic, and Pacific provinces. The Platform group consists of the Arctic, Hudson, Interior, and St. Lawrence Provinces. The Orogen group consists of the Innuitian, Cordilleran, and Appalachian provinces. And the Shield group consists of Grenville, Churchill, Southern, Bear, Superior, Slave, and Nutak provinces.

The Shelves group corresponds to the ocean coasts, the Platforms to the plains regions, the Orogen group to the mountainous areas, and the Shield group to the border of Hudson Bay.

7. *Why is the Canadian Shield called a shield?*
The Canadian Shield is also called the Laurentian Shield or the Precambrian Shield. The region is called a shield because it forms, as it were, a rock-hard breastplate around Hudson Bay.

The largest of the five main geographical zones of the country, the Shield covers about 42 percent of the land area and has less than 10 percent of the country's population. The Shield is a rolling, lake-dotted region of rock, forest, and water. The rock reaches a thickness of 3,000 metres, or 10,000 feet, and some of it is as much as 3.8 billion years old. The rocks are exposed throughout most of the North and contain most of the country's metallic minerals.

8. *How old is Canada? How old is the universe?*

Canada could be said to be 3.8 billion years old. In that epoch the Precambrian rocks were laid down and the continents directly ancestral to our own were formed. Yet familiar sights are not that old. It is said that the Rocky Mountains were formed only 70 million years ago. Niagara Falls is more recent than that. It was formed with the retreat of the last Ice Age some 10,000 years ago.

How old is the universe and everything in it? Following the scenario suggested by Isaac Asimov in 1983, the universe came into being with the Big Bang, which occurred perhaps 20 billion years ago. The galaxies, including our solar system with its single sun and the planet Earth, took shape some 4.5 billion years ago. The continents acquired known forms about 3.8 billion years ago. Life on the planet Earth commenced perhaps 3 billion years ago. The first hominid ancestors appeared 4 million years ago, and *Homo sapiens* were walking about 50,000 years ago.

It is suggested that in 5 billion years our sun will swell into a Red Giant and then collapse into a White Dwarf. In 9 billion years' time, the universe will be swallowed up by the Cosmic Collapse.

9. *When was the last ice age?*

There is geological evidence to show that there were four ice ages. The northern half of the North American continent was covered by continental ice sheets on four occasions in the distant past. The first of the ice ages commenced some 2 million years ago; the last concluded about 10,000 years ago.

The last ice age was called the Wisconsin Glaciation. The Canadian Shield was buried to a depth of up to 3 km, or 2 miles. When the temperature rose, the ice retreated about 30 km, or 20 miles, a century, creating the great landmarks — the Great Lakes, Niagara Falls, Lake Winnipeg, etc. Some geologists and climatologists maintain that the warm, ice-free weather enjoyed today is but an interglacial reprieve, and that the ice will begin to advance again in some 10,000 years.

10. *What is the Continental Divide?*

The Continental Divide is the height of land that separates the drainage basins of the North American continent. It corresponds to the Rocky Mountain Range, which extends from south of the 49th parallel to a region north of the Yellowhead Pass in the Northwest Territories in Canada. Thus, in part, it corresponds to the boundary between Alberta and British Columbia. It has been noted that there is one spot — an ice cap — where the drainage is divided among three oceans. The ice cap is Snow Dome, where Banff National Park meets Jasper National Park. One's cup of tea, if spilled, would flow eventually into the Arctic Ocean, the Pacific Ocean, and the Atlantic Ocean (via Hudson Bay).

11. *Are there many meteorite craters in Canada?*

Almost one third of the world's largest meteorite craters have been found in this country, which has more than two dozen such craters measuring a kilometre (half a mile) or more in diameter. Some are considerably larger. The three largest meteorite craters found in the country are at Sudbury, Ont., 140 km, or 87 miles, in diameter; Manicouagan, Que., 70 km, or 44 miles, in diameter; and Charlevoix, Que., 46 km, or 29 miles, in diameter. They were created by impact at points in time ranging from 1,840 million years ago to 210 million years ago.

12. *What are Canada's highest and lowest recorded temperatures?*

The country's highest recorded temperature was reported at Midale and Yellow Grass, Sask. On July 5, 1937, it was 45°C, or 113°F.

The country's lowest recorded temperature was reported at Snag, N.W.T. On February 5, 1947, it was −63°C, or −81°F.

13. *What are some other record-setting climatic extremes?*
The following extremes in climate are officially recorded.

Greatest annual precipitation: Henderson Lake, B.C., 1931, 812.24 cm, or approximately 320 inches.

Heaviest seasonal snowfall: Revelstoke/Mt. Copeland, B.C., 1971–72 season, 2,446.53 cm, or approximately 980 inches.

Highest wind speed (for one hour): Cape Hopes Advance, Que., November 18, 1931, 203 km/h, or approximately 126 mph.

Most fogbound place: Grand Bank, Nfld., with fog an average of 120 days a year.

14. *Which cities are the coldest and warmest?*
The coldest city is Yellowknife, N.W.T., the mean annual temperature being −5.6°C, or approximately 22°F. The warmest city is Vancouver, B.C., the mean annual temperature being 9.8°C, or approximately 50°F.

15. *Is it true that Ottawa is the world's coldest capital?*
No. Ottawa is the world's coldest capital — with the exception of Ulan Bator, capital of Outer Mongolia. Ottawa's coldest recorded temperature was −38.3°C, or −36.9°F, on February 17, 1934.

16. *What is a chinook?*
A chinook is a dry and warm southwest wind in southern Alberta and British Columbia. During the winter, it causes a rapid rise in temperature, a welcome break from subzero winter temperatures. Fur traders, who observed the wind to come from the direction of villages of the Chinook Indians, named it after them. It is similar to the Swiss föhn or the sirocco of the Sahara.

17. *How often is the census taken?*

The Canadian census is taken every ten years, with a mini-census every five years. The 1871 census was compiled by fifty clerks; the 1981 census involved seven years of planning and 42,000 employees of Statistics Canada, the federal body charged with the responsibility of regular information gathering.

18. *What is the population of Canada?*

Statistics Canada estimated the population of Canada on October 1, 1985, to be 25,444,900. The population increased from 25,208,900 a year earlier, continuing the annual growth rate in recent years of about 1 percent.

Here are Statistics Canada's population estimates for the provinces and territories. Newfoundland, 581,100. Prince Edward Island, 127,700. Nova Scotia, 883,400. New Brunswick, 719,400. Quebec, 6,597,700. Ontario, 9,111,100. Manitoba, 1,072,400. Saskatchewan, 1,020,100. Alberta, 2,357,600. British Columbia, 2,900,400. Yukon Territory, 22,800. Northwest Territories, 51,200.

19. *What are the population figures for the two dozen largest cities in Canada?*

The population figures for the two dozen largest cities in the country appear below. The information comes from the census of 1981 which distinguishes between cities per se and Census Metropolitan Areas (hence Ottawa-Hull). The total population of these cities comes to 13,546,700, or approximately 56.1 percent of the total 1981 population of 24,341,700.

Calgary, Alta.	592,600
Chicoutimi-Jonquière, Que.	135,200
Edmonton, Alta.	656,900
Halifax, N.S.	277,700
Hamilton, Ont.	542,100

Kitchener, Ont.	287,800
London, Ont.	283,700
Montreal, Que.	2,828,300
Oshawa, Ont.	154,200
Ottawa-Hull	718,000
Quebec City, Que.	576,000
Regina, Sask.	164,300
St. Catharines-Niagara Falls, Ont.	304,400
Saint John, N.B.	114,000
St. John's, Nfld.	154,800
Saskatoon, Sask.	154,200
Sudbury, Ont.	149,900
Thunder Bay, Ont.	121,400
Toronto, Ont.	2,998,700
Trois-Rivières, Que.	111,500
Vancouver, B.C.	1,268,100
Victoria, B.C.	233,500
Windsor, Ont.	246,100
Winnipeg, Man.	584,800

20. *What is Canada's population density?*
It is estimated that Canada's population density is six people per square mile. If there are 25 million people in Canada and 5 billion people on earth, Canada's population is 0.5 percent of the earth's. Canada covers nearly 7 percent of the earth's surface. Therefore 0.5 percent of the earth's population occupies 7 percent of its surface.

21. *How much of Canada is occupied?*
There is no permanent settlement in approximately 89 percent of Canada. Only the smallest province, Prince Edward Island, is completely occupied. About one third of Canada's area is developed; less than 8 percent is occupied farm land and about 27 percent productive forests.

22. Where do most Canadians live?

About 58 percent of Canada's population lives in the rough triangle formed by the Great Lakes system and an east-west line
1,046 km, or 650 miles, in length drawn from Quebec City to
Sault Ste. Marie. The eight largest cities in this block—Montreal,
Toronto, Hamilton, Ottawa, London, Windsor, Quebec City,
Kitchener — account for more than one third of the total population of the country.

23. What percentage of Canadians live within 320 km, or 200 miles, of the Canada–United States border?

It is estimated that 90 percent of all Canadians live within 320 km,
or 200 miles, of the international border.

It is further estimated that 75 percent of all Canadians live
within 160 km, or 100 miles, of the international border. (Inter-
estingly, only 12 percent of Americans live within 160 km, or 100
miles, of the border with Canada.)

24. Are Canadians country dwellers or city dwellers?

The majority of Canadians live in cities rather than in the country.
Over 75 percent of the population lives in an urban rather than a
rural environment.

25. Which country has the longest coastline of any in the world?

The Soviet Union. Canada comes second with 241,402 km, or
approximately 150,000 miles, of coastline. That is a lot of continental shelf, over half of it formed by islands. The mainland
coastline measures only 17,860 km, or 28,742 miles.

26. When did Canada assert the 200-mile (320-km) limit?

The Canadian government asserted its sovereignty and jurisdiction over coastal waters to the offshore limit of 200 miles, or

320 km, on January 1, 1977. Canada was the first country to do so. By creating this "economic zone," Canada was better able to protect its fisheries from overfishing and to ensure control of offshore oil reserves.

27. *What is Canada's longest river?*
The country's longest river is the Mackenzie River. It is 4,241 km, or 2,635 miles, in length.

The second- and third-longest rivers in Canada are the Yukon River and the St. Lawrence River. The only river on the North American continent to exceed the Mackenzie in length is the Mississippi-Missouri-Red Rock river system in the United States.

28. *Is it true that New Brunswick has the world's highest tides?*
The *Guinness Book of World Records* (1971) accepts the claim, recording that "the greatest tides in the world occur in the Bay of Fundy, which separates Nova Scotia from Maine and the Canadian province of New Brunswick. Burncoat Head in the Minas Basin, N.S., has the greatest mean spring range from 47.5 feet [14 m], and an extreme range of 53.5 feet [16 m]."

29. *Where are the world's strongest currents?*
It is believed that the world's strongest currents flow over the Natwakto Rapids at Slingsby Channel, B.C. The flow rate has reached 16 knots, or 18.4 mph.

30. *Which country has the most lakes?*
There are probably more lakes in Canada than in any other country. It has been estimated that almost 8 percent of Canada's total area is covered by lakes. Water covers approximately 70 percent of the Earth's surface.

31. What part of Canada has been described as "one of the most distinctive and predominant water features on the entire planet when viewed from space"?
The description applies to Hudson Bay, which is a "bay" of neither the Arctic nor the Atlantic ocean, but rather an "inland sea" in its own right. It was discovered by Henry Hudson, the English navigator, in 1611.

32. What is the largest fresh-water lake totally confined within Canada?
The largest fresh-water lake totally confined within Canada is Great Bear Lake in the Northwest Territories. It has an area of 31,080 square kilometres, or 12,000 square miles.

33. Who first described the Great Lakes as "great"?
The French explorer Pierre-Esprit Radisson was so impressed by their size that in 1665 he called them "these great lakes." He had good reason to be impressed, for the Great Lakes comprise the world's largest body of fresh water.

There are five Great Lakes in the system, and the mnemonic "HOMES" is helpful in recalling their names: H stands for Lake Huron, O for Lake Ontario, M for Lake Michigan, E for Lake Erie, and S for Lake Superior. Although large enough to be a lake in its own right, Georgian Bay is considered part of Lake Huron. Lake St. Clair, which lies between Lake Huron and Lake Ontario, is too small to be considered "great."

34. If Niagara Falls is not the highest waterfall in the world, why is it the best known?
Niagara Falls is certainly not the world's highest waterfall. The highest is Venezuela's Angel Falls, with a drop of 979 m, or 3,212 feet. Niagara Falls is not even the highest in Canada, that record being held by British Columbia's Della Falls, with a drop of

440 m, or 1,443 feet. Niagara, with its two cascades — the American falls at 64 metres, or approximately 210 feet; the Canadian (or Horseshoe) falls at 54 metres, or approximately 180 feet — hardly compares.

Nor is Niagara the world leader in annual flow. It is exceeded by Sete Quedas Falls, between Brazil and Paraguay, over which water flows at the rate of 13,300 cubic metres per second, or 470,000 cubic feet per second. Niagara's rate is a mere trickle at 60,088 cubic metres per second, or 212,200 cubic feet per second.

Yet Niagara Falls exceeds all the world's other waterfalls in fame because of its history, its beauty, its accessibility to tourists, its reputation (as "the honeymoon capital of the world"), and its combination of height and flow. It was first mentioned in print by the missionary explorer Louis Hennepin who, on December 6, 1678, described Niagara as "an incredible cataract or waterfall," and so it is.

35. *Does Canada have a reversing falls?*

There are three so-called reversing falls. This natural phenomenon is created by tidal action. During low tide, inland waters race over a rocky shelf. During high tide, sea water forces its way back. In both instances, the rocky shelf creates eddies, whirlpools, and rapids which resemble a waterfall. The best-known instance of reversing falls is the St. John River in the Bay of Fundy, N.B. The others are in the Northwest Territories: Wager Bay, Ford Lake; Banner Inlet, Hudson Strait.

36. *Which is the larger island, Baffin Island or Newfoundland?*

The largest island in Canada is Baffin Island, N.W.T. It is 507,451 square kilometres, or 195,928 square miles. It is followed in size by Victoria Island and Ellesmere Island, all Arctic islands. The fourth-largest is the island of Newfoundland, which is 108,860 square kilometres, or 42,031 square miles.

37. *What are the so-called Badlands, where are they located, and what are they noted for?*

The Badlands are an arid and desert-like expanse of land in southern Alberta. Deep gullies, sharp ridges, flat tops, and tall columns caused by erosion are characteristic of the region, which is rich in fossils of dinosaurs and other long-dead prehistoric creatures. Dinosaur Provincial Park, where fossil skeletons may be viewed, is located in the Badlands, northeast of Brooks, Alta.

38. *Where are the Barren Lands and are they barren of life?*

The Barren Lands are an expanse of arctic and subarctic tundra in the Northwest Territories. The area is roughly triangular, two sides of the triangle being Hudson Bay and the Arctic Coast, the hypotenuse being an imaginary line from Churchill, Man., to the shore of Coronation Gulf. The region was described as ''barren'' by the explorer Samuel Hearne in the 1770s, but there is much life here. The region may be treeless but there is considerable plant and animal life and tens of thousands of lakes and rivers. Before he starved to death in the Barrens, the trapper and adventurer John Hornby described the region as ''the land of feast and famine.''

39. *What is the difference between tundra and muskeg?*

Tundra is characteristic of the Far North, muskeg of the North. Tundra is a treeless plain found on the arctic prairie. It supports a wide variety of animal life and, in the summer, a varied range of flora. The word is Lapp for ''hill.''

Muskeg is swamp or marsh or bogland, where decaying plant life achieves a considerable undrained depth and makes summer transportation almost impossible. *Muskeg* is the Algonkian word for ''swamp.''

40. *What is Canada's highest mountain?*

The highest mountain in Canada is Mount Logan. It is a somewhat featureless peak in the mighty St. Elias Mountains of the Yukon Territory and the centrepiece of Kluane National Park. Mount Logan is 5,949 m, or 19,523 feet, above sea level. After Mount McKinley in Alaska, it is the highest peak in North America.

As mountains go, Mount Logan may set a Canadian record, but it hardly stacks up globally. It is, for instance, two-thirds the height of Mount Everest in Asia, the world's highest mountain. And to put Everest in perspective, the highest peak known to man is not on the Earth at all but on the planet Mars. Olympus Mons, the largest known planetary feature in the solar system, is estimated to be 27,000 m, or 88,560 feet, in height, three times the height of Everest.

Mount Logan bears the name of William E. Logan (1798–1875), the famous geologist who served in 1842–70 as the first head of the Geological Survey of Canada.

41. *What is the purpose of Geological Survey of Canada?*
The Geological Survey of Canada is an organization within the Department of Energy, Mines and Resources that maps and studies the geology of Canada. It mounts about 100 expeditions each year to various regions to examine the potential and probable distribution of the country's natural resources and ways to preserve the natural environment. The Surveys and Mapping Branch has produced topographical maps of the whole country and has led the world in rapid mapping techniques.

42. *What minerals does Canada produce?*
From Canadian mines and smelters come some sixty minerals. The most valuable minerals are crude petroleum, natural gas, iron ore, nickel, zinc, asbestos, and potash. Canada is the world's leading producer of nickel and zinc; the country comes second in molybdenum and silver; it is among the leaders in the production of copper, gold, lead, and aluminum.

Here is a list of eighteen major minerals and the provinces and territories in which they are found.

Asbestos is mined in Quebec, Newfoundland, Ontario, British

Columbia, and the Yukon. **Coal** is mined mainly in Alberta and British Columbia, followed by Nova Scotia, Saskatchewan, and New Brunswick. **Cobalt** is produced in Manitoba and Ontario. **Copper** is mined mainly in Ontario, British Columbia, and Quebec, but also in all territories and provinces except Prince Edward Island, Alberta, and Nova Scotia. **Fluorspar** is mined in Newfoundland. **Gold** is presently produced in every province and territory except Prince Edward Island, Nova Scotia, and Alberta. **Gypsum** is mined primarily in Nova Scotia, but also in Ontario, Newfoundland, British Columbia, Manitoba, and New Brunswick. **Iron ore** is mined chiefly in Newfoundland, followed in order by Ontario, Quebec, and British Columbia. **Lead** is mined chiefly in the Yukon, British Columbia, and the Northwest Territories, as well as in all provinces except Prince Edward Island, Nova Scotia, Saskatchewan, and Alberta. **Molybdenum** is produced in British Columbia and Quebec. **Nepheline syenite** is mined in Ontario. **Nickel** is mined in Ontario and Manitoba. **Potash** is mined in Saskatchewan, with known reserves in Manitoba, Alberta, New Brunswick, and Nova Scotia. **Salt** has been found but not mined in all provinces and territories except British Columbia and the Yukon; Ontario is the leading producer. **Silver** is mined in both territories and in all provinces except Prince Edward Island, Nova Scotia, and Alberta. **Titanium** is produced in Quebec. **Uranium** is mined in Ontario and Saskatchewan. **Zinc** is produced in both territories and in all provinces except Prince Edward Island, Nova Scotia, and Alberta.

43. *How does Canada rank in terms of world mineral production?*
Canada comes third in world mineral production, following the United States and the Soviet Union. However, it ranks first in terms of diversity of mineral production.

The Province of Alberta has led all other provinces in mineral production since 1960. Alberta produces almost half of all the minerals mined in Canada.

44. *Which are the most important manufacturing provinces?*
Ontario and Quebec are the most important manufacturing provinces. Ontario produces 55 percent of the country's manufactured goods, and Quebec produces 30 percent.

45. *Which province is Canada's most active exporting province?*
Although Ontario produces 55 percent of Canada's manufactured goods, the most active exporting province is British Columbia. Nearly 40 percent of the West Coast province's products leave the country, including most of its pulp, newsprint, lumber, and fish.

46. *Is Canada rich in fauna?*
Indeed. Darryl Stewart writes in *The Canadian Wildlife Almanac* (1981), "This huge country, the second largest in the world, is consequently blessed with 524 species of birds, 192 species of mammals, 43 species of reptiles, 37 species of amphibians, and 182 species of freshwater fish." He calls the country a "varied habitat . . . a veritable paradise for the naturalist."

47. *What is the largest creature that has ever lived in Canada?*
The largest creature that has ever lived on earth is the blue whale (*Balaenoptera musculus*), which exceeds even the largest dinosaur in size. It inhabits Canadian northern waters. A large specimen may attain a length of 30 m, or 100 feet, and a weight of up to 145,150 kg, or 160 tons. Many of the globe's largest animals make their homes in Canada, but their numbers are rapidly dwindling. These great whales are an endangered species. Despite this they are relentlessly hunted by man and needlessly slaughtered. Species of whales found in Canadian waters include the blue whale, fin whale, minke whale, humpback whale, right whale, and bottlenose whale.

48. *What is the country's largest native land animal?*
The largest native land animal is the wood bison (*Bison bison athabascae*), which can weigh up to 900 kg, or 2,000 pounds.

Two of the world's largest carnivores are also found in Canada: the polar bear (*Ursus maritimus*) and the grizzly bear (*Ursus arctos horribilis*).

49. *What is the difference between the bison and the buffalo?*
The bison and the buffalo are both large, hoofed animals of the cattle family. The bison (*Bison bison*), the larger of the two, roams the prairies and plains of North America. The buffalo (*Bubalus bubalis*, or water buffalo) is found in Asia and Africa where it is domesticated. However, in North America, the word "buffalo" is commonly applied to the bison.

Scientifically speaking, William F. Cody, the American sharpshooter, should be nicknamed "Bison Bill" instead of "Buffalo Bill." Because of sharpshooters like Cody, the bison, which once formed the largest mammal congregations on earth, almost became extinct in the 1870s.

50. *Are there polar bears at the North Pole?*
The North Pole is too far north for even the polar bear (*Ursus maritimus*). Its natural habitat is subarctic rather than arctic. Polar Bear Provincial Park in northern Ontario was named after its bulky inhabitant.

51. *What are the names of some members of the deer family found in Canada?*
The deer is a ruminant mammal of the *Cervidae* family found in most parts of the world. Here are the names of some members of the deer family found in Canada.

The reindeer (*Rangifer tarandus*) is a large deer with branching horns that lives in the arctic and subarctic regions of the world.

(The "rein" of "reindeer" is a reference to the reins used to harness the animal to draw a sledge.)

The caribou (*Rangifer tarandus pearyi*, or Peary's caribou) is a type of deer native only to Canada and Greenland. It is an endangered species. (The word "caribou" comes from the Algonkian word for "pawer," a reference to the animal's habit of pawing snow in search of grass.)

The moose (*Alces alces*) is the largest North American member of the deer family. (The word "moose" derives from the language of the Narragansett Indians.)

The elk, or wapiti (*Cervus canadensis*), is another large North American deer. (The word "wapiti" is derived from the Algonquian word for "white," a reference to the deer's white-coloured rump.)

52. *How big is a herd of caribou?*
The Porcupine herd is the biggest and it has about 150,000 members. The total number of caribou is around 500,000. The barren land caribou, by far the most numerous, winter in Alaska and the Yukon, give birth near the shores of the Beaufort Sea, and move across the tundra all summer long.

53. *What is a musk ox?*
The musk ox (*Ovibos moschatus*) is the northernmost of the cattle family, being found in arctic America and Greenland. It is a large mammal with a shaggy coat and a strong, musky smell. Built like an ox, it looks like a gigantic sheep. When threatened, the musk ox herd forms a circle, horns pointed outward, with the young in the centre. Its chief enemy, besides the Inuit and Indians who hunt it for its flesh and fur, is the wolf.

54. *Are wolves dangerous to man?*
Wolves are not, by nature, dangerous to man and only rarely to livestock. Yet the wolf's mournful howl sent shivers up and down

the spines of early settlers. Like almost any animal, they will not attack humans, unless provoked. There is no authentic case of a timber wolf (*Canis lupus*) ever seriously harming a human on this continent. James W. Curran, editor of the Sault Ste. Marie *Daily Star* in the 1940s, used to maintain, "The man that says he's been et by a wolf is a liar." Farley Mowat wrote *Never Cry Wolf* (1963) to dispel the entrenched belief that wolves are dangerous to man. Yet naturalists like David Grainger classify the wolf among the ten most dangerous animals in Canada! Wolves live in 90 percent of Canada and are absent only from the Atlantic provinces and the settled southern areas.

55. *Which dog is associated with the Eskimos?*
The breed of dog associated with the Eskimos is officially known as the Canadian Eskimo Dog. The native name for this breed is Qimmiq, or Kingmik. It was introduced to the Canadian Arctic from Greenland almost one thousand years ago. Not as swift as the Siberian husky or as strong as the Alaskan malamute, it is nevertheless a powerful and friendly beast and is used to pull sleds in winter and packs in summer. It can transport up to 80 kg, or 176 pounds, 112 km, or 70 miles, a day. The stock declined to 200 purebreds so in the 1970s the Eskimo Dog Research Foundation of the Northwest Territories was established to ensure its survival.

56. *Does the Labrador retriever come from Labrador?*
The Labrador retriever, a fine sporting dog, came originally from Europe but was introduced to Newfoundland (not specifically Labrador) by early explorers and settlers. The breed was found to make excellent hunters and retrievers, and was officially recognized by the Kennel Club (England) in 1903. Widely used as a police and guide dog for the blind, the Labrador retriever remains England's most popular gun dog. The large, heavy-coated animal is called the Newfoundland dog; the smaller, lighter-coated animal the Black Water dog or the St. John's dog.

57. *What is unique about the Vancouver Island marmot?*
A close relative of the familiar groundhog, the Vancouver Island marmot (*Marmota vancouverensis*) is the only species of mammal whose entire population is found within the boundaries of Canada. Its habitat is entirely restricted to Vancouver Island's alpine and subalpine regions. It is officially designated an endangered species.

58. *Why did the EEC ban the sale of seal pup skins?*
The European Economic Community voted to impose a two-year ban on the sale in member countries of seal pup skins, effective October 1, 1983. The decision was taken to protest the traditional methods of the Seal Hunt as practised in Atlantic Canada. Council members felt that the slaughtering of seal pups was inhumane considering that the skins are used for luxury goods. The ban marked a reprieve for the grey seal, which is the largest of Canadian seals, and the harp seal, which is distinguished by the dark, harp-shaped mark found on its back. The market for seal skins markedly declined. The hunt is held each March by sealers in Atlantic Canada, but on a much reduced scale.

59. *What are the most dangerous animals in Canada?*
According to naturalist David Grainger, author of *Animals in Peril* (1978), Canadians should take special care to avoid the following ten animals and reptiles, for they are exceedingly dangerous: polar bear, grizzly bear, black bear, prairie rattlesnake, massasauga rattlesnake, cougar, wolverine, timber wolf, bison, and walrus.

60. *What are the most endangered animals in Canada?*
According to David Grainger, author of *Animals in Peril* (1978), the ten most endangered Canadian animals are the following: northern kit fox, black-footed ferret, Vancouver Island marmot, black-tailed prairie dog, Newfoundland pine marten, California

bighorn sheep, wood bison, eastern cougar, northern sea otter, and Roosevelt elk.

61. What are the most endangered Canadian birds?

According to John P. S. Mackenzie, author of *Birds in Peril* (1977), the ten most endangered Canadian birds are the following: whooping crane, bald eagle, prairie falcon, peregrine falcon, Aleutian Canada goose, Eskimo curlew, Hudsonian godwit, prairie chicken, Kirkland's warbler, and Ipswich sparrow.

62. What are some of Canada's extinct species of birds and animals?

According to Darryl Stewart in *Canadian Endangered Species* (1974), the following birds and animals have become extinct. These species died out between the 1840s and the 1970s: passenger pigeon, great auk, Labrador duck, wild turkey, sea mink, eastern elk, Queen Charlotte Island caribou, great plains wolf, Newfoundland wolf.

63. What is the largest of Canadian birds?

The white pelican (*Pelecanus erythrorhynchos*) is the largest of all Canadian birds. It has a wingspan approaching 3 m, or 10 feet.

The smallest Canadian bird is the calliope hummingbird (*Stellula calliope*) from British Columbia. It rarely attains a length of more than 70 mm, or 2.75 inches.

64. What is the scientific name of the Canada Goose?

The scientific name of the Canada Goose is *Branta canadensis*. This wild North American bird has a characteristic honk and, when migrating, flies in the familiar V-formation. It has established migratory patterns that take it twice over Point Pelee National Park, reaching its peak heading south on or about October 20, and heading north on or about April 20.

The naturalist Jack Miner once observed the following: "Canada Geese conduct themselves with dignity, never fight unless it's absolutely necessary to protect their families — and then their wrath is terrible. The gander takes only one mate in a lifetime, and I've never known one to make application for divorce."

65. *Are there dangerous snakes in Canada?*
Of the twenty-four species of snakes native to Canada there are three (all rattlesnakes) that are dangerous to man. The dangerous varieties are the northern Pacific rattlesnake (*Crotalus viridis oreganus*), the prairie rattlesnake (*Crotalus viridis viridis*), and the eastern massasauga rattlesnake (*Sistrurus catenatus catenatus*). These venomous varieties have a series of bony plates or rattles on the ends of their tails and should be avoided.

66. *How much of the country has soil suitable for farming?*
It is estimated that one eighth of the land is suitable for agriculture.

67. *What role does agriculture play in the economy?*
Agriculture accounts for more than one quarter of the country's economy. Farm exports earn 20 percent of the country's foreign exchange. The prairie provinces account for 80 percent of the country's improved farm land. Major crops are wheat, oats, barley, canola, flaxseed, and rye. The prairies also support ranching. The prairie provinces are sometimes called "the breadbasket of the world."

68. *There is a saying that a Russian peasant can produce enough food to feed three Russian generals. How many people can a Canadian farmer feed?*
One Canadian farmer can produce enough food to feed fifty-five people.

69. *Which country is the world's largest wheat producer?*
The Soviet Union is the largest wheat-producing country in the world. Yet, with all its production, the Soviet Union cannot meet its own needs, so it is a major buyer of Canadian and world wheat. Canada is the second-largest wheat-producing nation on Earth.

70. *Which province grows most of Canada's wheat?*
Saskatchewan ranks first in wheat production and grows two thirds of Canada's crop.

71. *What are the wheat pools?*
The wheat pools are farmers' co-operatives. They were formed in each of the three prairie provinces in the mid-1920s to act as grain-handling co-operatives. They acquired grain elevators and handled the marketing of grain, though the latter is now the concern of the Canadian Wheat Board.

72. *What is Marquis wheat?*
Marquis wheat, a fast-maturing strain of wheat ideal for prairie growing conditions, was developed by Charles E. Saunders, appointed Dominion Cerealist in Ottawa in 1903. It revolutionized the growing of grain in Canada. The Marquis strain, ideal for baking and milling, matured ten days earlier than other types of wheat.

73. *Where is the world's largest wheat field?*
According to the *Guinness Book of World Records* (1971), "The world's largest single wheat field was probably one of more than 35,000 acres [14,000 ha], sown in 1951 near Lethbridge, Alberta, Canada."

74. *What is rapeseed now called?*

Rapeseed, the seed of the brilliant yellow rape plant, was renamed canola in 1974. It was renamed for two reasons. Because of its name, rapeseed was the butt of countless jokes; also, new varieties were devised by the scientist Baldur Stefansson. They differ from the old in that they contain less fatty acid. All rapeseed grown in Canada is now known as canola, a combination of the words Canada and oil. It is an important source of edible oil and, after wheat and barley, is Canada's most valuable crop. For years Tisdale, Sask., located in the heart of fields of rapeseed and apiaries, was known as "The Land of Rape and Honey."

75. *Do the plants* **Sarracenia purpurea** *and* **Bougainvillaea** *have special connections to Canada?*

These two plants were named after talented French naturalists with Canadian connections. *Sarracenia purpurea*, the scientific name of the pitcher plant, was so called after Michel Sarrazin (1659–1734), a physician and naturalist in New France who published a treatise on plant life in the New World.

Bougainvillaea is the scientific name of the bougainvillea, an exotic plant found in the tropics. It bears the name of Comte de Bougainville (1729–1811), a Frenchman of many talents who, before leading a scientific voyage that took him around the world, served in Quebec as aide-de-camp to Montcalm.

76. *What is ginseng?*

Ginseng is a wild plant, native to Canada, the root of which was and is highly prized in China for its medicinal effects. The mandrake-like root is held to be a tonic that restores virility. The root sold for its weight in silver in twelfth-century China. Its value and scarcity were stressed in reports by Jesuits in Canton, and these were studied by Jesuits in Quebec, who undertook a search for the plant in the forests around Montreal. Found in profusion in 1718, it was harvested and exported to China. In one year, 1752, the crop brought 20,000 pounds sterling. Today ginseng is grown in Quebec, Ontario, and Nova Scotia and exported to China. Related to parsley and sarsaparilla, it is sometimes called the red-berry. Wild ginseng (*Panax quinquefolius*) has five parted leaves; dwarf ginseng (*Panax trifolius*) has three parted leaves.

77. *What is* Zizania aquatica*?*

This is the scientific name of wild rice, also called riz sauvage and Canada rice, a tall aquatic grass with long, flat leaf blades. It produces a rice with a nutty flavour which tastes delicious especially when served with wild duck. Wild rice is grown extensively in the vicinity of Peterborough, Ont., but also in the Rainy River–Lake of the Woods region and the Whiteshell Forest area of Manitoba.

78. *Which fruit and vegetable grown in Canada hold the most economic importance?*

Measuring in dollar crop value, the most important fruit grown in the country is the apple, and the most important vegetable is the potato.

79. *What is the most distinctive apple grown in the country?*

The most distinctive Canadian apple is the McIntosh red, which sprang from a chance seedling transplanted by John McIntosh at Dundela, Ont., in 1796. The apple resembles those of the Fameuse trees brought to Quebec from Normandy in the 1600s.

80. *How much of the country is covered in trees?*

More than one third of the total area of Canada is covered in trees. Forests are estimated to cover 906 million ha, or 2,264 million acres, of land. There are more than 14.5 ha, or 36 acres, of forest for every man, woman, and child in the country. More than 90 percent of this vast forest is publicly owned. It is administered by the provinces, which lease sections of it to pulp and paper companies.

Nine forest regions are recognized, and these are the Boreal Forest, the Coast Forest, the Subalpine Forest, the Montane Forest, the Columbia Forest, the Deciduous Forest, the Great Lakes–St. Lawrence Forest, the Acadian Forest, and the Grasslands.

There are 140 species of trees, and these divide into the softwoods (conifers) and the hardwoods (deciduous). Among the softwoods are pines, larches, spruces, hemlocks, Douglas firs, and arbor vitae. Among the hardwoods are willows, poplars, walnuts, birches, alders, maples, and sumacs.

81. *Where do the tallest trees grow?*
The country's tallest trees grow in Cathedral Grove in Macmillan Provincial Park on the western slope of Vancouver Island. Here the Douglas firs attain heights in the neighbourhood of 83 m, or 275 feet, with a circumference at the base of 9 m, or 30 feet. The oldest is 800 years old. The Douglas fir, no matter where it grows, is a giant among trees, exceeded in height on this continent only by the redwood.

82. *How does Canada rank in forestry products?*
Canada is the world's largest exporter of pulp and paper. The pulp and paper industry is the country's leading manufacturer in terms of production and employment. Its annual production is valued at about $8 million, of which about 80 percent is exported. Forty percent of the world's newspaper pages are printed on Canadian newsprint.

83. *What plant is most characteristic of the arctic tundra?*
The most characteristic single genus of the arctic tundra is the reindeer moss. Actually, it is not a moss but a lichen, and its technical name is *Cladonia*. The species *Cladonia rangiferina*

grows a few centimetres, or inches, tall. It is grey in colour, branched like a diminutive shrub, and grazed upon by caribou.

84. *How long does it take an arctic flower to bloom?*
It takes many years to move from germination to first flowering. There are at least 834 different flowering plants in the Arctic, and they do the best they can in the short summer. There are no climbing plants, none with spines or thorns, and none that sting.

85. *What is the popular name of the edible frond of the ostrich fern?*
The edible frond of the ostrich fern (*Matteuccia struthiopteris*) is popularly called the fiddlehead. The green spring vegetable bears a striking resemblance to the curled head of a fiddle. Although fiddleheads grow in various parts of North America, it is claimed that the most delicious are found in New Brunswick.

86. *What is the country's oldest continuing industry?*
For thousands of years the native peoples hunted and fished the lands and waters of Canada. Almost a thousand years ago there were Norsemen fishing off the East Coast, and centuries later Basque fishermen plied the Grand Banks of Newfoundland. All this economic activity predated the voyages of Columbus, Cabot, and Cartier. Although hunting for survival and trade was eventually replaced by agriculture, fishing continues to this day to be one of our most important industries. So fishing is the country's oldest continuing industry.

87. *Which country is the world's largest exporter of fish?*
Canada is the largest exporter of fish. Its fishermen annually harvest over 1 million tonnes, or 1.1 million tons, of fish. More than two thirds of the catch is sold abroad, making Canada, since

1979, when it re-established this position, the world's largest fish exporter.

88. *What fish are caught by the Atlantic fisheries?*

More than 80 percent of the fish landed in Canada is taken in the Atlantic provinces and Quebec. There are some 30 kinds of fish, shellfish (clams, scallops, oysters), and marine crustaceans (lobsters). The principal fish are cod and "groundfish" (like haddock and pollock) which feed on the sea bottom. Cod and lobster are the most valuable economically.

89. *What species of fish are taken from Canada's inland waters?*

Canada's lakes, rivers, and streams comprise half the world's available fresh water. Located in seven provinces, they support commercial fisheries that harvest more than a dozen species of fish. Half the total landed value is accounted for by whitefish, yellow perch, and walleye. Locally important species include Manitoba saugers, Ontario lake trout, and Quebec eels.

90. *What are the five types of Pacific salmon?*

The five types of Pacific salmon are chinook, coho, chum, pink, and sockeye. Pacific salmon accounts for about 70 percent of the West Coast catch.

91. *Who was the first person to attain the North Pole?*

The North Pole is the northern point of the Earth's rotation on its axis. It corresponds to a polar ice cap north of Ellesmere Island where latitude and longitude meet. Here the coordinates read "latitude 90° north, longitude 0°." The North Pole was first reached — the technical term is "attained" — by one of two claimants. Even after more than eighty years it is still uncertain whether the first person to reach the North Pole was Frederick A.

Cook on April 21, 1908, or Robert E. Peary on April 6, 1909. The two American explorers each claimed to be "the only first."

92. *Who first attained the North Magnetic Pole?*

The North Magnetic Pole was first attained by Sir James Clark Ross on June 1, 1831. Ten years later Ross, who specialized in polar exploration, made an unsuccessful attempt to reach the South Pole. To mark the site of the North Magnetic Pole he erected a cairn at Cape Adelaide on the west coast of Boothia Peninsula. The sponsor of his expedition aboard the paddle steamer *Victory* was not the British Admiralty, but Felix Booth, the distiller of Booth's Gin.

93. *What is the present position of the North Magnetic Pole?*

The North Magnetic Pole is that point on the Earth's surface where the Earth's magnetic field is vertical. Since the pole was first attained in 1831, the point has drifted across the Arctic in a northwesterly direction. Its current rate of drift is approximately 11.5 km, or 7.1 miles a year. In addition, there is a daily displacement from its mean position of 60 km, or 36 miles, or more.

The Earth Physics Branch of Energy, Mines and Resources Canada conducted a survey to redetermine its average position. The 1984 North Magnetic Pole Survey established that its present position is on the southeast tip of Lougheed Island in the eastern Arctic. The extrapolated position for 1985 was 77.1° north, 102.4° west.

2. HISTORY

94. *Who really discovered Canada?*

Nobody knows. There is no record, written or otherwise, about the first human being who set foot on what is now Canadian soil. The Manitoba-born Arctic explorer Vilhjalmur Stefansson once quipped: "A land may be said to be discovered the first time a European, preferably an Englishman, sets foot on it."

Scientists believe that the first human beings arrived on the North American continent from Siberia between 10,000 and 25,000 years ago. Ancestors of today's native people crossed Beringia (as geologists term the Bering Sea when referring to the region in the distant past) and made their way from the Old World to the New. These Asiatic nomads were the discoverers of Canada. So the Inuit and the Indians are descendants of the first inhabitants of North America.

95. *Did the Chinese or the Phoenicians visit early Canada?*

There is much conjecture and speculation concerning the pre-Columbian exploration of Canada. It has been suggested that a Chinese Buddhist monk named Hoei Shin missionized and explored the West Coast about A.D. 500. Another suggestion is that about the same time there was a Phoenician voyage of discovery under a Lord Hiram which sailed up the St. Lawrence. Such notions flourish in the absence of firm evidence.

96. *What was the* **Brendan** *voyage?*

Did St. Brendan the Navigator, the Irish abbot and missionary who lived about A.D. 500, sail from Ireland to the New World in a canvas coracle? The modern-day explorer and writer, Tim Severin, undertook to re-create St. Brendan's voyage via Iceland and Greenland in just such a coracle, which he named the *Brendan*. He succeeded, and landed at Peckford Island, Nfld., on June 26, 1977. There is no doubt that St. Brendan could have made the trip but no proof that he actually did.

97. *Who were the first known Europeans to colonize the country known today as Canada?*

The Norsemen, or Vikings, were the first known Europeans to colonize any part of the North American continent. They made their expeditions to the eastern coast of Canada from Greenland, and established colonies in the New World which, for a variety of known and unknown reasons, died out. Leif Ericsson, called Leif the Lucky, is the first known European to land on mainland North America, and this occurred around A.D. 1000. According to an old saga, Leif visited Helluland (identified with Cape Dyer, Baffin Island, N.W.T.), Markland (perhaps Cape Porcupine, Labrador), and Vinland (L'Anse aux Meadows, Nfld.), where he established his principal colony.

98. *What proof exists that the Norsemen established the colony they called Vinland about A.D. 1000 at L'Anse aux Meadows, Nfld.?*

Remains of the only indisputable Norse settlement found in North America were unearthed in the summer of 1960 by an expedition headed by the Norwegian explorer Helge Ingstad, whose work was underwritten by the Norwegian Research Council for Science and the Humanities and the National Geographic Society. Further archaeological work uncovered eight house sites, a smithy, four boatsheds, plus additional evidence of pre-Columbian Norse occupation. Carbon-14 tests dated some of the findings at about A.D. 1000.

The settlement site, a remote fishing village called L'Anse aux Meadows on the northeast tip of Newfoundland, is now known as L'Anse aux Meadows National Historic Park and may be visited.

99. *Are there grape vines at Vinland?*

No. "Grape vines" are a misnomer for Vinland or Vineland, according to Helge Ingstad, the discoverer of the Norse colony at L'Anse aux Meadows, Nfld. Ingstad maintains that the Old Norse word *vin* means "meadow" or "pasture," not "grapes" or "vines."

100. *Who were the original "Red Indians" or "Redskins"?*

The original "Red Indians" or "Redskins" were the Beothuk, a group of Indians who lived in Newfoundland for centuries before being exterminated by the Europeans and the Micmacs. There were never more than a few thousand Beothuk at any one time. Shanawdithit, a woman who died in St. John's in 1829, was the last of the Beothuk.

The Beothuk, who greeted the Europeans who arrived on their shores to fish and then to settle, had the custom of dyeing their bodies red (rather in the manner of the early Britons who dyed themselves blue). This custom led to the application of the term "Red Indians" or "Redskins" to all North American Indians.

101. *What did John Cabot discover?*

No one is certain what was discovered by John Cabot (1450–1498), the Venetian who sailed from Bristol, England, in 1497, five years after Columbus made his epic voyage. Cabot coasted along the seaboard of Maine and Nova Scotia, it is believed, and probably made a landfall on June 24 at Cape Race, Nfld., thinking he had reached Asia. In 1498, he set out on a second voyage to the New World, from which he did not return.

102. *Which European explorer is generally credited with the discovery of Canada?*
Jacques Cartier (1491–1557), the navigator from Saint-Malo, France, is credited with the discovery of the St. Lawrence River, hence, of Canada. He crossed the Atlantic in twenty days in search of a route to Asia, passed by the coast of Labrador, and explored the Gulf of St. Lawrence. On July 24, 1534, he raised a thirty-foot cross on the Gaspé Peninsula, and, despite protests from the Iroquois chief Donnacona, claimed the land for France. He visited Stadacona (Quebec City) and the island of Hochelaga (Montreal) on his second voyage in 1535, and made his third and last voyage in 1541. His only rival for the claim of discoverer of Canada is the Venetian mariner and explorer, John Cabot.

103. *What is one of the earliest and most imaginative descriptions of Canada?*
Jacques Cartier described the appearance of the north shore of the Gulf of St. Lawrence, today's Labrador and Quebec, this way: "In fine," he wrote during the summer of 1534, "I am rather inclined to believe that this is the land God gave to Cain." He found it so bleak he had to refer to biblical imagery to find a parallel.

104. *Who named Mount Royal?*
Mount Royal was named by Jacques Cartier, the navigator, who in 1535 visited the Indian village of Hochelaga, which corresponds to the present-day site of Montreal, and climbed the mountain behind the village. At its summit he named it "Mont Royale." The name stuck and evolved into Montreal. The mountain is actually an extinct volcano, which rises 233 m, or 764 feet, above sea level.

105. *Who was Sir Humphrey Gilbert? Why was he significant?*
The Elizabethan explorer, Sir Humphrey Gilbert, claimed New-

foundland as England's first overseas colony. Then he set sail aboard the *Squirrel*, but his small vessel sank in the Atlantic off the Grand Banks on September 9, 1583. Before the ship went down, he was overheard by the crew aboard his companion ship to comfort his own crew by stating: "We are as near to heaven by sea as by land!"

106. *Who is regarded as "the first farmer of the Americas"?*
The first farmers of North and South America were the native people, of course, but the first known European farmer in today's Canada was the French apothecary, Louis Hébert (1575–1627), who in 1617 brought his wife and three children to settle at Quebec. The industrious Frenchman was the first Canadian settler to support himself from the soil. He cultivated the earth with handtools. The plough he planned to use did not arrive in New France until a few months after his death.

107. *What are the dates of New France?*
New France was the name given to all the land discovered, explored, settled, or claimed by the French in North America. The colony may be dated from 1524, when Giovanni da Verrazzano reached the Atlantic coast, to 1803, when Louisiana, the last French colony on mainland North America, was sold to the United States. At its height, in 1712, New France covered nearly three quarters of the American continent, stretching from the Gulf of St. Lawrence to beyond Lake Superior, including Newfoundland, Acadia, the Iroquois country, and the Mississippi valley as far as the Gulf of Mexico.

108. *Who was called "the Father of New France," and why?*
Posterity has granted this title to Samuel de Champlain (1570–1635), the native of France who established the first French colonies in Acadia in 1604 and in Quebec in 1608. He laid the founda-

tions for the prosperous colony of New France, explored the western extremes of the colony, and died in Quebec on Christmas Day, 1635.

109. *Who were the first and last governors of New France?*

The first governor of New France was Samuel de Champlain, who assumed the position in 1612. The last governor was Pierre de Rigaud, Marquis de Vaudreuil-Cavagnal, who resigned in 1760 when Montreal was surrendered to the British. Between the first and the last governors, about two dozen men held the position for close to a century and a half. The best-known of them was Louis de Buade, Comte de Frontenac, who served twice as governor (1672–82, 1689–98).

110. *Who were the best-liked and least-liked intendants?*

The intendant of New France was responsible, under the governor, for commerce, finance, and the police. Between 1665 and 1760, there were one dozen intendants of New France. The best-liked was Jean Talon (1626–1694), the first. He was called "the Great Intendant" for his expansionist policies. The least-liked and last was François Bigot (1703–1778), who resigned in 1760 when the British assumed power and was found guilty by the King of France of embezzlement and profiteering on a gargantuan scale.

111. *Who were* les filles du roi?

Les filles du roi were "the king's girls" — orphan girls of good families who, as wards of the King of France, were sent out to New France in 1665–71 as brides for settlers and soldiers. In this way the King encouraged the population growth of the colony. There was also a dowry when the girl consented to marry — an ox, a cow, two chickens, two barrels of salted meat, two pigs, and eleven crowns. More than eight hundred young women came to Canada as *les filles du roi*.

112. *Who were the* habitants *and* seigneurs *in New France?*
In New France, the *habitants* were the farmers or peasants who worked on the land granted to the *seigneurs*. In the French language, the word *habitant* means "inhabitant," and the word *seigneur* means "senior" or "lord." The farmers cleared the land, lived on it, and paid the owner annual dues. The owner was obliged to build a mill, establish a court for minor disputes, etc., in exchange for the seigneurial tenure from the French Crown. The system was semi-feudal and survived until 1854, long after the dissolution of New France.

113. *How do the Habitation and Habitat differ?*
There are many differences between the Habitation and Habitat, although both obviously are derived from the same root meaning to frequent or dwell in a place. One is old, the other new; one was the residence of a developing colony, the other a development complex.

Habitation is the French word for "residence" or "dwelling." It is also the word used by Samuel de Champlain to describe the small wooden fortress he constructed at Port Royal to house his colony in 1605. The original Habitation, long since destroyed, has been reconstructed and may be visited by tourists at Lower Granville, N.S.

Habitat is the name given the multilevel apartment complex that was the star attraction of Expo 67 in Montreal. The modular construction and modernistic design were devised by the architect Moshe Safdie. Today, Habitat is used as a fashionable residential apartment building.

114. *Which institutions did Marie de l'Incarnation and Mère d'Youville establish in Quebec?*
The two remarkable women founded religious orders for Roman Catholic women in New France. Marie de l'Incarnation (1599–1672) established a branch of the Ursuline order in Que-

bec in 1639. She founded the convent that was the first private school for girls on the North American continent, and her correspondence, vivid and varied, is of considerable historical and literary interest.

Mère d'Youville (1701–1771) was the founder of the congregation of nuns called, officially, Order of Sisters of Charity and, popularly, Les Soeurs Grises (Grey Nuns). The order was established in Montreal in 1755. Members wear a grey habit and are dedicated to social service.

115. *What happened to Champlain's astrolabe?*

The French explorer Samuel de Champlain recorded the loss of his astrolabe in his journal on June 7, 1613. An astrolabe is a circular instrument, formerly used for measuring latitude. Champlain's was made of brass and measured about 15 cm, or 6 inches, in diameter. He lost it while travelling overland between the Muskrat and Green lakes. In 1867, a youngster uncovered it near Pembroke, Ont. Since 1943, it has been in the collection of the New York Historical Society.

116. *What was the name of the first European settlement in the interior of North America?*

The name of the first inland settlement by a European was Huronia, and it was established by the Jesuit missionary Jean de Brébeuf (1593–1649) in 1626. The principal mission post, Sainte-Marie Among the Hurons, near present-day Midland, Ont., was a palisaded settlement of some size. Destroyed by fire in 1649, it has now been reconstructed.

117. *What are the names of the Jesuit martyrs in North America?*

The Jesuit missionaries from France who died at the hands of the Indians in 1642–49 while in Huronia or Iroquois territory are Jean de Brébeuf, Noël Chabanel, Antoine Daniel, Charles Garnier,

Gabriel Lalemant, René Goupil, Isaac Jogues, and Jean de la Lande. The first five died in what is now Ontario, the last three in present-day New York State. All eight were canonized by the Pope in 1930 and are honoured at the Martyrs' Shrine which overlooks Sainte-Marie Among the Hurons near Midland, Ont.

118. *Who led the defence at Long Sault?*
Adam Dollard (1635–1660) has been called "the Hero of New France" because of the courageous stand he took at Long Sault, which may have saved the colony of Ville Marie (today's Montreal) from Iroquois attack. With sixteen companions plus Hurons and Algonquins, he held the abandoned fort at Long Sault on the Ottawa River for ten days in May, 1660. A vastly superior force of Iroquois finally took the fort, and Dollard and his companions died in the siege. Historians have cast doubt on the strategic importance of the defence, but social and religious figures in New France and later Quebec turned the exploit into a deed of daring and devotion.

119. *What was the original name of the Hudson's Bay Company?*
The original name of the Hudson's Bay Company was "Governor and Company of Adventurers of England Trading into Hudson's Bay." The full title appears on the letters patent, signed on May 2, 1670.

The Hudson's Bay Company is considered the oldest active company in the world. It began as a fur trading operation with control of Rupert's Land, the immense wilderness area drained by rivers flowing into Hudson Bay. The area corresponds to the Canadian northwest which, two centuries later, in 1870, was acquired by the newly formed Dominion of Canada in what has been described as the largest real estate transaction in history. Over the centuries, the H.B.C. or the Bay (as it is known) evolved into a diversified corporation ultimately acquired by the Thomson empire.

120. *What were* voyageurs *and* coureurs de bois?

French-Canadian fur traders who manned canoes and boats and assisted the factors of the great fur companies in the seventeenth and eighteenth centuries in New France were called *voyageurs* and *coureurs de bois*. The former were in effect licensed traders, the latter unlicensed traders. Both played an important part in the development of the fur trade and the exploration of Canada. A *voyageur* is, of course, a "voyager" or "traveller." A *coureur de bois* is, literally, a "runner of the woods," a kind of scout.

121. *Who were "Radishes and Gooseberries"?*

The two seventeenth-century explorers with the sobriquets "Radishes and Gooseberries" were Pierre-Esprit Radisson (1640–1710) and Sieur des Groseilliers (1618–1686). Radisson and his brother-in-law Groseilliers were French-born *coureurs de bois* who, in the employ of the Hudson's Bay Company, made journeys to Lake Michigan, Lake Superior, and Hudson Bay.

122. *What was Comte de Frontenac's reply to the order to surrender Quebec forthwith?*

The Governor General of New France, Comte de Frontenac (1622–1698), did not mince words. "I have no reply to make to your general," he informed the courier for the British envoy, Sir William Phips, who had ordered him to surrender Quebec, October 15, 1690, "other than from the mouths of my cannon and muskets."

123. *Who was "the Heroine of New France"?*

Madeleine de Verchères (1678–1747) was fourteen years old on October 22, 1692, when the Iroquois raided the family's seigniory on the south shore of the St. Lawrence River northeast of Montreal. The siege lasted eight days, with Madeleine almost alone organizing the defence. It was lifted only when relief arrived.

The defence earned Madeleine the title "the Heroine of New France" and a permanent place in the annals of Quebec and Canada. An arresting bronze statue of Madeleine, executed by Louis-Philippe Hébert, was erected at Verchères, Que., in 1913.

124. *What was the largest fortress in North America?*

The largest fortress ever built in North America was Louisbourg, which was named in honour of Louis XV of France, who commissioned it and constantly complained of its cost. The gigantic garrison was erected in 1713 near the eastern tip of Cape Breton Island, N.S., to house 4,000 soldiers. There was one cannon for every ten inhabitants.

Louisbourg was twice taken by the British, who finally levelled it in 1760. But, as unlikely as it may seem, the fortress of Louisbourg is rising from the original foundations. One quarter of the original citadel has been returned to its former eighteenth-century glory by the federal government. The work of historical reconstruction, commenced in 1961 and still underway, is the largest and most complex restoration project in North America after colonial Williamsburg in Virginia.

125. *What was the darkest day in Acadian history?*

The Acadians of today are descendants of the French inhabitants of Acadia, the name given by France to its possessions in the Maritimes. When the British assumed control of the area under the Treaty of Utrecht, they felt the inhabitants to be dangerous. Consequently, on Friday, September 5, 1755, at the Church of St. Charles at Grand Pré, now Grand Pré National Historic Park, the order of expulsion was read. Between 12,000 and 15,000 French colonists, mainly farmers and their families, were ordered dispersed among other British colonies in North America. Kith and kin were parted. Though many of the Acadians eventually returned to their land, it was the darkest day in the history of the Acadian people.

126. *Who was Evangeline?*

Evangeline was the name chosen by Henry Wadsworth Longfellow, the American poet, for the heroine of his book-length narrative poem, the full title of which is *Evangeline: A Tale of Acadie* (1847). Longfellow based his poem on an incident that occurred during the Expulsion of the Acadians in 1755. He describes how two lovers, whom he called Evangeline Bellefontaine and Gabriel Lajeunesse, are separated. Evangeline cannot rest until she finds Gabriel, but when she locates him in Louisiana, he is engaged to marry another woman. Although Evangeline never lived, the poignant tale was so popular that a statue of her was raised at Grand Pré. The bronze figure was so sculpted by Philippe and Henri Hébert that, as the observer moves around it, the young Evangeline seems to grow gradually older and sadder. Another statue was raised to Evangeline at St. Martinville, Louisiana.

127. *How numerous were the Loyalists?*

The Loyalists were citizens of the Thirteen Colonies who, wishing to remain loyal or true to British institutions, emigrated to the provinces of British North America during or immediately after the American Revolution of 1775–83. Approximately 70,000 people left the Colonies rather than become Americans. Some 60,000 settled in what would become Canada, 5,000 went to the West Indies, and another 5,000 returned to Great Britain. The Loyalists who came to Canada settled in today's Nova Scotia, Quebec, and Ontario.

128. *What was the purpose of the Constitutional Act of 1791?*

This act of the British Parliament divided Quebec into the provinces of Upper Canada and Lower Canada, today's Ontario and Quebec. It provided them with government institutions along the British line. It was enacted to accommodate the immigration of some 10,000 Loyalists into Quebec following the American Revolution.

129. *Who was the navigator who took possession of the west coast of Canada for Great Britain?*
Captain James Cook (1728–1779), master in the Royal Navy, explored the west coast of Canada as far north as the Bering Strait. He entered Nootka Sound, on the west coast of Vancouver Island, and on March 29, 1778, took possession of the land for Great Britain. Rivals for the land were Spain and Russia.

130. *Who was held captive at Nootka Sound?*
Nootka Sound is an inlet on the west coast of Vancouver Island. It was discovered by Captain James Cook in 1778. Here, in 1803, the Boston sailor, John R. Jewitt (1783–1821), was taken prisoner by Maquinna, chief of the Nootkas, who held him captive for two and a half years. Jewitt recounted his experiences in a journal, published in 1807. James Houston based his novel *Eagle Song* (1983) on Jewitt's captivity narrative.

131. *What is the fabled Northwest Passage?*
The Northwest Passage is the sea route between the Atlantic and Pacific oceans, through the islands that lie between Baffin Island and the Beaufort Sea. Among the explorers who searched for the passage as a presumed route to Asia were Sir Humphrey Gilbert, Martin Frobisher, John Davis, Henry Hudson, William Baffin, Sir John Franklin, John Rae, and John McClintock. The search for the route kept navigators busy mapping the Arctic coast from the sixteenth to the nineteenth century.

132. *Who was the first explorer to negotiate the Northwest Passage?*
The Northwest Passage was not negotiated or traversed until the Norwegian explorer Roald Amundsen sailed from east to west in the *Gjoa* in 1903–06. Sergeant Henry Larsen in the RCMP patrol vessel *St. Roch* sailed from east to west in 1940–42, and from

west to east in 1944, the first vessel to twice traverse the Passage. In 1969–70, the U.S. supertanker *Manhattan* completed the first commercial passage from the Beaufort Sea to Atlantic ports.

As well as being the first explorer to negotiate the Northwest Passage, Amundsen was the first person to reach the South Pole, which he attained on December 14, 1911.

133. *Where were the principal battles fought in the Seven Years' War?*

The Seven Years' War between Britain and France lasted from 1756 to 1763. During the seven years of hostilities, there were a number of military engagements in North America. The principal ones were battles at Fort Carillon (1758), Louisbourg (1758), Plains of Abraham (1759), and Sainte-Foy (1760). In the Treaty of Paris, which concluded the hostilities, France ceded New France to Britain.

134. *Who said, "Gentlemen, I would rather have written those lines than take Quebec tomorrow"?*

The remark is attributed to James Wolfe (1727–1759), the English general, after giving an impromptu recital of Gray's "Elegy, Written in a Country Churchyard," on September 12, 1759, the evening before he died on the Plains of Abraham securing Quebec for the British.

135. *Where are the Plains of Abraham?*

The Plains of Abraham are an extent of rolling land west of Quebec City immediately beyond the old walls. The plains were named after their first owner, Abraham Martin, a ship's pilot, who held the deed in 1635. On these plains on September 13, 1759, the British forces under Wolfe defeated the French forces under Montcalm. The Plains are now a National Historic Park.

136. *What is the importance of Anse au Foulon?*

Anse au Foulon, sometimes called Wolfe's Cove, is of military importance. This break in the cliff, southwest of Cape Diamond, leads from the St. Lawrence River to the Plains of Abraham. It was the route to the conquest of Quebec taken by General James Wolfe.

Anse au Foulon was lightly guarded by the French. In the early hours of September 13, 1759, Wolfe led his English troops to the cove. They scaled the cliff and gained the Plains of Abraham where 4,800 men presented the French with a problem. The French leader, the Marquis de Montcalm, was taken by surprise. He had to decide whether to attack the English or to wait for reinforcements. He decided to attack and within twenty minutes his soldiers had scattered and dispersed. Wolfe was killed and Montcalm was mortally wounded. Four days later, Quebec capitulated and the English were masters of Canada.

137. *Was Quebec ever envisioned as the Fourteenth Colony?*

General Richard Montgomery (1738–1775) led an American invasion of Canada and captured Montreal on November 13, 1775. He later died in an unsuccessful assault on Quebec, December 31, 1775. His dying words were the rallying cry: "Push on, brave boys, Quebec is ours!" Thus ended the attempt of the Continental Congress to annex Quebec as "the Fourteenth Colony."

138. *What, in general terms, was British North America?*

British North America was the collective name for the British colonies in North America. The term was used from 1783, the year Britain acknowledged the independence of the United States, to 1867, the year Britain proclaimed the creation of the Dominion of Canada.

139. *What are the early names for Ontario and Quebec?*

The Province of Quebec was created by the Proclamation of 1763, and the area included parts of present-day Quebec and Ontario. The area was divided into the provinces of Upper Canada and Lower Canada by the Constitutional Act of 1791. Upper Canada was generally the area west of the Ottawa River. The provinces retained these names until the creation of the Province of Canada on February 10, 1841, which gave the name Canada West to Upper Canada, and the name Canada East to Lower Canada. This arrangement lasted until the creation of the Dominion of Canada, July 1, 1867, when the Province of Ontario and the Province of Quebec were so named.

140. *What message did Sir Alexander Mackenzie inscribe on a boulder at Dean Channel, Bella Coola River, British Columbia?*
In large characters he wrote: ''Alexander Mackenzie, from Canada, by land, July 22, 1793.'' This inscription on a boulder overlooking the Pacific marked the completion of the first overland trek of the northern half of the North American continent. The inscription is preserved to this day.

141. *Who founded the Red River Settlement?*
The Red River Settlement, a colony at the junction of the Red and Assiniboine rivers, was founded by the Scots colonist Thomas Douglas, Lord Selkirk (1771–1820), in 1812. It was established on land granted by the Hudson's Bay Company. The colony grew into the city of Winnipeg.

142. *What caused the Massacre of Seven Oaks?*
Rivalry between two fur trading companies resulted in the massacre at Seven Oaks on June 19, 1816. Métis and Indians under the leadership of Cuthbert Grant of the North West Company killed the governor and settlers of the Red River Settlement, which was sponsored by the Hudson's Bay Company. A plaque in downtown Winnipeg marks the spot where the massacre took place.

143. *Who won the War of 1812?*
Both Great Britain and the United States claimed to be victors of the War of 1812. But the Treaty of Ghent, signed in Belgium on December 24, 1814, which brought an end to the hostilities, restored the status quo. To the extent that the United States failed to make territorial gains, the British and the Canadians were the victors. It is sometimes said that the War of 1812 is the first war the Americans lost.

144. *Who was Sir Isaac Brock?*
Sir Isaac Brock (1769–1812) was the popular leader of the British forces in the War of 1812 who fell during the Battle of Queenston Heights, October 13, 1812. It was once believed that his dying words were the ringing command, "Push on, brave York Volunteers!" Historians now doubt that his last thoughts were directed to the charge of the York (Toronto) Volunteers, but there is no general agreement as to his last utterance.

145. *Is there a connection between the city of Toronto and the White House of Washington, D.C.?*
During the War of 1812, there were acts of sacking and burning committed by both British and American troops. On April 30, 1813, American invaders sacked and burnt the town of York, the future city of Toronto. On August 24, 1814, in direct retaliation, British troops set fire to the Capitol building in Washington, D.C., and also to the White House, the official residence of the American President. The exterior of the presidential mansion was scorched and required repainting.

The official Mace, taken from the legislature of York in 1813, was returned by U.S. President Franklin D. Roosevelt 121 years later.

146. *Who was Laura Secord and why did she trek through the woods at night?*

Laura Secord (1775–1868) was a thirty-eight-year-old United Empire Loyalist housewife living in Queenston, in the Niagara district, when she learned of a planned attack on Beaver Dam by American soldiers billeted in her house. To warn the British commander, she trekked nineteen miles through the woods in the dead of night, June 21–2, 1813. Contrary to popular belief, she made the trek alone, not in the company of her cow. The British commander, forewarned of the attack both by Mrs. Secord and by Indians, won the Battle of Beaver Dam, a minor engagement in the War of 1812. Mrs. Secord's trek earned her the title "the Heroine of the War of 1812," but it was not until 1860, and the visit of the Prince of Wales, that her heroism was properly acknowledged. The Prince, later King Edward VII, presented her with his personal cheque for one hundred pounds. In 1969, the Laura Secord candy company restored the Secord homestead, from which the trek began, at Queenston, Ont.

147. *Who led the Rebellions of 1837 in Upper and Lower Canada?*

The rebellion in Lower Canada (Quebec) was led by Louis-Joseph Papineau (1786–1871). The rebellion in Upper Canada (Ontario) was led by William Lyon Mackenzie (1795–1861). Papineau was a lawyer and Mackenzie was a journalist. Both rebelled against conservative-minded appointed officials who controlled policy and patronage in the colonial administrations.

148. *Who described the French and the English in Canada as "two nations warring in the bosom of a single state"?*

That was the celebrated observation of Lord Durham in his official *Report on the Affairs of British North America* (1839). Sent by the British Parliament to report on the condition of colonists in Upper and Lower Canada, Lord Durham wrote: "I expected to find a contest between a government and a people: I found two nations warring in the bosom of a single state."

149. *What was or is Responsible Government?*
Simply put, Responsible Government is the system of government
Canadians enjoy today. In that system, government ministers are
elected and not appointed, and they are ultimately responsible to
the legislature. This was not the case in Upper and Lower Canada
in the early nineteenth century, when the executive was appointed
and in no way bound by the will of the elected legislature. The
notion that the executive should be "responsible" or responsive
to the legislature was put forward by Dr. William Warren Baldwin
in 1828 and developed by his son Robert Baldwin in 1836. It was a
key recommendation of Lord Durham's *Report* (1839) and it was
eventually implemented.

150. *What is the meaning of the rallying cry "Rep by Pop"?*
"Rep by Pop" was the rallying cry of George Brown and others
in 1851 in Canada West (Ontario) when its population exceeded
that of Canada East (Quebec). It called for "representation by
population" in the House of Commons, instead of equal representation by district or province. A compromise was achieved in
Confederation, with representation by population coupled with
guarantees of limits of representation to Quebec and the smaller
provinces.

151. *Who are the Grits and the Tories?*
The Grits are members of the Liberal Party and the Tories are
members of the Progressive Conservative Party. Both terms are
traditional. "Grits" derives from the reformers in Canada West
(Ontario) in the 1840s and refers specifically to strength of character, as in the expression "true grit." Tories are conservative-
minded; the word derives from British parliamentary history.

152. *What is the significance of the slogan "Fifty-four Forty, or
Fight"?*
This slogan, which expressed the demands of the United States in

the Oregon Dispute, is attributed to William Allen, who spoke in
the U.S. Senate on the question in 1844. He pressed the American
claim that the boundary between Canada and the District of Oregon (now the states of Oregon and Washington) should include the
whole Pacific coast north to Alaska (or 54°40′ north). Four years
later the present western boundary between Canada and the United
States (the 49th parallel) was established. The slogan was wrong;
it was neither fifty-four forty nor fight.

153. *What was the Underground Railroad?*
The Underground Railroad was an undercover organization that
transported Black slaves from the American South to safety in the
American North. When, in 1850, it became illegal to harbour
runaway slaves anywhere in the United States, the last stop on the
Underground Railroad was extended north across the border. There
was no slavery in Upper and Lower Canada, as the practice had
been outlawed in the British Empire as early as 1784. It is possible
the Underground Railroad was so named in an allusion to the
''underground railroad'' (a type of subway for trains) being planned
for London, England.

154. *Was Uncle Tom a Canadian?*
Uncle Tom's Cabin (1852), one of the most influential novels of
all time, was written by Harriet Beecher Stowe. The American
author showed the inhumanity of slavery, and she based her hero,
Uncle Tom, in part on the life and work of Josiah Henson
(1789–1883). Henson was a Black slave in Kentucky when he
learned that his family was to be broken up. He escaped on the
Underground Railroad to Upper Canada with his wife and four
small children in 1830. Near Dresden, Ont., he founded a settlement for runaway slaves, and became a spokesman for freedom.
He talked at length with Mrs. Stowe, who modelled the good
Uncle Tom on Henson. His tulipwood cabin is a museum at Dresden, north of Chatham, Ont. He died a British subject.

155. *What was the Province of Canada?*
The combined districts of Canada West and Canada East from 1841 to 1867 were known as the Province of Canada. Upper Canada became Canada West and Lower Canada became Canada East by the Act of Union of 1841. With Confederation in 1867, Canada West became Ontario and Canada East became Quebec.

156. *Who were the Fenians who invaded Canada in 1866?*
In ancient Ireland, the Fenians were roving mercenary soldiers who served the High Kings. In the United States in the 1860s, the Fenians belonged to a secret brotherhood or movement of Civil War veterans of Irish-American background intent upon lending aid to Ireland in its struggle against England. To this end they mounted several raids on the English in Canada. The Battle of Ridgeway, their principal raid, took place on June 2, 1866. Eight hundred Fenians attacked the village of Ridgeway, west of Fort Erie, Ont., but were repulsed. Over seven hundred were subsequently arrested by U.S. authorities. The result of the Fenian threat was the urgency of uniting the British provinces into Confederation.

157. *What is the British North America Act of 1867?*
This statute was passed by the Parliament of Great Britain in February, 1867. It created "one Dominion under the name of Canada" out of the colonies of Canada, Nova Scotia, and New Brunswick, dividing them into four provinces named Ontario, Quebec, Nova Scotia, and New Brunswick. The bill received royal assent on March 29, 1867, and became effective on July 1, 1867. This statute or act resulted in Confederation.

158. *In what order did the provinces and territories enter Confederation?*
Confederation was the result of the federal union of Quebec,

Ontario, New Brunswick, and Nova Scotia on July 1, 1867. Manitoba and the Northwest Territories joined on July 15, 1870. British Columbia joined on July 20, 1871. Prince Edward Island joined on July 1, 1873. Yukon Territory joined on June 13, 1898. Saskatchewan and Alberta joined on September 1, 1905. Newfoundland joined on March 31, 1949.

159. *Who were the Fathers of Confederation?*
The Fathers of Confederation were the delegates of the British North American colonies who attended one or more of the conferences at which the terms of Confederation were agreed upon. The conferences were held in Charlottetown (September 1, 1864), Quebec City (October 10–29, 1864), and London (December 4, 1866, and thereafter). The names of the thirty-six Fathers of Confederation — there were no Mothers among them — are listed below in alphabetical order with the abbreviation of the region that each delegate represented.

Adams G. Archibald, N.S.
George Brown, Canada
Alexander Campbell, Canada
Frederick B. T. Carter, Nfld.
George-Etienne Cartier, Canada
Edward B. Chandler, N.B.
Jean-Charles Chapais, Canada
James Cockburn, Canada
George H. Coles, P.E.I.
Robert B. Dickey, N.S.
Charles Fisher, N.B.
A. T. Galt, Canada
John Hamilton Gray, N.B.
John Hamilton Gray, P.E.I.
Thomas Heath Haviland, P.E.I.
William A. Henry, N.S.
William P. Howland, Canada

Jonathan McCulley, N.S.
A.A. Macdonald, P.E.I.
John A. Macdonald, Canada
William McDougall, Canada
Thomas D'Arcy McGee,
   Canada
Peter Mitchell, N.B.
Oliver Mowat, Canada
Edward Palmer, P.E.I.
William H. Pope, P.E.I.
John W. Ritchie, N.S.
J. Ambrose Shea, Nfld.
William H. Steeves, N.B.
Sir Etienne-Paschal Taché,
   Canada
Samuel Leonard Tilley, N.B.
Charles Tupper, N.S.

John M. Johnson, N.B.   Edward Whelan, P.E.I.
Hector L. Langevin, Canada   R. D. Wilmot, N.B.

160. *One occasionally hears the words "Canada First." What do they signify?*

"Canada First" was the name of a political, social, and literary movement founded in Ottawa in 1868 by a group of enthusiasts who wanted to foster national pride. It was a response to Confederation, which had occurred one year earlier, and the immediate result was a flowering of poetry written on national themes and expressing patriotic sentiments. Such writers as Sir Charles G. D. Roberts, Bliss Carman, W. W. Campbell, Archibald Lampman, and Duncan Campbell Scott responded to the felt need. The political leader Edward Blake delivered his noted "Aurora Speech" in 1874 at Aurora, Ont., about the need for national ideals. The educator George Munro Grant travelled across the country and wrote an inspired travelogue, *Ocean to Ocean* (1873), which is perhaps the peak of the Canada First movement's influence. The spark glowed for a decade or so and then died out, never to be long rekindled.

161. *Who are the Métis? What is the meaning of the word?*

The Métis are people of the prairies who trace their descent back to Cree and Ojibwa women and French fur traders. The French called them Métis, or "half-breed." They were also known among the French as the *bois-brûlés*, the "charred-wood" people because of their characteristic swarthy complexion. Engaged in the primary occupations — fishing, hunting, trapping, agriculture — they sought to preserve their traditional way of life by asserting territorial rights in the Red River Rebellion in 1870 and the North West Rebellion of 1884–85.

Today, the Métis are recognized, along with the Inuit and the Indians, as a "founding people." The term "Métis" is now applied to any Indian of mixed blood.

162. *When did the two so-called Riel rebellions occur?*

The two rebellions of the Métis people led by Louis Riel are properly called the Red River Rebellion and the North West Rebellion. Riel and his followers occupied Fort Garry in January, 1870, four months before the incorporation into Canada of the Province of Manitoba. With the arrival of the expeditionary force under General Garnet Wolseley in August, the Rebellion collapsed.

The North West Rebellion may be dated from Riel's arrival in Batoche in July, 1884. Here he established his Métis headquarters, more than two decades before the creation of the Province of Saskatchewan. Hostilities broke out in March, 1885. There were a number of skirmishes and pitched battles with the forces of General Frederick Middleton. But in two months the Rebellion was over.

163. *Was Louis Riel mad?*

Louis Riel (1844–1885), the Métis leader, was the central figure in the Red River Rebellion and the North West Rebellion. There is no easy answer to the question of his sanity, although he did spend some time in a mental hospital. The feeling in English Canada was that Riel was crazy to rebel against civil authority. The feeling in French Canada was that his actions, however precipitous, represented French interests in the West. The Métis responded to his charismatic leadership, and he saw himself as divinely inspired and "the Prophet of the New World." As well, he was a poet, a mystic, and a man with an overriding sense of mission. It has been argued that he did not act treasonously during the Red River Rebellion, as the Canadian government had no legal claim on the Métis land. It has also been argued that he should not have been hanged following the North West Rebellion, as he was an American and not a Canadian citizen at the time. The federal government, while recognizing his unique importance to Canada as an exemplar of minority rights, has steadfastly refused to pardon him for his acts.

164. *Should Louis Riel be posthumously pardoned?*

In 1979 the Association of Métis and Non-Status Indians of Saskatchewan petitioned the federal government to grant a posthumous pardon to Louis Riel. The association advanced nine reasons why the government should show mercy. These ranged from the fact that Riel acted out of conviction that he was advancing the recognition of the rights of his people to the suggestion that a pardon would renew the faith of the Métis people in their quest for social justice.

The government chose not to act on the petition. Should Riel be pardoned for his act of high treason? The question was asked by Thomas Flanagan in *Riel and the Rebellion of 1885 Reconsidered* (1983). "My opinion is that such a pardon would be a mistake," he wrote, arguing that such an act would be a "sentimental gesture" at best. In Flanagan's view, Riel was guilty of the offence of high treason, as he could have acted otherwise in the circumstances, and he did receive a fair trial.

165. *Who was Gabriel Dumont?*

The colourful Gabriel Dumont (1838–1906) was Riel's "adjutant general" in the North West Rebellion, gaining victories against the British regulars and Canadian militia in skirmishes at Duck Lake and Fish Creek in 1885. Dumont has been acknowledged to be a brilliant strategist and tactician. With the collapse of the Rebellion, he fled to the United States, where he became a star performer in Buffalo Bill's Wild West Show. Following the general amnesty, he returned to western Canada and died at Batoche, the headquarters at the time of the Rebellion.

166. *What is the meaning of the rallying cry, "Stand fast, Craigellachie!"?*

When George Stephen, president of the CPR, was in England encountering difficulty raising badly needed capital, he received this message, cabled to him in November, 1884, by Donald Smith (later Lord Strathcona), a CPR director in Montreal. It referred to the mighty rock near their birthplaces in northern Scotland. It bolstered Stephen's confidence until the funding came through. Consequently, the spot where the Last Spike was driven home was named Craigellachie.

167. What was the Pacific Scandal?

The Pacific Scandal was the controversy concerning corruption in the awarding of the charter to construct the Canadian Pacific Railway. Liberals charged that railroad financier Sir Hugh Allan received the charter in exchange for a secret donation of $179,000 to the Conservatives in the 1872 election, and a royal commission substantiated the charge. Prime Minister Sir John A. Macdonald, the Conservative leader, spoke in the House of Commons on November 3, 1873, in his own defence, but resigned two days later. It was — and remains — the most scandalous of Canadian scandals.

168. What was "the National Dream"?

The construction of the Canadian Pacific Railway across the western half of the North American continent in the 1880s was described by Pierre Berton as the realization of "the National Dream." The grand undertaking is the subject of his two-volume history, *The National Dream* (1970) and *The Last Spike* (1971).

The Canadian Pacific Railway was incorporated on February 16, 1881. The Last Spike was driven home on November 7, 1885. One of the terms on which British Columbia agreed to enter Confederation was the construction of a transcontinental railway.

169. What was the fate of the original "Last Spike"?

No one is certain of its whereabouts, although Pierre Berton in his CPR history tells of its possible fate. There were two plain iron spikes associated with the driving-home ceremony that marked the completion of the CPR at Craigellachie, B.C., November 7, 1885. Donald Smith, misjudging his blow, bent the first. He expropriated the spike and had it cut into strips and presented them to wives of the dignitaries present at the ceremony.

Smith drove the second spike home. In order to foil souvenir hunters, the roadmaster removed it after the ceremony and passed it on to CPR president Edward Beatty. It was stolen from his desk. There is a possibility that the last spike is in the possession of a resident of Yellowknife known to Berton but that it has been reworked into the shape of a carving knife.

170. *In which three areas did Sir John A. Macdonald's National Policy supply a federal initiative?*

Tariffs, the railway, and immigration were the three main areas affected by Prime Minister Sir John A. Macdonald's National Policy, first advocated in the House of Commons on March 12, 1878. It proposed to introduce protective tariffs to foster local agriculture, mining, and manufacturing; it promised to complete the transcontinental railway to promote a national economy; it sought to encourage immigration to the West to build up markets for Canadian manufactured goods.

171. *When did mass settlement of the prairies begin?*

Mass settlement of the virgin lands of the prairies may be symbolically dated with the arrival of a group of 107 settlers from the Ukraine at Quebec City, April 30, 1896. They were led by Joseph Oleskiw, who took them by train to the Northwest. These were the first immigrants from Eastern Europe — "the men in sheepskin coats" — to farm in the West.

172. *When did the Klondike Gold Rush begin?*

The Klondike Gold Rush of 1896 drew thousands of prospectors

and adventurers to the Yukon. It began with the discovery of gold
on the bank of Bonanza Creek, a tributary of the Klondike River,
August 17, 1896. The three prospectors who made the strike were
George Carmack, Skookum Jim, and Tagish Charlie.

173. What was the Alaska Boundary Award and why was it so controversial and contentious an issue?

Alaska was acquired by the United States from Russia in 1867,
but the boundary line between the Alaska Panhandle and the west
coast of British Columbia remained unclear. This became a matter
of some moment during the Klondike Gold Rush in 1896 when
both the American and Canadian governments sought jurisdiction. An international joint commission was established in 1903 to
decide the issue. Its "six impartial jurists of repute" consisted of
three American members, two Canadian members, and the British commissioner, Lord Alverstone. Two of the three American
members expressed their pro-American views in advance and
threatened the use of force if they were not met. Alverstone
deferred, the Canadian members dissented, and the Award went
to the United States. The decision of the commission was resented
and regarded as a British betrayal of Canadian interests to Americans. Alverstone's name was turned into a verb. To be "Alver-
stoned" was to be sold out.

174. What is the significance in Canadian life of the British military cry, "Ready, aye, ready"?

The traditional British answer to the call to arms is "Ready, aye,
ready." It was sounded in Canada in 1896, in 1914, and in 1922,
when the British government turned to the Canadian government
for military solidarity. During the Chanak Crisis of 1922 in Turkey, Britain cabled Ottawa to ask for troops. The Mackenzie King
administration cabled no reply, and no war broke out, but Opposition leader Arthur Meighen complained: "When Britain's message came, then Canada should have said: 'Ready, aye, ready; we

stand by you.' " The phrase, today at least, smacks of militaristic jingoism.

175. *What was the greatest Canadian battle of World War I?*

According to military historian George F. G. Stanley, "The battle of Vimy Ridge was the first of the great assaults of 1917 in which the Canadians took part. For Canada it was the greatest battle of the war. Vimy Ridge may not have been the hardest fought or the most strategically significant battle of the War of 1914–18, but it was important to Canada as the first exclusively Canadian victory. For the first time a major operation was carried out by the Canadian Corps with all four divisions attacking simultaneously. Its success was a tribute to officers and men alike to their cohesion and *esprit de corps*, to the careful planning, the co-ordination of all arms, the thorough training and rehearsal which preceded the launching of the assault." Vimy Ridge, in northern France, was taken on Easter Monday, April 9, 1917.

176. *Were there more Canadian casualties in World War I or in World War II?*

There were more casualties in World War I than in World War II. Of the 626,636 Canadian officers and men from all services who fought in the Great War, 59,769 lost their lives. Of the total 730,625 men and women who saw service with the Canadian Army, the Royal Canadian Navy, and the Royal Canadian Air Force during World War II, the total casualties were 41,992.

177. *When was Prohibition?*

Prohibition was the period during which the sale of alcoholic beverages was prohibited in Canada. It commenced as a temporary war measure with an Act to Amend the Canada Temperance Act, given assent May 18, 1916. Bootlegging and speakeasies were the order of the day. The provinces individually returned to the sale of liquor under provincial licence and local option in the 1920s. The province to hold out the longest was Prince Edward Island, which restricted the sale of alcoholic beverages until 1948.

178. When did the Winnipeg General Strike break out?

The Winnipeg General Strike began on May 15, and ended on June 26, 1919. A strike over union recognition and collective bargaining escalated until over twenty-two thousand workers, including civic and government employees, left their jobs. Although the strike collapsed with the intervention of the Mounted Police, it marked a new western radical spirit. It was the only general strike to occur in Canadian history.

179. What was the Balfour Report and how did it affect Canada?

The Balfour Report was a resolution that defined Great Britain and the self-governing dominions as "autonomous communities within the British Empire, equal in status." It was moved by the British parliamentarian Arthur Balfour and adopted at the Imperial Conference on November 18, 1926. The notion of autonomy and equality of status was embodied in the Statute of Westminster of 1931.

180. In what ways did the Depression affect Canada?

The economy of Canada and of the world was severely affected by the Depression, which commenced with the crash of the stock market on Wall Street on October 29, 1929, and concluded a decade later with the outbreak of World War II. Canadians were hit hard, especially those in the West. At the same time, the prairies suffered an unprecedented drought that produced "dust bowl" conditions. These years were indeed "the Dirty Thirties."

Farmers were ruined, labourers were unemployed. Many single men ended up in relief camps. An On-to-Ottawa Trek was organized in 1935 to protest these conditions. The thirties saw the birth of such political parties as Social Credit and the CCF.

181. *When did the British Empire become the Commonwealth of Nations?*

The British Empire, a collective term for territories under the British Crown, is generally dated from 1583, when Sir Humphrey Gilbert claimed Newfoundland as England's first overseas colony, to the passing of the Statute of Westminster in 1931. The latter date is taken to be the inception of the Commonwealth of Nations, a free association of sovereign independent states — together with colonies, protectorates, protected states, mandated and trust territories — united by a common allegiance to the British Crown.

The Commonwealth embraces more than forty-nine sovereign states and covers one quarter of the earth's land surface. Annual Commonwealth Conferences and Games are held. "The sun never sets on the British Empire," it used to be said. Malcolm Muggeridge, the English writer, added, "And it never rose on the Commonwealth."

182. *Who were the Mac-Paps?*

The Mac-Paps were members of the Mackenzie-Papineau Battalion of the XVth International Brigade of the Spanish Republican Army which battled Franco's fight for total control of Spain. The Battalion was formed of Canadian volunteers as part of the Popular Front against the Nationalist forces in 1937. When the Spanish Civil War was lost, members of the Battalion returned to Canada in 1939. Because the Republican Army was believed to be a revolutionary force and because Spain's political alignment was unclear, the Mac-Paps have been denied veteran status to this day and at one time were incorrectly branded as communists. The Battalion's name honoured the nineteenth-century rebels William Lyon Mackenzie and Louis-Joseph Papineau. Approximately 1,250 idealistic Canadians fought in the Spanish Civil War.

183. *Who is the best-known Canadian in China?*

The most famous Canadian in the People's Republic of China is

Norman Bethune (1890–1939). The medical doctor was born in Gravenhurst, Ont., practised medicine in Montreal, and served in the Spanish Civil War. In Madrid, he organized the world's first mobile blood-transfusion service. Early in 1938, he joined the Eighth Route Army of the Chinese Communists in the hills of Yenan, where he formed the world's first mobile medical unit. He died of an infection from operating. With the formation of the People's Republic of China a decade later, and the publication by Mao Tse-tung of an essay which extols Bethune's "boundless sense of responsibility," the Canadian doctor emerged as a leading hero and martyr. There are monuments and memorials to him throughout China. In Canada, the family home in Gravenhurst is now a museum, and the Chinese government donated a statue of Bethune which stands in downtown Montreal.

184. Was Canada invaded during World War II?

Canada was not invaded during World War II, but the country was attacked. A Japanese submarine fired shells at the lighthouse on Estevan Point, on the west coast of Vancouver Island, on June 20, 1942. Later that summer, two German U-boats wreaked havoc in the St. Lawrence River. Japanese weather balloons loaded with explosives were carried over the West Coast, some landing in British Columbia and the prairies. A German submarine landed at Martin Bay on the northern tip of Labrador in late 1943, where technicians established a battery-operated weather station. It provided Germany with weather-pattern reports about North Atlantic shipping lanes. The station relayed information for a three-month period before its batteries went dead. The remains were located on August 1, 1981, by an expedition mounted by the Department of National Defence, which was contacted by one of the surviving U-boat officers who was curious about the fate of the installation.

185. *What expression of Mackenzie King's is associated with conscription?*

Conscription, or the compulsory drafting of people for military service, was a divisive issue during the two world wars. The feeling, particularly in Quebec, was that the government should rely on volunteers, not the draft, for manpower. Prime Minister Mackenzie King tried to appease both proponents and opponents of conscription in the House of Commons on June 10, 1942, when he first used his celebrated expression, "Not necessarily conscription, but conscription if necessary."

186. *What tragedy occurred on August 19, 1942?*

August 19, 1942, was the date of the Dieppe raid. On that day 4,963 officers and men of the 2nd Canadian Division, accompanied by more than a thousand British Commandos, launched a full-scale raid on the German-held seaport of Dieppe in northern France. The raid lacked surprise and the invading force withdrew under fire. The German 302nd Division counted 333 casualties. The total Canadian casualties were 3,367 and 946 Canadians were taken prisoner. The codename was Operation Jubilee. It was truly "a brave and bitter day."

187. *Which ship typified the Royal Canadian Navy in the Battle of the Atlantic?*

The corvette, a class of coastal escort ship developed early in World War II, came to typify the Royal Canadian Navy in the Battle of the Atlantic. Its sea-keeping qualities rendered it invaluable in its unintended role as an ocean escort vessel. A typical unit was 62 m, or 205 feet, in length with the main armament one 4-inch gun. In all, 123 corvettes served with the RCN.

188. *Who attended the two Quebec Conferences?*

The Quebec Conferences were top-level meetings held in Quebec City during World War II. The first was held in August, 1943, the second in September, 1944. These summits were attended by the British and American wartime leaders — Prime Minister Winston Churchill and President Franklin Delano Roosevelt — as Combined Chiefs of Staff. Canada was not represented but Prime Minister Mackenzie King attended as "host."

189. *When did the Cold War begin and what was Canada's role?*

The beginning of the so-called Cold War between the Soviet Union and the Western World may be symbolically dated from the evening of September 5, 1945, when Igor Gouzenko (1919–1984), a Russian cipher clerk, defected from the Soviet Embassy in Ottawa, taking with him 109 carefully selected documents. They established the existence of a Soviet spy ring operating in North America and led to the conviction of several supposed agents. Gouzenko's autobiography, *This Was My Choice* (1948), was filmed later that year as *The Iron Curtain*, with Dana Andrews as Gouzenko.

190. *Who is "the only living Father of Confederation"?*

The Fathers of Confederation total thirty-six — thirty-seven with the inclusion of Joseph R. (Joey) Smallwood (b. 1900). He led the pro-Confederation forces in his native Newfoundland and saw the Great Island cease to be Britain's oldest colony and become Canada's youngest province on March 31, 1949. He became its first premier and served in that capacity until 1971. He was dubbed "the only living Father of Confederation" by the St. John's humorist Ray Guy.

191. *What was the slogan of Quebec's Quiet Revolution?*

The so-called Quiet Revolution, identified with the administration

(1960–66) of Jean Lesage, saw the transformation of Quebec society. Its slogan was *Maîtres chez nous*, which means "Masters in our own house." Adoption of the slogan is attributed to one of Lesage's chief ministers, René Lévesque.

192. *Who were the Three Wise Men of Quebec?*
The so-called Three Wise Men of Quebec were Jean Marchand, Gérard Pelletier, and Pierre Elliott Trudeau, leading intellectual figures in Quebec. They held federalist rather than separatist views. In order to represent Quebec's best interest in Confederation, they entered federal politics in the early 1960s. Their brand of federalism is associated with the early years of the Trudeau administration, which commenced in 1968.

193. *What was Charles de Gaulle's celebrated utterance from the balcony of Montreal's City Hall?*
The President of the French Republic used the following words in a speech from the balcony of Montreal's City Hall on July 24, 1967: "Vive le Québec! Vive le Québec libre!" In doing so, he voiced the Quebec separatist slogan which translates: "Long live a free Quebec!" The use of the slogan in an official speech seemed to signify the French Republic's acceptance of the separatist claim that Quebec was oppressed and unfree.

194. *What was the FLQ? What were its objectives?*
The FLQ — *Le Front de Libération du Québec* (The Quebec Liberation Front) — was a terrorist organization dedicated to obtaining at any cost the independence of Quebec from the rest of Canada. It was formed in secret in Montreal in 1960. In April, 1963, it issued its manifesto, which called for an end to "Anglo-Saxon colonization" of French Canada and "Revolution by the people, for the people, independence or death." Mailboxes in Montreal's Westmount district and federal buildings were blown up. It is doubtful that the FLQ had many members, but many

outside the clandestine organization approved of its objectives if not of its methods.

195. *What was the October Crisis?*

The October Crisis was a two-month period of terror in Quebec. It began on October 5, 1970, when a cell of the FLQ kidnapped James Cross, a British consular official, from his Montreal home and demanded, among other things, the release of terrorists held in custody. On October 10, a second FLQ cell seized Pierre Laporte, Quebec Minister of Labour. On October 16, the federal government invoked the War Measures Act, banning the FLQ, sending the armed forces into Quebec, and arresting and detaining great numbers of known and suspected separatists, FLQ supporters, and other citizens. The following day, Laporte was strangled. Gradually the federal forces gained the upper hand. Cross was released on December 3, with the provision of safe passage for the kidnappers to Cuba. Members of the second cell were captured later that month and charged with murder.

196. *During the October Crisis, the government invoked the War Measures Act. What is the purpose of the Act?*

The War Measures Act grants the government emergency powers in the event of "war, invasion, or insurrection, real or apprehended." It rests on a section of the BNA Act that states that the government has the power to make laws for "peace, order, and good government," and it grants the federal cabinet authority to override provincial authority and civil liberties for the duration of the emergency.

Although the War Measures Act was invoked for the duration of the two world wars, the only time it has been used in peacetime was during the October Crisis of 1970. The government justified its course of action by maintaining that a state of "apprehended insurrection" existed. Critics of the government's action could find no proof to justify the extreme measures taken. The irony is that the government was headed by Prime Minister Pierre Elliott Trudeau, a noted civil libertarian. The issue is still a lively one and widely debated.

197. *What was the Canadian Caper?*

The Canadian Caper is one part of the Iranian hostage incident. The U.S. Embassy in Teheran was occupied by student radicals on November 4, 1979. Six American citizens, fearful of arrest, appealed to Canadian authorities for asylum. Kenneth Taylor, Canada's ambassador, sheltered them as ''houseguests'' for two months until he was able to spirit them out of the country with Canadian passports. He then closed the Canadian Embassy. The Canadian Caper was revealed to the world on January 29, 1980.

198. *What act grants access to government records?*

The Access to Information Act, passed in 1983, is the statute by which any Canadian citizen or permanent resident of Canada has the right to examine and obtain copies of records held by federal government institutions. Exempt or excluded from scrutiny is information on national security, trade secrets, Cabinet documents, and otherwise readily available facts and figures. The Act creates the office of the Information Commissioner. Libraries and post offices have an Access Register, which describes and locates government records, and information request forms.

The Privacy Act, also passed in 1983, is the statute that sets conditions for the collection, retention, and disposal of personal information by federal government institutions. It also provides a useful disclosure code for the protection of this information, thus establishing the confidentiality of information in government records. It permits the individual to request a correction of untrue or misleading information. Prohibited by the act is the disclosure of information concerned with national security and law enforcement. The Privacy Act creates the position of the Privacy Commissioner.

3. PLACES

199. *Is there a place called Canada in Canada?*

There is no place called Canada in the Dominion of Canada, but there is a Canada Bay on the eastern shore of northern Newfoundland, as well as three Canada Creeks in the Maritimes (in New Brunswick's Albert County, in Nova Scotia near Kentville, and in the Tyre Valley of Prince Edward Island).

Elsewhere in the world there are other Canadas. In New York State, there is the town of Canadaway as well as Canada Lake, Canadarego Lake, and West Canadian River. A town in Pennsylvania is called Canadensis. Canadian is the name of a town in Texas located on the Canadian River.

Cañada de Gomez, Cañada Honda, and Cañada Verde are three towns in central Argentina. These are not references to our Canada, for the word *cañada* in Spanish means "canyon."

Kanada is the name of a district in southwest India, the name of the Dravidian language spoken by its 18 million people, and the name of a second-century Hindu philosopher.

Finally, *Kanaka* is a Polynesian word used by the Polynesians to describe themselves. It means "man."

200. *What are provinces and territories?*

A province is one of the political divisions of Canada. In figurative terms, a "realm" is divided into "provinces." The concept of a province having certain rights and sharing others with a federal government dates from Confederation.

In addition, Canada has two territories. A "territory" is a

region which has yet to achieve the status of a province, being administered directly by the federal government.

The head of a provincial government is a premier. The head of a territorial government is a commissioner.

201. What is the shortest official place name in Canada? The longest?

There is no single shortest official place name. The shortest are single-letter names of geographical features, and there are a number of these, including A Lake in New Brunswick and Lac Y in Quebec. The shortest place names for populated places are three-letter place names, and these are numerous, including Ayr and Emo, both in Ontario.

Longest official place names may be divided into those that are multiple-word and those that are single-word. The longest multiple-word place name is for the New Brunswick river: Lower North Branch Little Southwest Miramichi River. The longest single-word place name record-holder is the body of water in northern Manitoba called: Pekwachnamaykoskwaskwaypinwanik Lake. The name is thirty-one letters long.

202. Four provinces have names derived from Indian words. What do the words mean?

The four provinces with names derived from Indian words are Manitoba, Ontario, Quebec, and Saskatchewan.

Manitoba comes from the Cree *manito-wapow*, "the strait of the spirit" (a reference to the narrows of Lake Manitoba). Ontario derives from an Algonkian word — either *Onitariio*, meaning "beautiful lake," or *Kanadario*, "sparkling water." Quebec recalls *kebek*, the Algonkian word for "strait" or "narrow passage." Saskatchewan comes from the Cree *Kisiskatchewani Sipi*, meaning "swift current." (Thus the province and the city of Swift Current derive from the same Cree place name.)

203. *Are there any World Heritage Sites in Canada?*
World Heritage Sites are regions recognized by the United Nations Educational, Scientific, and Cultural Organization (UNESCO) as possessing national and cultural properties of outstanding universal value. UNESCO recognized 164 sites in seventy-eight countries by 1984. There are eight Canadian World Heritage Sites: L'Anse aux Meadows National Historic Park, Nfld.; Dinosaur Provincial Park, Alta.; Head-Smashed-in Bison Jump, Alta.; Wood Buffalo National Park, Alta. and N.W.T.; Anthony Island Provincial Park, B.C.; Burgess Shale, Yoho National Park, B.C.; Kluane National Park, Y.T.; Nahanni National Park, N.W.T.

204. *Is there a difference between the Maritime provinces and the Atlantic provinces?*
Yes, there is a difference. The Maritime provinces is a collective term for three provinces (Nova Scotia, New Brunswick, Prince Edward Island), whereas the Atlantic provinces is a collective term, in use since the mid-1900s, for four provinces (the above three plus Newfoundland).

205. *Which is Canada's most easterly province?*
Canada's most easterly province is Newfoundland. Once Britain's oldest overseas colony, it became Canada's tenth and youngest province on March 31, 1949.

206. *Which is the most easterly city in North America?*
The most easterly city in North America is St. John's, which is located on the east coast of Newfoundland, of which it is the capital. Founded in 1583, it was incorporated as a city in 1888. It claims to be the oldest inhabited town in North America.

207. *What is Newfoundland's second-largest city?*
Corner Brook, situated at the mouth of the Humber River on the

west coast of the island, is Newfoundland's largest city after St. John's.

208. *What are outports?*

Outports are small, isolated fishing villages that dot the coast of Newfoundland. Many of these communities have been abandoned or closed down. It was provincial government policy in the 1950s and 1960s to relocate villagers of some of the more remote outports. Some five hundred outports remain to this day.

Perhaps the best-known outport (to mainlanders, at least) is Burgeo, a community of 2,500 on the south coast. Farley Mowat and his wife Claire wrote books about their life there in the mid-1960s.

209. *Why does every Newfoundlander know Cape St. Mary's?*

Newfoundlanders know about Cape St. Mary's, the small fishing community on the southwest tip of the Avalon Peninsula, because the outport is celebrated in one of the most moving and popular of Newfoundland songs. "Let Me Fish off Cape St. Mary's" was written in 1947 by Otto Kelland, the balladeer. The final verse runs: "Take me back to that snug green cover/Where the seas roll up their thunder./There let me rest in the earth's cool breast,/Where the stars shine out their wonder,/And the seas roll up their thunder."

210. *Newfoundland is famed for its peculiar place names. What are some of them?*

Perhaps the most astonishing of place names is Dildo, a village west of Bay Roberts in the Avalon Peninsula. In addition to plain Dildo, there are Dildo Arm, Dildo Cove, Dildo Islands, Dildo Pond, Dildo Run, and Dildo South.

Nearby will be found such features as Spread Eagle Bay, Tickle Bay, Broad Cove, Heart's Delight, Heart's Desire, Fitter's Cove, and Breakheart Point.

Finally, in the vicinity of Conception Bay, are such names as Blow Me Down Bluff, Burnt Stump, Ballyhack, Cupids, Pick Eyes, and Bareneed. Hibbs Hole, considered too indelicate even for Newfoundlanders, was officially changed to Hibbs Cove.

"Great Islanders" are uninhibited poets when it comes to place names.

211. Is Labrador part of Newfoundland or Quebec?

Politically Labrador is part of Newfoundland, but geographically it is part of Quebec. It has been under Newfoundland's jurisdiction since 1763, except when annexed to Quebec in 1774–1809. The present boundaries were established by the British Privy Council in 1927. The "British" decision still rankles in Quebec.

212. What is the easternmost of the mainland provinces?

Nova Scotia, the easternmost of the mainland provinces, consists of a peninsula off the mainland and Cape Breton Island, which is connected to the peninsula by the Canso Causeway. It became part of the newly created Dominion of Canada on July 1, 1867.

213. Who described Halifax as "The Warden of the North"?

An important naval port and military base, as well as the capital of Nova Scotia, Halifax was described as a "Warden" by Rudyard Kipling. In a poem called "The Song of the Cities" published in 1896, he referred to Halifax as "The Warden of the Honour of the North." It is the largest city in the Atlantic provinces.

214. Which city is linked with Halifax by a ferry system and two bridges?

Dartmouth, which lies across the harbour from Halifax, is linked with the Nova Scotian capital by a ferry system and two bridges. Dartmouth became a city in 1961.

215. *In which province will the Cabot Trail be found?*
The Cabot Trail, one of the most scenic drives in North America, skirts the northern half of Cape Breton Island, N.S. It offers tourists vistas of sea and highland, Acadian and Scottish settlements, and excursions to Baddeck, Glace Bay, and Louisbourg. The trail is about 457 km, or 284 miles, long and was named after the explorer John Cabot, who first sighted the Cape Breton coast in 1497.

216. *Is there buried treasure on Oak Island?*
No one knows whether there is buried treasure on Oak Island. Certainly no known treasure cache has ever been found, but some evidence has been excavated to suggest that there once was a wooden well or "money pit" on the island. Excavations have gone on intermittently since 1795. The theory is that the buccaneer Captain Kidd, who was hanged for piracy in 1701, buried his treasure cache on Oak Island, which lies in Mahone Bay off the Atlantic coast of Nova Scotia, southwest of Halifax. But this is only a theory. No doubt speculation — and excavation — will continue.

217. *Where is the most picturesque spot in the country?*
By common agreement among painters and photographers, the most picturesque spot in the country is Peggys Cove, a small fishing village southwest of Halifax, N.S. The sea, wharfs, trim cottages, and slender sailing vessels combine to create a charming picture. Most painters and photographers spell the place name "Peggy's Cove," with an apostrophe, but not the Canadian Permanent Committee on Geographical Names, which officially spells it without the apostrophe.

218. *Which island is known as "the graveyard of the Atlantic"?*
Sable Island, in the Atlantic Ocean east of Halifax, is known as

"the graveyard of the Atlantic" because so many ships have been wrecked there owing to unexpected shallows and the storms common in the area.

Anticosti Island, in the Gulf of St. Lawrence, is known as "the graveyard of the Gulf" for the same reasons.

219. *Which is the largest city on Cape Breton Island?*
The largest city on Cape Breton Island is Sydney, N.S., on the northeastern coast.

220. *Which province shares boundaries with Quebec and the State of Maine?*
New Brunswick is bounded by Quebec to the north and by the State of Maine on the west. It is connected to Nova Scotia by the narrow Chignecto Isthmus. New Brunswick was one of the four original colonies that formed the Dominion of Canada on July 1, 1867.

221. *Which New Brunswick city was originally known as Sainte-Anne?*
Fredericton, the capital of New Brunswick, was originally an Acadian settlement called Sainte-Anne. With the arrival of the Loyalists it was named Fredericktown. (The "k" and the "w" were soon dropped.) Fredericton was incorporated in 1848.

222. *Which Canadian city was the first to be incorporated?*
The first city to be incorporated was Saint John, N.B., which received its articles of incorporation in 1785. It is the largest city in New Brunswick. The spelling of its name is frequently confused with that of St. John's, the capital of Newfoundland.

223. *Where is Campobello Island and with which American president is it associated?*
Campobello Island is the largest of a group of small islands in Passamaquoddy Bay, which flows into the Bay of Fundy. Although politically part of New Brunswick, the island is closer to the United States than to Canada and is linked with Maine by the Roosevelt International Bridge. The southern portion of the island is known as Roosevelt Campobello International Park, for here, in a thirty-two-room summer home, U.S. President Franklin Delano Roosevelt (1882–1945) spent the summers of his youth. He always referred to Campobello as his ''Beloved Island.''

224. *Which province has only one city?*
Prince Edward Island has numerous towns and villages but only one city. That city is its capital, Charlottetown, the ''Cradle of Confederation.'' Here, in 1864, the first of the pre-Confederation conferences was held. The province is known as the Garden of the Gulf both for its strong agricultural base and for its position in the Gulf of St. Lawrence.

225. *Where will you find the following familiar lines: "Providence being their guide/They builded better than they knew"?*
These lines are inscribed on the bronze plaque, unveiled July 1, 1927, to mark the place in the Legislative Chamber, Government House, Charlottetown, P.E.I., where the basis was established for the confederation of the British North American colonies. Above the lines this explanation appears: ''In the hearts and minds of the delegates who assembled in this room on September 1, 1864, was born the Dominion of Canada.'' Then follow the familiar lines, a powerful pastiche of words taken from the English poet John Milton and the American essayist Ralph Waldo Emerson.

226. *Which is the oldest and largest of the provinces?*
Quebec, the oldest of the provinces, was proclaimed a province
by the British in 1763. The largest of the provinces, it became part
of the Dominion of Canada on July 1, 1867. The capital is Quebec
City, founded by the Indians as Stadacona, and settled by the
French as Quebec. It is the only walled city in North America
north of Mexico.

227. *Who gave the St. Lawrence River its name?*
The honour of naming the St. Lawrence River must go to Jacques
Cartier, the navigator, who gave the name St-Laurent to a small
bay in the Gulf of St. Lawrence. He named the bay after the saint
whose feast was celebrated on the day of its naming, August 10,
1535.

St. Lawrence was a martyr. To the Romans who were roasting
him alive on a gridiron, he exclaimed: "My flesh is well cooked
on one side; turn the other, and eat."

228. *What is the Micmac word for "end" or "extremity"?*
The Micmac word for "end" or "extremity" is *Gaspé*, which
has been applied to a number of features, including a peninsula,
cape, bay, basin, town, and county in southeastern Quebec. Off
the Gaspé Peninsula is Percé Rock.

229. *What is the meaning of* percé, *as in Percé Rock?*
Percé is French for "pierced." The rock off the eastern tip of
Gaspé Peninsula was so described by Samuel de Champlain in
1607. He used the word "pierced" to describe the gap in the rock
at water level.

230. *Where were Stadacona and Hochelaga?*
Stadacona and Hochelaga were Iroquois settlements visited by

Jacques Cartier on his second voyage of 1535. Stadacona was located on the site of Quebec City, and Hochelaga on the site of Montreal. Both words survive as names of municipal and electoral districts.

231. *What is so historic about Jacquet House in Quebec City?*
Jacquet House, built 1675–76, is the oldest house in Quebec City. The thick-walled residence was once occupied by the literary figure Philippe-Joseph Aubert de Gaspé and for many years has housed Aux Anciens Canadiens, a restaurant that specializes in authentic French-Canadian cuisine.

232. *What is the symbol of the Quebec Winter Carnival?*
The symbol of the Quebec Winter Carnival is a two-metre, or seven-foot, snowman named variously Jean Bonhomme or Bonhomme Carnaval. The figure is carried through the streets of Quebec City, and a statue of him stands before the central tourism office. The Quebec *Carnaval* was first held in 1894. Current festivities, held in late February or early March, date from the revival in 1954.

233. *How many rivers are there at Trois-Rivières?*
Only two. The descriptive place name derives from the fact that Trois-Rivières, Que., is located at the point where the St. Maurice River meets the St. Lawrence River. The St. Maurice forms a delta with three branches, described as "rivers." The city is an important pulp and paper centre.

234. *Is there really a place called Saint-Louis-du-Ha! Ha!?*
A community on the south shore of the St. Lawrence, inland from Rivière-du-Loup, Que., bears this unusual name. It was named to honour St. Louis and the memory of Louis Marquis, the first

settler. It has been suggested that Saint-Louis-du-Ha! Ha! is the only place name in the world with an official designation that includes two exclamation marks.

235. *How high is Montreal's Mount Royal?*
Montreal is dominated by Mount Royal, an extinct volcano, which rises above sea level 233 m, or 764 feet. Atop the mountain, which overlooks the Island of Montreal, is a giant illuminated cross visible from up to 80 km, or 50 miles.

236. *What is the Château Ramezay?*
The Château Ramezay, in Old Montreal, is an old and pleasing stone building built in 1705 by Governor Claude de Ramezay. It served as the official residence of the governor and then the intendant; as the headquarters for the army of the Continental Congress which occupied Montreal; as quarters for Université Laval; and now as an historical museum devoted to its many uses.

237. *What is Montreal's oldest standing monument?*
The Nelson Column in Old Montreal is the city's oldest standing monument. Erected in 1809 in honour of Lord Horatio Nelson, it was, ironically, the first tribute paid anywhere to the English admiral who was victorious over the French.

238. *Where are Westmount and Outremont?*
Westmount and Outremont are affluent residential districts in Montreal. They take their names from their position in regard to Mount Royal, Westmount being on the western slope, Outremont being on the northern slope. Traditionally, the former is Anglo-Saxon, the latter French.

239. *What is Place Ville Marie?*
Place Ville Marie is one of the largest integrated office and shop-ping complexes in North America. It is in downtown Montreal and was designed by I. M. Pei for William Zeckendorf and the Royal Bank of Canada. It opened in 1962. Three times the size of New York's Rockefeller Plaza, the entire complex contains more rental space than the Empire State Building. The daytime ''popu-lation'' of the underground concourse and the forty-two-storey, cruciform Royal Bank Building is 25,000.

240. *What are Quebec's Eastern Townships east of?*
Quebec's picturesque Eastern Townships are eleven townships east of the Richelieu River and south of the St. Lawrence River. The region of rural charm is known in French as *Les Cantons de l'Estrie.*

241. *Which province has the greatest population?*
Although second in size to Quebec, Ontario is the first of the provinces in population. Ontario became part of the Dominion of Canada on July 1, 1867. The capital is Toronto, the largest city in Canada.

242. *What is the meaning of the name Ottawa?*
Ottawa, the nation's capital, takes its name from the Algonkian word *adawe*, which means ''to trade'' or ''to barter.'' This seems an appropriate meaning for the name of the city which, above all others, is concerned with commerce and the economy, not to mention interests and influence.

243. *Who chose Ottawa to be the nation's capital?*
Queen Victoria selected Ottawa to be the permanent capital of the

Province of Canada on December 31, 1857. She is reported to have said, pointing to a map, "That is the place." The original name of Ottawa was Bytown, after Colonel John By of the Royal Engineers who built the Rideau Canal. It officially became Bytown in 1847, the city of Ottawa in 1855, a capital city in 1857, and the capital of Canada on July 1, 1867.

244. Which city was built to be the capital of Canada?

Kingston, on the St. Lawrence River, at the eastern end of Lake Ontario, was built to be the capital of Canada. In 1783 it was given the name Kingston to honour King George III.

245. How many Parliament Buildings are there?

There are three Parliament Buildings on Parliament Hill, the famous promontory in downtown Ottawa that overlooks the Ottawa River. Parliament Hill is the seat of government, and the government buildings are the Centre Block, the East Block, and the West Block.

The Centre Block contains the Peace Tower, the House of Commons, and the Senate Chamber, as well as the Library of Parliament. The East Block and the West Block were designed by Thomas Fuller in the neo-Gothic style and constructed in 1860–66. They are used today as offices. Across the street from Parliament Hill is the American Embassy, which social commentators jokingly refer to as "the South Block."

246. Which buildings on Parliament Hill escaped destruction in the Great Fire?

The Great Fire of February 3, 1916, destroyed most of the Centre Block of Parliament Hill but left unaffected the East Block, the West Block, and the Library of Parliament, the only part of the Centre Block to escape destruction. The Library is an impressive, high-domed circular area with a statue of Queen Victoria in the centre. It serves the information needs of elected and appointed officials and not the general public. The new Centre Block was rebuilt by J. A. Pearson in 1916–24.

247. *How high is the Peace Tower?*

The Peace Tower, one of the most symbolic of Canadian images, is the Gothic-style tower that rises 92 m, or 302 feet, above the Centre Block of the Parliament Buildings. It was dedicated in 1927. There is a carillon of fifty-three bells. The tower includes the Memorial Chamber with the Altar of Sacrifice upon which are displayed the Books of Remembrance, inscribed with the names of the 111,542 Canadians who died on active service in the two world wars.

248. *Who lives in Rideau Hall? Who lives at 24 Sussex Drive? Who lives in Stornoway?*

Rideau Hall is the popular name for Government House, the official residence of the Governor General of Canada. It is in the fashionable Rockcliffe Park area of Ottawa and across the street from 24 Sussex Drive. This is the street address and the name of the mansion that serves as the official residence of the Prime Minister of Canada. Elsewhere in Rockcliffe Park is Stornoway, the official residence of the leader of the Opposition.

249. *In which park will you find Kingsmere, Moorside, The Cloisters, Harrington Lake, and Meech Lake?*

These sites will be found in Gatineau Park, northwest of Ottawa. Unique among Canada's parks, Gatineau Park is neither a national nor a provincial park. Instead, it has been administered directly by the government since 1938. It is maintained by the National Capital Commission, which is responsible for public lands and federal buildings.

Kingsmere is the name of the estate in the park once owned by

Prime Minister Mackenzie King. Kingsmere includes Moorside, his summer home, which is now the home of the Speaker of the House of Commons. It is open to the public, as are the grounds of Kingsmere, which include The Cloisters, the ruin-like structure the late Prime Minister had constructed on the grounds.

A large summer home at Harrington Lake has served, since 1959, as the official summer residence of the Prime Minister. The French name of Harrington Lake is Lac-Mousseau.

Also in Gatineau Park is Meech Lake (Lac-Meech) with its large stone residence. In recent years it has served as a conference centre for senior officials, especially cabinet ministers.

250. What is the origin of Ottawa's Tulip Festival?

Ottawa provided wartime refuge to members of the Dutch royal family. Princess Juliana and her consort, Prince Bernhardt, resided at Stornoway in Ottawa from June, 1940, to May, 1945. In 1943, Juliana gave birth to Princess Margriet at the Ottawa Civic Hospital (which was temporarily declared Dutch territory). They returned to Holland and Juliana served as Queen of the Netherlands from 1948 to 1980.

Juliana remembered the kindness of the citizens of Ottawa. In 1946, in gratitude, she sent 20,000 tulip bulbs and over the years sent more than 100,000 Dutch bulbs. These were planted in the city's parks so that now, in late May, when the flowers bloom, tourists flock to see the profusion of tulips, hear concerts, tour exhibitions, etc. The official name of Ottawa's annual Tulip Festival is the Festival of Spring.

251. Which national capital city is the most distant from Ottawa?

The national capital city that is most distant from Ottawa is Canberra, capital of Australia.

252. Are there really a thousand islands in the Thousand Islands?

The Thousand Islands is a resort area in the St. Lawrence River at the eastern end of Lake Ontario. There are actually fifteen hundred islands in the group.

253. *What city, midway between Montreal and Toronto, has been called Cataraqui, Fort Frontenac, and King's Town?*

Kingston, Ont., is on the north shore of the St. Lawrence River, between Montreal and Toronto. It was called Cataraqui by the Iroquois, Fort Frontenac by the French, and King's Town by the English. It became the city of Kingston in 1846.

254. *Where is "Steel City"?*

"Steel City" is the nickname of Hamilton, Ont., which is the home of two immense iron and steel plants, Stelco and Dofasco. Hamilton became a city in 1846. It is the third-largest industrial centre in Canada (Toronto and Montreal are larger) and is often compared to Pittsburgh, Pennsylvania, the centre of the U.S. steel industry.

255. *What is the meaning of the word "Toronto"?*

The official explanation is that the word "Toronto" derives from the Huron word that means "place of meeting." However, it may derive from the Wyandot word that means "place of plenty." The British called it York in 1794, but it was renamed Toronto when incorporated in 1834.

256. *What are Bay Street and Queen's Park?*

Toronto's Bay Street is the financial centre of the city and the country. Queen's Park, not far from Bay Street, is the location of the Ontario legislature.

257. *Why is Punkeydoodles Corners notable?*

Punkeydoodles Corners is the actual name of a dispersed rural community located southwest of Kitchener, Ont. Voters here are often questioned to determine trends in voting patterns in the country. In 1982, one reporter described the community as consisting of fourteen inhabitants, three houses, and one barn.

258. Which Ontario city is sometimes called "the Hartford of Canada"?

The head offices of a number of insurance companies are located in London, Ont., so it came to be called "the Hartford of Canada." Hartford, Connecticut, is a city with an unusually high concentration of home offices for the insurance business. In the nineteenth century, to distinguish it from London, England, it was called "London the Lesser." It was incorporated in 1855.

259. Which Canadian place name is misspelled more often than any other?

The dubious distinction of having the most misspelled name most likely goes to St. Catharines. Two orthographical points are peculiar about the spelling of the Ontario city's name. To the dismay of students, the name is spelled with two *a*'s rather than two *e*'s, and there is no apostrophe before the *s*. It was named in 1809 by the merchant Robert Hamilton to honour his wife Catharine Askin Hamilton. Even the Irish poet William Butler Yeats, who lectured there in 1914, misspelled its name.

260. What is Canada's most southern city?

The most southern city in the country is Windsor, Ont. It is on the same approximate latitude as Sofia and Tashkent. Indeed, Windsor lies south of the American city of Detroit. It shares with Detroit the concerns of the North American automobile industry. Windsor became a city in 1892.

261. *What is exceptional about Manitoulin Island?*
Manitoulin Island, in Lake Huron, made the *Guinness Book of Records* (1983). The entry reads: "The largest island in a lake is Manitoulin Island (1,068 sq. mi. [2,766 square kilometres]) in the Canadian (Ontario) section of Lake Huron. The island itself has a lake of 41.09 sq. mi. [106.42 square kilometres] on it, called Manitou Lake, which is the world's largest lake within a lake, and in that lake are a number of islands."

262. *Is there really a place in Ontario named Swastika?*
Swastika is the name given in 1906 to a small mining community near Kirkland Lake, Ont. Today Swastika is part of Kirkland Lake, but in 1940, when the two were separate places, there was a movement to change Swastika's name to Winston, to honour British war leader Winston Churchill and to affirm the patriotism of the townsfolk who did not wish to be identified with the hated emblem of Hitler's Nazi party. However, other townsfolk pointed out that Ontario's use of the name (actually the Sanskrit word for a kind of cross) predated Germany's and would outlast Hitler, so the name was retained.

263. *Why is Wawa notable?*
The world's largest sculpture of a goose stands just south of the Ontario community of Wawa. The sculpture is made of steel and is 9 m, or 30 feet, long. *Wawa* is the Algonkian word for "goose," and is onomatopoeic for the sound a goose makes. The sculpture distinguishes Wawa from similar mining and pulp and paper communities on the north shore of Lake Superior.

264. *Which two communities amalgamated in 1970 to form Thunder Bay?*
Thunder Bay, the Ontario community at the head of Lake Supe-

rior, was formed in 1970 with the amalgamation of Fort William and Port Arthur.

The humorist Stephen Leacock anticipated the amalgamation in 1937 when he wrote: "When I say Fort William I include with it the adjoining city of Port Arthur. They ought to be joined and called Fwather, or Port Arthliam. One can't keep saying both."

265. *Is there a difference between the prairie provinces and the western provinces?*
Yes, there is a difference. The prairie provinces is a collective term for three provinces (Manitoba, Saskatchewan, Alberta), whereas the western provinces is a collective term for four provinces (the above three plus British Columbia).

266. *Where are the prairies?*
The prairies are the gently rolling hill country of southern Alberta, southern Saskatchewan, and southwestern Manitoba. The Canadian prairies are an extension of the Great Plains of the United States. The word "prairies" is the plural form of the French noun for "meadow." In the United States the preferred word is "plains."

267. *Why was Manitoba once described as "the postage stamp province"?*
The original shape of Manitoba was rectilinear, rather like a postage stamp. From its creation in 1870 to the extension of its boundaries northward in 1881, Manitoba was "the postage stamp province."

268. *What does the Indian word* **Winnipeg** *mean?*
In Cree, the word *Win-nipi* was applied to Lake Winnipeg. It has the unfortunate meaning of "dirty water" or "murky water." In the same way, Lake Winnipegosis derives from the Cree for

"little muddy water." Thus the root meaning of the name of the capital of Manitoba is "dirty water."

Winnipeg, Manitoba's capital and largest city, was incorporated in 1873.

269. *What is Winnipeg's* **Golden Boy?**

Golden Boy is the gilded bronze figure of a youth carrying a torch in his right hand and a sheaf of wheat in his left. The statue is perched atop the dome of the Manitoba Legislature Building in Winnipeg. The 4-m, or 13.5-foot-high figure represents "Eternal Youth" and "The Spirit of Adventure." It has been a landmark since the opening of the Legislature Building in July, 1920.

270. *Where is the windiest place in Canada?*

The windiest place in all of Canada is said to be the intersection of Portage and Main in downtown Winnipeg. This is lore, of course, but anyone who has ever stood at the intersection of Portage Avenue and Main Street in the depths of winter will appreciate its essential truth.

271. *Where is the largest Icelandic community in Canada?*

The largest Icelandic community in Canada — indeed, the largest anywhere in the world outside Iceland — is on the west shore of Lake Winnipeg at Gimli, Man. Two hundred and eighty-five Icelandics arrived here in 1875. The population of the area today is approximately 4,000. Gimli was named after the home of the gods in Norse mythology.

272. *What Canadian city is named after the hero of a dime novel?*

The mining community of Flin Flon bears the nickname of the hero of a dime novel. (Dime novels were pocket books that sold for ten cents apiece and were popular at the turn of the century.) The dime novel is *The Sunless City* (1905), written by the English author of adventure fiction J. E. Preston-Muddock, and it tells of a fantastic adventure — how Professor Josiah Flintabbatey Flonatin (nicknamed Flin Flon) discovered a "sunless city" rich in gold beneath the surface of the Earth. A prospector in northern Manitoba found a copy of the dime novel, read of Flin Flon's fabulous adventures, and when he staked a claim in the area, named the district Flin Flon. Two years later, in 1915, it became the community's official name. In the Flin Flon Public Library there is a dog-eared copy of the novel. A statue of Flin Flon, designed by the cartoonist Al Capp in 1962, stands outside the city of Flin Flon, which is in northern Manitoba on the Saskatchewan border.

273. *Where is Palliser's Triangle?*
Palliser's Triangle is an area that includes most of the southern part of present-day Alberta and Saskatchewan. It was named after Captain John Palliser, who in 1857–60 led an expedition that explored the prairies, dividing the region into a "fertile belt" and an "arid belt" that was roughly triangular in shape. Palliser's Triangle is the driest part of the prairie land.

274. *Which is the middle of the three prairie provinces?*
Saskatchewan is between Manitoba on the east and Alberta on the west. It became a province on September 1, 1905. Its capital and largest city is Regina.

275. *What was the original name of Regina?*
Regina, the capital of Saskatchewan, was originally called Pile o' Bones, a literal translation of *Wascana*, the Cree word for the place where buffalo bones were stacked. In 1882, it was renamed by the Governor General, the Marquess of Lorne, in honour of Queen Victoria, who happened to be his mother-in-law.

276. What city was named for an edible red berry?
Saskatoon, after Regina the largest city in Saskatchewan, takes its name from the Cree word *Mis-sask-quah-too-min* for an edible red berry, the serviceberry (*Amelanchier alnifolia*), which grows near the South Saskatchewan River. Saskatoon became a city in 1906.

277. Which is the most westerly of the prairie provinces?
The province of Alberta, which lies west of Saskatchewan and east of British Columbia, is the most westerly of the prairie provinces. Alberta became a province in 1905.

278. Which of Canada's major cities is the most northerly?
Edmonton, the capital of Alberta, is so far north it is sometimes called the "Gateway to the North." It occupies the same latitude as Liverpool and Hamburg. Edmonton was incorporated as a city in 1904.

279. What is Alberta's second-largest city?
The largest city in Alberta is Edmonton; the second-largest city, Calgary. It is in the foothills of the Rockies and is the centre of the country's petroleum industry.

280. Who was the first known European to view the Rocky Mountains?
Anthony Henday, the explorer, was the first known European to view the Rocky Mountains. He called them the "shining mountains," based on an Indian description of them. The sighting occurred near present-day Innisfail, Alta., on October 17, 1754.

281. Which is the oldest of Canada's National Parks?
Banff National Park, established in 1885, is the oldest of the

national parks. The system of federal parklands, established and
maintained by Parks Canada within Environment Canada, preserves areas representative of the natural heritage of the country
for purposes connected with conservation, education, and recreation. The system has grown and, in 1986, embraces thirty-one
National Parks. There are plans to develop twenty more national
parks, ten of them in the North.

In addition to the system of National Parks, Parks Canada
maintains the National Historic Parks and Sites, the program of
preserving, restoring, and reconstructing sites and artifacts
commemorating persons, places, or events of major significance
in the historical development of Canada. From 1911 to 1986, the
system has grown to include sixty National Historic Parks and 900
National Historic Sites.

282. Was one of the Rocky Mountains named after Dwight D. Eisenhower?

Yes. From 1946 to 1979, Castle Mountain in Banff National Park,
Alta., bore the name Mount Eisenhower. The decision to honour
Dwight D. Eisenhower, Supreme Allied Commander in World
War II, was made in 1946 by Prime Minister Mackenzie King. It
was an unpopular decision, as it set aside a ninety-nine-year-old
name. One of Joe Clark's last acts as Prime Minister was reversing the decision, reserving Eisenhower's name for a prominent
peak on Castle Mountain.

283. How did Kicking Horse Pass get its name?

Kicking Horse Pass in the Rocky Mountains got its name on
August 29, 1858, when Sir James Hector, M.D., a member of the
Palliser expedition, was kicked in the chest by a pack horse he was
attempting to pull out of the river. He was rendered senseless for
some time and the party was delayed three days.

284. Which province is "the first one on the left"?

This amusing reference to the Province of British Columbia was made by Vancouver humorist Eric Nicol, who had in mind the practice of reading from left to right. British Columbia is, indeed, "the first one on the left," being Canada's westernmost province. It is also known as the Pacific coast province. It entered Confederation in 1871. Nicol went on to suggest that it was "railroaded" into Confederation, since completion of the national railway was a condition of its joining the Dominion.

285. Which city is the capital of British Columbia?

Victoria is the capital of British Columbia. It is on the southeastern extremity of Vancouver Island, overlooking the Strait of Juan de Fuca. It became a city in 1862.

286. Which is the third-largest city in the country?

The third-largest city in the country is Vancouver. The largest city in British Columbia, it is located on Burrard Inlet at the mouth of the Fraser River. It is exceeded in size by Toronto and Montreal. Vancouver was incorporated in 1886.

287. Where is the largest fresh-water port on Canada's Pacific coast?

New Westminster, located on the north bank of the Fraser River, is the largest fresh-water port on Canada's Pacific coast. New Westminster is part of greater Vancouver.

288. What is meant by the term Pacific northwest?

The Pacific northwest is the part of Canada west of the Rockies, corresponding to British Columbia. In North American terms, the designation includes, as well, the Pacific coast of Alaska, the two northern Pacific states (Washington and Oregon), and sometimes three landlocked states (Idaho, Montana, and Wyoming).

289. *When was the Yukon created?*
The Yukon Territory entered Confederation on June 13, 1898. The Klondike Gold Rush of 1896 brought prospectors into this most northwesterly part of Canada. The land was originally acquired from the Hudson's Bay Company in 1870. Dawson was the original gold rush capital. Whitehorse has been the territorial capital since 1953.

290. *On which river is Whitehorse situated?*
Whitehorse, the capital of the Yukon Territory, is situated on the Yukon River. The city was named for the nearby Whitehorse Rapids, part of the river system that has played so important a role in the development of the territory.

291. *What is the country's most celebrated "ghost town"?*
Dawson City boasted a population of 25,000 at the height of the Klondike Gold Rush in the late 1890s. When the gold ran out, so did the prospectors and their suppliers. Today, no longer a city, it is plain Dawson, Y.T. The seven hundred or so permanent residents are mainly employed in the tourist industry.

292. *What is the most northern settlement in the Yukon Territory?*
Old Crow is the most northern settlement in the Yukon. It is 112 km, or 70 miles, north of the Arctic Circle, not far from the border with Alaska. Since 1926, Old Crow has had a post office, an RCMP detachment, and a mission. The population is about two hundred and twenty.

293. *Which city is the capital of the Northwest Territories?*
Yellowknife is the capital of the Northwest Territories. It is on the north shore of Great Slave Lake and is only 512 km, or 320 miles, south of the Arctic Circle. The name Yellowknife derives not from the colour of the gold found in the region but from the colour of copper deposits once worked by the Athapaskan Indians. Yellowknife was incorporated as a city in 1970.

294. *Who or what inspired the names of the three districts that constitute the Northwest Territories?*
The three districts are named Mackenzie, Keewatin, and Franklin. The District of Mackenzie, the western one, was named for Sir Alexander Mackenzie (1764–1820), who explored much of the region. The District of Keewatin, the eastern one, takes its name from the Cree word for "the north wind." The District of Franklin, the northern one, commemorates the Arctic explorer Sir John Franklin (1786–1847). The present boundaries date from 1920.

295. *What is the name of the first settlement designed and built for permanent residence in the Far North?*
Inuvik, on the Mackenzie River delta north of the Arctic Circle in the Northwest Territories, was the first settlement so designed and built. It was established in 1955 to replace Aklavik as the administrative and service centre. In the Inuktitut language of the Inuit, Inuvik means "the place of man."

296. *Where is the largest park in the world?*
The largest park in the world is Wood Buffalo National Park, which is partly in northern Alberta and partly in the Northwest Territories. Established in 1922, it has an area of 44,800 square kilometres, or 17,300 square miles.

297. What is the name of the world's most northern settlement?
The most northern settlement in the world is Alert, N.W.T. It is a
weather and signals station located on the northern tip of Ellesmere
Island overlooking the Arctic Ocean. Located some eight hundred
kilometres, or five hundred miles, from the North Pole, it is
closer to Moscow than to Montreal. It was established by the
government in 1950 for undefined communications and military
purposes. It was named after the HMS *Alert*, flagship of the
British survey expedition to the Arctic in 1875–76.

**298. What is the difference between North of Sixty and the
Arctic Circle?**
There is a considerable difference between North of Sixty, which
is the region north of the 60th parallel, and the Arctic Circle,
which is the parallel of latitude at 66°32′ north. The 60th parallel
corresponds to the southern boundary of the Northwest Territories and the Yukon. The Arctic Circle represents the most southerly point at which, during a twenty-four-hour day, the sun does
not rise (December 22) or set (June 21). North of Sixty is a
convenient political and geographical reference, whereas the Arctic Circle corresponds to a solar characteristic.

**299. Which country claims jurisdiction over the Arctic Archi-
pelago and the Northwest Passage?**
Canada's jurisdiction over the Arctic Archipelago — the islands of
the Arctic Ocean — is questioned by no other country. What is
questioned is Canada's jurisdiction over the Northwest Passage —
the waters between the islands. Is the historic route an international waterway? The Canadian claim is resisted by the U.S.
government. Two U.S. oil tankers have traversed the Passage
without permission: the *Manhattan* in 1969 and the *Polar Sea* in
1985, although the former was "escorted" by a Canadian icebreaker and the latter took on board Canadian Coast Guard cap-
tains (as advisers, according to Ottawa; as guests, according to
Washington).

Canada's claim to sovereignty over the land, sea, and air between the northern coast of Canada and the North Pole, enclosed by longitudinal lines drawn from the eastern and western extremities of the coastline, is based on the Sectorial Theory of 1909. In 1970, the Trudeau administration extended Canada's claim to sovereignty over arctic waters from 5 km, or 3 miles, to 19 km, or 12 miles, and passed the Arctic Waters Pollution Prevention Act, which envisaged a 160-km, or 100-mile environmental control zone. The Mulroney administration signed a Cabinet order on September 10, 1985, declaring Canadian jurisdiction and sovereignty over the internal waters and offshore areas of the Arctic.

300. *Which is the largest of the arctic islands?*

The largest of the arctic islands, as well as the most eastern, is Baffin Island, N.W.T. It was named after the seventeenth-century explorer William Baffin.

301. *What are Nunavut and Denendeh?*

These are names proposed by native groups that favour the division of the Northwest Territories into two territories or provinces. The line of division would run diagonally across the Northwest Territories from the Mackenzie Delta in the northwest to the southeastern-most point of the territories.

Nunavut, the name for the northeastern portion, including the arctic islands, means "our land" in Inuktitut. The name was proposed in a land claim presented to the federal government by the Inuit Tapirisat of Canada on February 27, 1976.

Denendeh, the name for the southwestern portion, means "the land of the people" in the language of the Athapaskan Indians. Meeting at Fort Simpson on July 19, 1975, the Indian Brotherhood of the Northwest Territories argued for the recognition of the Dene Nation — "Dene" (pronounced dennay) means "the people," and embraces the Chipewyan, Dogrib, Slavey, Hare, and Loucheux Indians. The Dene Nation chose the name Denendeh in 1978.

302. *In which of the provinces is the capital city not the largest city?*
In Quebec, New Brunswick, and British Columbia, the largest cities are not the capital cities. Montreal exceeds the size of Quebec City, the capital of Quebec. The capital of New Brunswick is Fredericton, which is much smaller than Saint John. Vancouver is the largest city in British Columbia, much larger than the capital city, Victoria.

303. *Which three provinces do not border on American states?*
Newfoundland, Nova Scotia, and Prince Edward Island are the only provinces that do not border on any of the American states.

304. *Which American state borders on one of the two territories?*
The State of Alaska borders on the Yukon Territory. Alaska is the largest but least populous of the American states. Its capital is Juneau.

305. *What is the busiest border crossing?*
The busiest border crossing between Canada and the United States is the Peace Bridge between Fort Erie, Ont., and Buffalo, N.Y. The bridge was built in 1927 to celebrate one century of peace. In 1984, the Peace Bridge acted as a point of entry or departure for 5,194,751 vehicles and 6,750,140 passengers (two thirds of them Americans). The only rival to the Peace Bridge is the Windsor Tunnel and Bridge, between Windsor, Ont., and Detroit, Mich., which came in second in terms of vehicle and passenger volume in 1984.

306. *How long is the Canada–United States border?*
There are two borders to measure. The length of the southern border with the United States is 6,416 km, or 3,986.8 miles. The

length of the border with Alaska is 2,478 km, or 1,539.8 miles. Thus the combined border lengths are 8,894 km, or 5,526.6 miles.

307. *What are the "nine nations" of North America?*

The notion that North America consists of "nine nations" rather than three countries (Canada, the United States, and Mexico) is associated with the book *The Nine Nations of North America* (1981) by the American journalist Joel Garreau. Disregarding national and provincial or state boundaries, Garreau divided the continent into utilitarian regions, each with its own distinctive character and capital city, arguing that each region displays the characteristics of a "nation."

The "nine nations" are the following: New England, The Foundry, Dixie, The Breadbasket, The Empty Quarter, Ectopia, MexAmerica, Quebec, and The Islands. In this continental scheme of things, Quebec remains intact. The Atlantic Provinces become part of New England. Southern Ontario joins Illinois, Pennsylvania, and New York as part of The Foundry. Parts of the prairie provinces join the Midwestern American states as The Breadbasket. The Empty Quarter consists of the two territories, much of Alberta, and the west-central United States. Ectopia consists of the Pacific coast from Alaska to south of San Francisco. The other regions lie within the United States and Mexico except for The Islands which consists of the Caribbean (including Cuba).

308. *Canada is close to four foreign countries. What are they?*

Canada's four neighbouring countries are the following: United States (via Alaska and the southern-border states), Soviet Union (via Siberia), Denmark (via Greenland), and France (via St. Pierre and Miquelon).

309. *Are the Turks and Caicos Islands part of Canada?*

No, unfortunately. The Turks and Caicos Islands, geographically part of the Bahamas, are a British colony in the West Indies with no Canadian association. A private member's bill, introduced into the House of Commons by the late Max Saltsman in 1974, proposed the association of Canada and the Turks and Caicos Islands for no other purpose than to give Canadians a place in the winter sun. The motion was defeated. Reports suggest that the 6,000 residents of the islands favoured some form of association. The total area of the islands is 430 square kilometres, or 166 square miles. The capital is Grand Turk.

310. *Does France retain any North American possessions?*
Three quarters of the North American continent was at one time controlled by France. But the empire was lost and the last French possession on the continent, Louisiana, was purchased by the United States in 1803, joining the American Union in 1812. Inhabitants of its delta region continue to recall their French past, referring to themselves as "Cajuns," a corruption of "Acadians."

Although Louisiana may be the last French possession on the continent, it is not the last possession in North America. In the West Indies, Guadeloupe and Martinique remain French Overseas Departments. Closer to Canada, the islands of St. Pierre and Miquelon, in the Gulf of St. Lawrence, off Newfoundland's Burin Peninsula, remain French possessions. In 1984, they became a Territorial Collectivity, a status intermediate between that of a Department and an Overseas Territory. Their capital is St. Pierre and a deputy and a senator are elected to the French Parliament.

The ferry to St. Pierre and Miquelon leaves from Fortune Bay, Nfld.

311. *How does Canada compare in size with other countries?*
Canada is the second-largest country in the world. Canada comprises 9,976,139 square kilometres, or 3,851,809 square miles. It is smaller than the Soviet Union (22,396,271 square kilometres, or 8,647,249 square miles) but larger than China (9,558,470 square kilometres, or 3,690,546 square miles).

Here is how the provinces and the territories compare in size with some countries of the world. Alberta is larger than Somalia but smaller than Afghanistan. British Columbia is larger than Venezuela but smaller than Tanzania. Manitoba is about the same size as France. New Brunswick is larger than Ireland but smaller than Scotland. Newfoundland is larger than the Congo but smaller than Zimbabwe. Nova Scotia is larger than Costa Rica but smaller than Togo. Ontario is larger than Turkey but smaller than Nigeria. Prince Edward Island is larger than Trinidad and Tobago but smaller than Cyprus. Quebec is larger than South Africa but smaller than Tibet. Saskatchewan is larger than Spain but smaller than Kenya. The Northwest Territories and the Yukon combined are somewhat larger than India.

312. *What are the Seven Natural Wonders of Canada?*

Ancient Greek travellers compiled lists of the Seven Wonders of the Ancient World. Their lists included man-made wonders like the pyramids of Egypt, the Hanging Gardens of Babylon, the Colossus of Rhodes, etc. Less common are lists of natural wonders. Here is a list of seven natural wonders associated with Canada.

1. aurora borealis
2. Precambrian Shield
3. Douglas fir
4. blue whale
5. polar bear
6. Niagara Falls
7. North Magnetic Pole

313. *What are the Seven Manmade Wonders of Canada?*

The previous question asked about natural wonders. This one inquires about manmade wonders. No list of this sort is ever more than suggestive of other lists, but here goes . . .

1. Norse ruins, L'Anse aux Meadows, Nfld.
2. Haida totem poles, Queen Charlotte Islands, B.C.
3. Quebec (Pierre Laporte) Bridge, Quebec City, Que.
4. Trans-Canada Highway, opened in 1962
5. Daniel Johnson Dam (Manic 5), Manicouagan River, Que.
6. CN Tower, Toronto, Ont.
7. Canadarm, designed and built by the National Research Council and Spar Aerospace, Toronto, Ont.

4. GOVERNMENT

314. Who or what has "authority of and over Canada"?
In the words of the BNA Act of 1867, "Authority of and over Canada is . . . vested in the Queen." Thus the Queen or King of Great Britain—the Crown—is the supreme executive authority in Canada. The Crown is a formal institution whose powers are exercised through responsible officials acting in the monarch's name. The individual sovereign is a Constitutional Monarch who acts with the authorization of constitutional advisers, the Cabinet, members of which are accountable to Parliament. In practice, the sovereign delegates most of the powers of the Crown to the Governor General.

315. Which British sovereigns have ruled Canada since 1867?
Six British sovereigns have ruled Canada. Queen Victoria, the last of the House of Hanover, ruled from 1837 to her death in 1901. King Edward VII, the sole member of the House of Saxe-Coburg and Gotha, ruled from 1901 to his death in 1910. King George V, the first of the House of Windsor, ruled from 1910 to his death in 1936. Edward VIII, the second of the House of Windsor, was never crowned. He was *de facto* king from January 20 to his abdication, December 11, 1936. King George VI, the third of the House of Windsor, ruled from 1936 to 1952. Queen Elizabeth II, the fourth of the House of Windsor, has ruled since 1952.

Princess Elizabeth married Philip Mountbatten, Duke of Edinburgh, on November 20, 1947. She acceded to the throne as

Elizabeth II on the death of her father in 1952, and was crowned at Westminster Abbey on June 2, 1953. The Queen and the Prince have four children: Prince Charles, Prince of Wales, born in 1948; Princess Anne, born in 1950; Prince Andrew, born in 1960; and Prince Edward, born in 1964.

316. What is the Queen's Royal Style and Title?

Queen Elizabeth II is the Queen of Canada. Parliament approved the official Royal Style and Title on February 3, 1953: "Elizabeth the Second, by the Grace of God, of the United Kingdom, Canada and Her other Realms and Territories, Queen, Head of the Commonwealth, Defender of the Faith." Similar designations apply in the United Kingdom, Australia, and New Zealand.

317. Who made the first royal visit?

A royal visit is the progress of the monarch or a member of the royal family through a dominion or colony. Many "royals" have visited Canada; some, like Queen Victoria's daughter, Princess Louise, have lived here. The first visit to Canada by a reigning monarch was that of King George VI, who crossed the country with his wife, the present Queen Mother, in 1939.

Queen Elizabeth II, as Princess Elizabeth, visited Canada in 1951. As a reigning monarch, she has made numerous royal visits, notably to celebrate the Centennial in 1967 and to sign the Constitution Act in 1982.

318. What is the role of the Governor General?

The Governor General is the representative of the Crown in Canada and the head of state. The office is symbolic of national unity and of the continuity of institutions and national life. The Governor General is appointed by the Queen, usually for five years, on the advice of the Cabinet. The office-holder, as CEO (chief executive officer) of the state, is "above politics." Governor General

Lord Tweedsmuir once quipped that as Governor General he was responsible for "governor-generalities."

319. *Who was the first native-born Governor General? Who was the first woman Governor General?*
The first native-born Canadian to be appointed Governor General was Vincent Massey. The appointment was made in 1952. The first woman to be appointed Governor General was Jeanne Sauvé. The appointment was made in 1984.

320. *Who are the men and women who have served as Governors General of Canada? What are their years of office?*
Here is a list of the Governors General of Canada with their years of office.

Lord Monck, 1867–68
Lord Lisgar, 1869–72
Lord Dufferin, 1872–78
Lord Lorne, 1878–83
Lord Lansdowne, 1883–88
Lord Stanley, 1888–93
Lord Aberdeen, 1893–98
Lord Minto, 1898–1904
Lord Grey, 1904–11
Duke of Connaught, 1911–16
Duke of Devonshire, 1916–21

Lord Byng, 1921–26
Lord Willingdon, 1926–31
Lord Bessborough, 1931–35
Lord Tweedsmuir, 1935–40
Lord Athlone, 1940–46
Lord Alexander, 1946–52
Vincent Massey, 1952–59
Georges P. Vanier, 1959–67
D. Roland Michener, 1967–74
Jules Léger, 1974–79
Edward Schreyer, 1979–84

Jeanne Sauvé, 1984–

321. *How do you greet the Governor General and other public figures?*
The style of address of the Governor General of Canada is "Excellency."

"Right Honourable" is the style of address of the Prime Minister of Canada — past or present, the Chief Justice of Canada, and all members of the United Kingdom Privy Council.

"Honourable" is the style of address of all members of the Privy Council, and they may use the initials P.C. after their names. Members of the Privy Council include all cabinet ministers, past and present, and speakers of the Senate and the House of Commons, plus appointed civilians. In addition, all senators, all premiers and members of the executive councils of the provinces, and all justices of the superior courts of Canada and of the provinces are styled "Honourable."

322. *What is the title of a representative of the Crown in a province of Canada?*

The representative of the Crown in a province of Canada is called a lieutenant-governor. The lieutenant-governor is appointed by the Queen, normally for five years, on the advice of the federal ministry. He or she is the chief executive officer of the provincial government and is "above politics."

Until 1974, all appointments were made to men. That year, Pauline McGibbon was appointed Lieutenant-Governor of Ontario. (The British pronunciation of "lieutenant" — "lef-tenant" is used, not the American pronunciation — "loo-tenant.")

323. *What is the title of the head of the federal government?*

The head of the federal government, and in practice the leader of the party in power in the House of Commons, is the Prime Minister.

324. *What are the names of the Prime Ministers of Canada, and how many people have served in this capacity?*

Brian Mulroney is the eighteenth Prime Minister of Canada. Here is a list of the Prime Ministers with the years of their administrations and their party affiliation (c, conservative; l, liberal).

Sir John A. Macdonald (c) 1867–73
Alexander Mackenzie (l) 1873–78
Sir John A. Macdonald (c) 1878–91
Sir John Abbott (c) 1891–92
Sir John Thompson (c) 1892–94
Sir Mackenzie Bowell (c) 1894–96
Sir Charles Tupper (c) 1896
Sir Wilfrid Laurier (l) 1896–1911
Sir Robert Borden (c) 1911–20
Arthur Meighen (c) 1920–21
W. L. Mackenzie King (l) 1921–26
Arthur Meighen (c) 1926
W. L. Mackenzie King (l) 1926–30
R. B. Bennett (c) 1930–35
W. L. Mackenzie King (l) 1935–48
Louis St. Laurent (l) 1948–57
John G. Diefenbaker (c) 1957–63
Lester B. Pearson (l) 1963–68
Pierre Elliott Trudeau (l) 1968–79
Joe Clark (c) 1979–80
Pierre Elliott Trudeau (l) 1980–84
John Turner (l) 1984
Brian Mulroney (c) 1984–

325. *Which Prime Ministers held office for the longest and the shortest terms?*

The longest-serving Prime Minister was W. L. Mackenzie King, who set a Canadian and Commonwealth record that holds to this day. He served in the highest elected office for 7,817 days. Next in line for the Canadian honours are Sir John A. Macdonald (6,719 days) and Pierre Elliott Trudeau (5,641 days).

The shortest-serving Prime Minister was Sir Charles Tupper, who lasted 69 days in 1896. He is followed by John Turner, who held on to power for 80 days in 1984, and then by Joe Clark, who was was Prime Minister for 275 days in 1979–80.

Another record, of sorts, is that twice Canada had three Prime Ministers in one calendar year. Mackenzie Bowell, Sir Charles Tupper, and Sir Wilfrid Laurier were all Prime Ministers in the year 1896. Pierre Elliott Trudeau, John Turner, and Brian Mulroney served as Prime Ministers in 1985.

326. *Who was the last Prime Minister to be born in the nineteenth century? Who was the first Prime Minister to be born in the twentieth century?*
Lester B. Pearson, who became Prime Minister in 1963, was the last Prime Minister to be born in the nineteenth century. He was born in 1897. Pierre Elliott Trudeau, who succeeded Pearson as Prime Minister in 1968, was the first Prime Minister to be born in the twentieth century. He was born in 1919.

327. *Fourteen of Canada's Prime Ministers are deceased. Where are they buried?*
In the list that follows, Canada's fourteen deceased Prime Ministers are arranged roughly in the order of their administrations. For each is given years of birth and death and location of final resting place.

Sir John A. Macdonald (1815–1891): Cataraqui Cemetery, Kingston, Ont. **Alexander Mackenzie** (1822–1892): Lakeview Cemetery, Sarnia, Ont. **Sir John Abbott** (1821–1893): Mount Royal Cemetery, Montreal, Que. **Sir John S. Thompson** (1844–1894): Holy Cross Cemetery of All Saints Cathedral, Halifax, N.S. **Sir Mackenzie Bowell** (1823–1917): Belleville Cemetery, Belleville, Ont. **Sir Charles Tupper** (1821–1915): St. John's Anglican Cemetery, Halifax, N.S. **Sir Wilfrid Laurier** (1841–1919): Notre Dame Cemetery, Ottawa, Ont. **Sir Robert Borden** (1854–1937): Beechwood Cemetery, Ottawa, Ont. **Arthur Meighen** (1874–1960): St. Mary's Cemetery, St. Mary's, Ont. **R. B. Bennett** (1870–1947): Graveyard, St. Michael's Anglican Church, Mickleham, Surrey, England. **W. L. Mackenzie King** (1874–1950): Mount Pleasant Cemetery, Toronto, Ont. **Louis St. Laurent**

(1882–1973): Cemetery of St. Thomas Aquinas, Compton, Que. **John G. Diefenbaker** (1895–1979): Grounds of the Diefenbaker Centre, University of Saskatchewan, Saskatoon, Sask. **Lester B. Pearson** (1897–1972): Maclaren Cemetery, Wakefield, Que.

328. *What is a premier?*

A premier is the head of a provincial government, and in practice the leader of the party in power in the provincial legislature.

329. *What are the names of the premiers of the provinces since Canada's Centennial?*

The names of the provincial premiers who have served since 1967 are listed below along with the years of their administrations and their political allegiances (C, Conservative; L, Liberal; NDP, New Democratic Party; PQ, Parti Québécois; SC, Social Credit; UN, Union Nationale).

ALBERTA
Ernest C. Manning (SC) 1943–68
Harry E. Strom (SC) 1968–71
Peter Lougheed (C) 1971–85
Don Getty (C) 1985–

BRITISH COLUMBIA
W. A. C. Bennett (SC) 1952–72
Dave Barrett (NDP) 1972–75
Bill Bennett (SC) 1975–

MANITOBA
Duff Roblin (C) 1958–67
Walter Weir (C) 1967–69
Edward R. Schreyer (NDP)
 1969–77
Sterling Lyon (C) 1977–81
Howard Pawley (NDP) 1981–

NEW BRUNSWICK
Louis J. Robichaud (L) 1960–70
Richard B. Hatfield (C) 1970–

NOVA SCOTIA
Robert Stanfield (C) 1956–67
George I. Smith (C) 1967–70
Gerald A. Regan (L) 1970–78
John M. Buchanan (C) 1978–

NEWFOUNDLAND
Joey Smallwood (L) 1949–72
Frank Moores (C) 1972–79
Brian Peckford (C) 1979–

ONTARIO
John P. Robarts (C) 1961–71
William G. Davis (C) 1971–85
Frank Miller (C) 1985
David Peterson (L) 1985–

PRINCE EDWARD ISLAND
Alex Campbell (L) 1966–78
W. B. Campbell (L) 1978–79
J. Angus MacLean (C) 1979–81
James M. Lee (C) 1981–86
Joseph Ghiz (L) 1986–

QUEBEC
Daniel Johnson (UN) 1966–68
Jean-Jacques Bertrand (UN)
   1968–70
Robert Bourassa (L) 1970–76
René Lévesque (PQ) 1976–85
Robert Bourassa (L) 1985–

SASKATCHEWAN
W. Ross Thatcher (L) 1964–71
A. E. Blakeney (NDP) 1971–82
Grant Devine (C) 1982–

330. *What is an M.P.? What is an M.L.A.?*
An M.P. is a member of Parliament, specifically a member of the
federal House of Commons.

An M.L.A. is a member of the legislative assembly of one of
eight provinces. Provincial parliamentarians are known as M.L.A.s
except in Quebec and Ontario. In Quebec, the designation M.A.N.
identifies a member of the Assemblée nationale. In Ontario, the
designation M.P.P. identifies a member of the provincial parliament.

331. *Which is the oldest of the federal political parties?*
The oldest continuing federal political party in this country is the
Progressive Conservative Party of Canada, known simply as the
Conservative Party. It goes back to the coalition of interests engi-
neered by Sir John A. Macdonald in 1854. The triumph of his
coalition was Confederation in 1867.

In 1942, the party was given its current name. Over the years it
has stood in opposition to liberal principles, so much so that it was
dubbed "the party of opposition" just as the Liberal Party was
dubbed "the party of government." Since World War II,
Progressive Conservative leaders who have formed federal governments are John G. Diefenbaker, Joe Clark, and Brian Mulroney.

332. *How and when did the Liberal Party form?*

The second-oldest continuing federal political party in the country is the Liberal Party of Canada. It traces its roots to the coalition of Clear Grits and independent reformers effected by George Brown in 1855, the year following the Conservative coalition under Sir John A. Macdonald. The first Liberal Prime Minister was Alexander Mackenzie, who formed his government in 1873.

The Liberals established their stronghold in Quebec under the leadership of Sir Wilfrid Laurier. The modern party and Canada's social welfare state took shape under W. L. Mackenzie King. Since his retirement in 1948, the Liberal leaders who have been called upon to form governments are Louis St. Laurent, Lester B. Pearson, Pierre Elliott Trudeau, and John Turner.

333. *How and when did the New Democratic Party form?*

The third-largest federal political party, after the Liberal Party and the Progressive Conservative Party, is the New Democratic Party. The NDP, founded in 1961 by the CCF and the New Party clubs, is committed to democratic socialism for Canada. The NDP has won the official support of organized labour (but not always its votes) and those members of the electorate who see the NDP as a "ginger group" — one which offers new ideas and initiatives. This has been its federal role. Provincially, the NDP parties have formed governments within recent memory in British Columbia, Saskatchewan, and Manitoba, and formed the official opposition in Ontario.

334. *What was the CCF?*

The CCF, or the Co-operative Commonwealth Federation, was a federal political party concerned with democratic socialism. Formed in Calgary in 1932, it was succeeded by the New Party clubs which led to the founding of the New Democratic Party in 1961. The conscience of the CCF was its first leader, J. S. Woodsworth. Federally, it was a source of new ideas but never the official opposition. Provincially, the CCF came to power in Saskatchewan under T. C. Douglas, and for some time in the 1940s it was the official opposition in British Columbia, Manitoba, and Ontario.

335. *What is Social Credit?*

Social Credit is a monetary theory about the redistribution of purchasing power. Developed in the 1920s by Major C. H. Douglas, an English engineer, it had a surprising political influence in western Canada and Quebec. To William Aberhart, an evangelist turned politician, the theory seemed a panacea for the ills caused by the Depression. He formed the world's first Social Credit government in Alberta in 1935. Using the ''Socred'' label, W. A. C. Bennett came to power in British Columbia in 1952, as did his son Bill Bennett in 1975. Réal Caouette led a contingent of Quebec Social Crediters, called Créditistes, in the House of Commons in 1962. Interest in Major Douglas's theories waned but the political labels continued.

336. *Is it against the law to be a member of the Communist Party of Canada?*

It is not illegal to be a member of the Communist Party of Canada, a national political party devoted to socialist and communist principles. Membership was not always legal. The party was founded in secret — in 1921 in a barn outside Guelph, Ont. — and it was banned in 1931–36 and again in 1940–45. During its history it elected one member to the House of Commons. The member was Fred Rose, who was identified by Igor Gouzenko as a Soviet spy. Its national leaders were Jack Macdonald (1922–29); Tim Buck (1929–62); Leslie Morris (1962–64); and William Kashtan (since 1964). The CPC is not to be confused with the CPC(M-L) — the Communist Party of Canada (Marxist-Leninist) — which adheres more closely to the policies of the People's Republic of China, than to those of Moscow.

337. *What is the Rhinoceros Party?*
The Rhinoceros Party was a quasi-political party founded in 1963 by Quebec writer Jacques Ferron. Its purpose was to ridicule the policies and promises of the mainline political parties and politicians generally. For instance, Rhino candidates in federal and provincial elections promised, if elected, to repeal the law of gravity; to scale down the arms race to a foot race; to supply tax credits to Canadians for sleeping; and to rebuild the Rocky Mountains, evening out the incline so Canadians could "coast to coast." The Rhinoceros Party was disbanded in April 1985, after Ferron's death.

The symbol of the party was Cornelius, a black rhinoceros born at the zoo in Granby, Quebec. The rhino was chosen because it is a slow-witted animal that can move fast when in danger. Over the years the party fielded about fifty candidates in federal and provincial elections. All lost their $200 deposits by receiving so few votes, but they succeeded in ridiculing the rhetoric of elections.

338. *What is a Red Tory?*
The political scientist Gad Horowitz, writing in the *Canadian Journal of Economics and Political Science*, May 1966, popularized the term "Red Tory," which he characterized as a person who is "a conscious ideological Conservative with some 'odd' socialist notions (W. L. Morton) or a conscious ideological socialist with some 'odd' tory notions (Eugene Forsey)."

339. *What do politicians mean when they talk about "loose fish" and "trained seals"?*
Sir John A. Macdonald used the term "loose fish" to describe members of Parliament not subject to party discipline, and hence troublesome people. Conservative leader George Drew coined the term "trained seals" to describe the behaviour of partisan backbenchers, who are, in effect, "yes men."

340. *Does Canada have a constitution?*
Yes. The Constitution of Canada is the supreme law of the land. Its legal title is Constitution Acts, 1867 to 1981. It is sometimes referred to as The New Constitution of Canada.

The Constitution of Canada consists, historically, of two acts with amendments of the British Parliament. In Britain these are called the British North America Act, 1867, and the Canada Act, 1981. The former act was patriated — that is, transferred from the British to the Canadian Parliament — and renamed the Constitution Act, 1867. The latter act is known in Canada as the Constitution Act, 1981. When Queen Elizabeth II, as Queen of Canada, proclaimed the Constitution Act, 1981, in Ottawa on April 17, 1982, she proclaimed, in effect, the Constitution of Canada. An important part of the Constitution Act, 1981, is the Canadian Charter of Rights and Freedoms.

341. *What is the Canadian Charter of Rights and Freedoms?*
The Canadian Charter of Rights and Freedoms is Schedule B of the Constitution Act, 1981, and hence an integral part of the Constitution of Canada. The Charter notes that Canada is "founded upon principles that recognize the supremacy of God and the rule of law."

The four "fundamental freedoms" guaranteed by the Charter are "freedom of conscience and religion; freedom of thought, belief, opinion and expression, including freedom of the press and other media of communication; freedom of peaceful assembly; and freedom of association."

342. *What is the Canadian Bill of Rights?*
The Canadian Bill of Rights is the short title of An Act for the Recognition and Protection of Human Rights and Fundamental Freedoms. An Act of Parliament given Royal Assent on August 10, 1960, it was close to the heart of Prime Minister John G. Diefenbaker and was an attempt to guarantee the rights of life,

liberty, security of person and enjoyment of property, equality before and protection of the law, freedom of religion, of speech, of assembly, and of the press, "without discrimination by reason of race, national origin, colour, religion, or sex." Its importance has been eclipsed by the Canadian Charter of Rights and Freedoms, 1981.

343. *What are the names and nicknames of the Houses of Parliament?*
The two houses of Parliament are the House of Commons and the Senate. The House of Commons is the lower house of the legislature, and the Senate is the upper house of the legislature.

Both houses of Parliament have nicknames. The House of Commons is traditionally called the Green Chamber, and the Senate is traditionally called the Red Chamber. Both terms derive from the colour of the carpets and other appointments in the two chambers. It is a point of procedure that the euphemism "the Other Place" is used when referring to the Senate in the House or the House in the Senate.

344. *How many seats are there in the House of Commons?*
There are 282 seats in the House of Commons. Each of the 282 constituencies or ridings in the country elects its representative or member of Parliament, who sits in the House.

After each general election, constituencies or ridings are redefined to better reflect population shifts. In 1985–86, the 282 constituencies or ridings, grouped provincially and territorially, were as follows: Newfoundland, 7; Nova Scotia, 11; New Brunswick, 10; Prince Edward Island, 4; Quebec, 75; Ontario, 95; Manitoba, 14; Saskatchewan, 14; Alberta, 21; British Columbia, 28; Yukon Territory, 1; Northwest Territories, 2.

345. *How many seats are there in the Senate?*
There are 104 seats in the Senate. Each seat is filled by a senator

appointed to represent a province or a territory, not a constituency or a riding.

Newfoundland has 6 senators; Nova Scotia, 10; New Brunswick, 10; Prince Edward Island, 4; Quebec, 24; Ontario, 24; Manitoba, 6; Saskatchewan, 6; Alberta, 6; British Columbia, 6; Yukon Territory, 1; Northwest Territories, 1.

346. *Is there a mandatory retirement age for senators?*

There never used to be, the result being that Canada had in the Senate some of the oldest legislators in the world. Now, senators are appointed to age seventy-five.

347. *Should the Senate be reformed or abolished?*

Reform of the Senate and even its abolition are issues that are raised from time to time. For a long time, appointments to the Senate have been viewed as patronage posts, and at times it seems the Senate does little more than rubber-stamp government legislation. But the Senate does act as a forum for the discussion of public issues, it may air grievances through its special committees, and it is said to take a "sober second look" at legislation originating in the House of Commons. Senate reform usually turns on such specific proposals as the suggestion made by Prime Minister Trudeau in 1978 that the Senate should be transformed into a House of the Provinces with equal representation given to all the provinces. Those who favour abolition of the Senate note that unicameral assemblies work more efficiently and are as democratic as bicameral assemblies.

348. *What are the functions of the Sergeant-at-Arms and the Gentleman Usher of the Black Rod?*

The Sergeant-at-Arms is the official charged with ceremonial functions and security duties in the House of Commons. The Sergeant carries the Mace in front of the Speaker of the House when so required.

The Gentleman Usher of the Black Rod is the ceremonial official of the Senate. One of the Gentleman's official duties is to summon members of the House of Commons to the Senate chamber to hear the Speech from the Throne at the opening of Parliament.

349. *Who is the Speaker?*

There is a speaker for both the Senate and the House of Commons. The Speaker of the Senate is appointed by the Governor General. The Speaker of the House of Commons is elected by the members at the beginning of each newly elected Parliament to act as its presiding officer and to conduct its business. By tradition, the Speaker is unwilling to assume his post and must be "assisted" into the chamber by the Prime Minister and the leader of the Opposition at the opening of a new Parliament. The reason for the feigned reluctance to enter the chamber derives from British parliamentary tradition when it was dangerous to be the Speaker. If the King disagreed with the actions of Parliament, he could summon the Speaker. If the Speaker didn't present Parliament's case well, the King might signal his disapproval by sending to Parliament, in way of reply, the Speaker's head.

350. *Who delivers the Speech from the Throne?*

The Speech from the Throne is the formal address delivered by the Governor General on behalf of the Queen in the Senate chamber to both houses at the opening of a new Parliament. It is written by the government and it refers to the measures it proposes to put before Parliament in the coming session.

351. *Who or what is* **Hansard***?*

Hansard refers to the printed record of the deliberations of Parliament. Reference is most often made to the *House of Commons Debates: Official Reports*, which appear daily in monograph form with minimal editing. The record takes its name from Luke

Hansard, the British printer who in 1774 began printing the proceedings of the British House of Commons.

352. What is the difference between a minority and a majority government?

A minority government in a provincial legislature or the federal House of Commons is one in which there are insufficient members of the governing party to ensure the passage of legislation without support from other parties. A majority government has sufficient members of the governing party to ensure the passage of legislation without help from other parties.

Majority governments are often considered more desirable than minority governments. Yet minority governments may be productive, and can be argued to be, in some senses, more democratic, as no single party can impose its will. Federally there have been Conservative minority governments in 1957, 1962, and 1979; and Liberal minority governments in 1921, 1925, 1926, 1963, 1965, and 1972.

353. What is the difference between a sitting and a session of the House of Commons?

A sitting of the House of Commons lasts one day; a session of the House lasts months. The Commons, when it is in session, generally sits five days a week. There must be at least one session of Parliament each year. In practice, sessions average 170 days a year. A session commences with the Speech from the Throne. A session concludes when it is prorogued until the next session.

354. Why is the newly opened Parliament's first business of the day always A Bill Respecting the Administration of Oaths of Office?

This is the title of Bill No. 1, which is always introduced by the Prime Minister and then allowed to lapse. It is tabled to assert the right of the Commons to discuss any business it sees fit.

355. *What is Standing Order 43?*

Standing Order 43 is a rule by which a member of the House of Commons, without prior notice, may make a motion, providing the matter is of some urgency. The order is frequently invoked by members of the Opposition to draw attention to issues of the day.

356. *What are the Statutes of Canada?*

The laws that govern the country are called the Statutes of Canada. They appear annually in tomes, bound in black, which collect the previous year's legislation passed by the Parliament of Canada. About every twenty years the annual volumes are collected and reprinted in consolidated form.

The abbreviation SC refers to the Statutes of Canada, and RSC refers to the Revised Statutes of Canada. A statute is composed of chapters (c.) and sections (s.). A citation is made in the following manner: The Canadian Bill of Rights, SC 1960, c. 44, s. 3.

357. *Must the Queen personally give royal assent to bills?*

It is not necessary for the sovereign or her representative to sign every bill into law. Royal assent may be given by one of her representatives or even by a deputy as long as assent is given in the presence of both houses of Parliament. The clerks of the houses then endorse the day on which assent was given. Royal assent has never been withheld.

358. *What is an Order-in-Council?*

An Order-in-Council is the formal instrument of decisions made by the Committee of the Privy Council or by the Cabinet acting as the Governor in Council. In the latter instance, it is the formal instrument for the legalizing of cabinet decisions undertaken with the formal approval of the Governor General. The government uses the Order-in-Council to enact technical regulations but also to push through controversial legislation.

359. What is the Privy Council?

The Privy Council is a body of senior elected and appointed officials; its purpose is to aid and advise the Crown. The Privy Council as a whole meets only on a few ceremonial occasions, so its constitutional responsibilities — to advise the Crown on matters respecting the government of Canada — are discharged by the Committee of the Privy Council, whose membership is identical to that of the Cabinet. Its instrument is the Order-in-Council. The Privy Council Office, a secretariat, publishes the *Canada Gazette* on a weekly basis for official notes, statutes, Orders-in-Council, etc.

360. Who is head of the Supreme Court of Canada?

The Supreme Court of Canada is the highest appeal court in the land. It is headed by the Chief Justice of Canada. The Chief Justice is chairman of the court of eight puisne (or junior) judges. The Chief Justice and the puisne judges are appointed by the Governor in Council. They may be removed from office by the Governor General. Judges hold office to the age of seventy-five.

361. Which judicial decision confirmed liberty of the press in early Canada?

The right to print without any previous licence, but subject to the consequences of the law, is part and parcel of British law. The right to a "free press" in early Canada was reaffirmed in May, 1835, when it took a jury ten minutes to acquit Joseph Howe of publishing libellous material in his newspaper the *Novascotian*.

362. What was the King-Byng Dispute?

This was a constitutional dispute concerning the role of the Governor General, the Crown's prerogative, and an appointed official's discretionary judgement. The dispute arose in 1926 when Governor General Lord Byng, having refused Prime Minister Mackenzie King's request for a dissolution of Parliament, granted the same request made by Arthur Meighen, King's successor as Prime Minister. King's request was made to avoid a vote of censure; Meighen's, following a vote of nonconfidence. In the general election later that year, King campaigned successfully, maintaining that there was an attempt to relegate Canada to colonial status.

363. *What was the celebrated Persons Case?*

This was the widely heralded decision of the Privy Council of Great Britain that women are "persons" and hence eligible to be summoned to the Senate of Canada. Five women from Alberta petitioned the Supreme Court of Canada, and then the Privy Council of Great Britain, for a ruling on the matter. The decision, rendered on October 18, 1929, declared that "the word persons includes members of the male and female sex." The five Alberta women were Emily Murphy, Nellie McClung, Louise McKinney, Irene Parlby, and Henrietta Edwards. The first woman to be summoned to the Senate was Cairine Wilson in 1930.

364. *What were the Padlock Law and the Roncarelli Case?*

Both were civil liberties issues in Quebec.

The so-called Padlock Law, passed in 1937, permitted the eviction of any person from a building and the padlocking of that building and the evicted person's belongings on the suspicion it was being used by Communists. The measure, opposed by civil libertarian F. R. Scott and others, was found to be *ultra vires* (a transgression of the power of the law) by the Supreme Court of Canada in 1957.

The Roncarelli Case concerned a Montreal restaurant owner named Frank Roncarelli, who, because he acted as a bondsman for Jehovah's Witnesses, had his restaurant's liquor licence cancelled in 1946 by the Quebec government. F. R. Scott and others took the case to the Supreme Court of Canada, which in 1959 established that the Quebec government had committed a "gross abuse" of legal power.

365. Who were — or are — Canada's "mandarins"?

Senior officials and counsellors of state in imperial China were known as mandarins. The same word is used in Canada to describe senior public servants, especially those who held the sway of power in Ottawa from 1935 to 1957. Historian J. L. Granatstein in *The Ottawa Men* (1982) named nineteen Ottawa mandarins of the period, notably O. D. Skelton (External Affairs), W. Clifford Clark (Finance), Graham Towers (Bank of Canada), Arnold Heeney (Privy Council Office), Dana Wilgress (Department of Trade and Commerce), and Lester B. Pearson (External Affairs — and later Prime Minister).

366. What is a deputy minister?

A deputy minister is a senior public servant who has been appointed to serve as the chief administrator of a government department or ministry. A deputy minister wields considerable power as manager of the department and adviser to the minister who is politically responsible for the department or ministry. The office is held at the pleasure of the government and the deputy minister must therefore have its confidence.

367. What is a Crown corporation?

A Crown corporation is a publicly owned corporation accountable to Parliament. Crown corporations are established by the government when it wishes to conduct some of its business through an independent corporation rather than through a federal department, a special board, or a commission. There are various types of Crown corporations, and some of them sell shares to the public.

Crown corporations are as diverse as the Unemployment Insurance Commission, the Royal Canadian Mint, Air Canada, and the Canada Council.

368. *When did the post office become a Crown corporation?*
The Canada Post Office Department became the Canada Post Corporation, a Crown corporation, on October 16, 1981.

369. *What is a royal commission?*
A royal commission is a commission appointed by the government to make an impartial inquiry into a problem. There are federal and provincial royal commissions. Commissioners, who hold their commissions from the Crown, have the power to hear witnesses, hold public hearings, and commission studies by experts. They transmit a report with recommendations for action to the government, but the government is not obligated to act on the report. Of the hundreds of royal commissions appointed since Confederation, many have been influential, among them Bilingual and Biculturalism, Status of Women, and the MacDonald Commission.

370. *What was the purpose of the Rowell-Sirois Commission?*
The Rowell-Sirois Commission is the popular name of the Royal Commission on Dominion-Provincial Relations, headed first by Newton Rowell and then by Joseph Sirois. It was charged with the mandate of examining the economic and financial basis of Confederation, especially the financial relations between the Dominion (or federal) and provincial governments. Among the recommendations of its report in 1940 was a scheme of national adjustment grants designed to maintain a national minimum of services across the country.

371. *What two principal actions were undertaken as the result of recommendations of the Massey Commission?*
The Massey Commission is the short title for the Royal Commission on National Development in the Arts, Letters, and Sciences, 1949–51, chaired by Vincent Massey (later Governor General). It was one of the most influential of royal commissions. Two actions

taken by the federal government in response to the Commission's recommendations were the establishment of the Canada Council in 1957 and a program of unrestricted grants to universities.

372. What is the purpose of the Canada Council?

The Canada Council is an independent body established by Parliament in 1957 to encourage the arts, humanities, and social sciences. (The latter two functions have in recent years been taken over by the Social Sciences and Humanities Research Council of Canada.) The Council advises the government on cultural concerns; maintains the Canadian commission for UNESCO; is responsible for the Governor General's Awards for Literature, the Molson Prize, and other honours; and administers a broad program of fellowships and grants to both individuals and institutions. The Council's influence on the arts has been enlightened and substantial.

373. What is the difference between a Green Paper and a White Paper?

Both the Green Paper and the White Paper are documents prepared by the government and tabled in the House of Commons, but there the similarity ends. The purpose of the Green Paper is to encourage discussion of a particular subject, whereas the purpose of the White Paper is to present government policy that will be translated into legislation.

374. What is "the thirty-year rule"?

Public access to Cabinet papers and other sensitive government documents is restricted for a period of thirty years, after which time the Privy Council Office routinely turns them over to the Public Archives for unrestricted use. The so-called thirty-year rule follows British practice.

Upon formal request under the Access to Information Act of 1983, copies of certain documents will be supplied after only twenty years. However, there are some documents that are not scheduled for release; these are those which may still be considered threatening to national security.

375. *What is a tax-sharing agreement called?*

A tax-sharing agreement, whereby a poorer province receives a larger share of tax revenue from the federal government than a wealthier province, is called an equalization payment. The principle is as old as the BNA Act, 1867, but the word "equalization" is said to date from 1956.

376. *What was the federal government's Anti-Inflation Program?*

The Anti-Inflation Program was a program initiated by the Trudeau administration, without prior provincial consultation, designed to reduce the rate of inflation through fiscal and monetary policies. The program provided for an Anti-Inflation Board which through "guidelines" attempted the regulation of wages and prices. The program had a modest impact on prices and profits but a substantial effect on wages. The program was in place from 1975 to 1978. It was followed some years later by the federal government's Six and Five Program which sought to limit wage increases to 6 percent in 1982 and 5 percent in 1983.

377. *What is a SIN?*

A SIN is a Social Insurance Number. Every taxpayer is issued an individual SIN. The nine-digit numbering system (e.g., 111 111 111) has been in use since 1964 for unemployment insurance, pensions, income tax, medical plans, etc. The first digit identifies one of five regional registration offices (1 is Atlantic; 2 is Quebec; 4 is Ontario; 6 is prairies; 7 is Pacific); the final digit is a check number; and the seven middle digits identify the specific number holder. The system permits 99 million combinations.

378. *Canadians enjoy Medicare. What is it?*
Medicare is the national comprehensive health and hospital insurance coverage enjoyed by Canadians. Sponsored by the federal government, it is operated by the provincial governments on a cost-sharing basis. Quarterly premiums are collected from subscribers. Medicare was first introduced in Saskatchewan in 1962.

Medicare covers visits to doctors and hospitals but not the cost of prescribed drugs or visits to dentists. A continuing controversy is whether medical practitioners should be permitted to "extra bill" — that is, charge Medicare for the scheduled fee and the patient for an amount in excess of that fee, to which the doctor feels entitled.

379. *How does unemployment insurance work?*
The Unemployment Insurance Commission was established in 1940 to ensure that regular payments are made to unemployed persons at a given rate for a stipulated period of time. All members of the work force who receive salaries or wages are entitled to benefits, as deductions are made from their income and contributions are made on their behalf by their employers.

380. *What is the "Baby Bonus"?*
The "Baby Bonus" is the popular name for "family allowance," the monthly payment to mothers of children under eighteen years of age. The first payments were made in July, 1945, under the Family Allowance Act. The payments come in the form of monthly cheques. They are taxable and indexed. In 1986, the payment to help in the raising of a child was approximately thirty dollars a month.

381. *What provisions has the government made for the economic well-being of Canadians once they reach the age of sixty-five?*
Sixty-five is the age of mandatory retirement, when one becomes

a "senior citizen" and a "pensioner." Once he or she reaches that age, a Canadian is generally entitled to receive benefits from the Canada Pension Plan, the Old Age Security Pension, and (if there is no other income) the Guaranteed Income Supplement. These plans are administered by the Department of National Health and Welfare.

382. What does "universality" mean in regard to social service programs?

"Universality" is the term used to describe those government social service programs which are available to all eligible Canadians regardless of income. Programs with "universality" include family allowance, old age pensions, and Medicare. Maintaining the universality of Medicare is considered by some governments a "sacred trust." Programs lacking in "universality" include programs aimed at the poor and based on the income of the recipient, such as allowances to be paid to senior citizens judged to need more than the basic pension.

383. When were lotteries legalized in Canada?

Lotteries were much opposed, being a form of gambling. Yet many Canadians covertly bought Irish Sweepstake tickets and engaged in on-track and off-track betting on sports events. In 1968, Jean Drapeau, mayor of Montreal, introduced a lottery in all but name to raise revenue to finance the Olympic Games. He called it a "voluntary tax contribution" but it was a sweepstake or lottery. The measure was so successful that federal legislation was passed to permit the provinces to establish their own lottery systems. This form of betting became legal on January 1, 1970. Revenues are usually earmarked for hospitals, culture, and special events.

384. What are some different kinds of correctional institutions?

There is no uniform nomenclature for correctional services, but the following terms had widespread application until the proclamation of the Young Offenders Act on December 2, 1985. Training Schools are institutions operated by the provinces for juvenile offenders, young people under the age of sixteen. Adult offenders may serve their sentences in reformatories or penitentiaries. Reformatories are operated by the provinces for offenders sentenced to terms of up to two years less one day; penitentiaries are operated by the federal government for offenders sentenced to terms of two years to life imprisonment (which generally means twenty-five years without parole). The Young Offenders Act replaced the term "juvenile offender" with the term "young offender," defined as a youth between the ages of fourteen and eighteen. Young offenders are sentenced to either "open custody" (a group home, for instance) or "secure custody." In 1985, the population at Canada's 455 prisons and jails was 24,889.

385. What is the status of capital punishment?

Capital punishment, commonly called the death penalty, has not been invoked since 1962 when, on December 11, at Toronto's Don Jail, two murderers, Ronald Turpin and Arthur Lucas, were simultaneously hanged. Capital punishment was formally abolished by Parliament in 1976 except for the premeditated murder of law-enforcement officers, so Canada is effectively abolitionist. Yet every decade or so the moral question of capital punishment is debated by Parliament with members voting free of party direction.

386. What is economic nationalism?

Economic nationalism is a movement, especially strong in the 1960s and 1970s, with economic, political, social, and cultural implications, to assert the country's sovereignty and independence, especially from the United States. Economic nationalists, like the former Liberal finance minister Walter L. Gordon, sought to slow down the rate of increase and reduce the amount of nonresident equity (or ownership) capital in the Canadian economy, thereby arresting or reversing the drift towards continentalism.

387. What is the "arm's length" relationship?

This is the principle that presumes a federally funded cultural agency will not be subject to the federal government for approval of its products or programs. Such organizations as the CBC and the NFB should be free from political influence and accountable to Parliament for their policies and procedures but not managed by the government of the day. The principle may be traced back to the Massey Commission's report of 1951.

388. What is the difference between an ambassador and a high commissioner?

An ambassador is the highest-ranking diplomatic representative sent by a Commonwealth country to a non-Commonwealth country. A high commissioner is the highest-ranking diplomatic representative sent by one Commonwealth country to another. Canada maintains more than a hundred ambassadors and more than thirty high commissioners abroad.

389. What is the classic statement of Canadian isolationism?

The classic statement of Canadian isolationism, expressing an unwillingness on the part of Canadians to involve themselves in world affairs, was uttered by Raoul Dandurand, Canadian delegate to the League of Nations Assembly, The Hague, October 2, 1924. On that occasion Dandurand said, "We live in a fire-proof house, far from inflammable materials."

390. What government organization is responsible for administering Canada's aid to developing countries?

The Canadian International Development Agency, known as CIDA, was established in 1960 and given its present name in 1968. It is headed by a president, who reports to Parliament through the Secretary of State for External Affairs. In 1985 its budget of close to $1 billion was spent on multilateral programs (involving grants, loans, and technical training for developing countries).

391. *Does Canada have an office of the ombudsman?*

There is no federal ombudsman, but many of the provinces have appointed ombudsmen to protect their citizens against bureaucratic abuse. The office originated in Sweden in 1809, but it was not until the mid-1960s that the provincial legislatures began to appoint officials to represent the citizenry in their dealings with the government and the public service. The ombudsman has no power to enforce his decisions but the office does exert moral force.

392. *What were the main provisions of the Official Languages Act?*

The Official Languages Act of 1969 declared French and English the official languages of Canada, enjoying equal status, rights, and privileges as to their use in all the institutions of Parliament and the Government of Canada. The Act called for the appointment of a Commission of Official Languages and for all federal departments and agencies to provide service in both official languages in designated bilingual districts.

393. *What was Bill 101?*

Bill 101 was called the Charter of the French Language. Drafted by the Parti Québécois, it was passed by the Quebec legislature in 1977. It proclaimed French the official language of Quebec and the sole language of the courts and legislature. It further sought to limit the role of English in public use, notably in the names of corporations. It limited access to English-language schools, established language-proficiency tests, and restricted the use of commercial signs in English. Many of its provisions were declared unconstitutional in a series of court decisions between 1977 and 1985.

394. *What was the wording of the Quebec Referendum?*
The Quebec Referendum on the issue of sovereignty-association was written by the Parti Québécois administration and offered to the electorate on May 20, 1980. It appeared in both French and English. The English text is as follows:

> The Government of Quebec has made public its proposal to negotiate a new agreement with the rest of Canada, based on the equality of nations.
>
> This agreement would enable Quebec to acquire the exclusive power to make its laws, levy its taxes, and establish relations abroad — in other words, sovereignty — and at the same time, to maintain with Canada an economic association including a common currency.
>
> No change in political status resulting from these negotiations will be effected without approval by the people through another referendum.
>
> On these terms, do you agree to give the Government of Quebec the mandate to negotiate the proposed agreement between Quebec and Canada?

The voter turnout was 85.6 percent. The results? The ''No'' vote was 2,187,991, or 59.36 percent. The ''Yes'' vote was 1,485,761, or 40.44 percent.

395. *Only one province has declared itself officially bilingual. Which is it?*
Although Canada is officially a bilingual country, only one province has declared itself officially bilingual. New Brunswick is the

sole province to declare English and French its official languages.

Quebec is not officially bilingual, although English and French are sanctioned for use in parliament and the courts. Neither is Manitoba officially bilingual. French was granted recognition in that province from its creation in 1870 until 1890, when provincial legislation called for the use of English only. It was not until 1979 that the Supreme Court of Canada struck down the 1890 statutes, and by 1986 all new Manitoba laws and regulations were being passed in both languages, with the promise that all government services would soon be available in the two languages. Although Ontario has never declared itself officially bilingual, it offers many government services in French.

396. What is meant by provincial autonomy, two nations, one Dominion, special status, separatism, and sovereignty-association?

Political catch phrases like these elude definition. Over the years they have been used to characterize the perceived relationship of French Canada to the rest of the country.

Provincial autonomy is associated with Quebec premier Maurice Duplessis, who died in office in 1959. He sought to protect provincial rights against the "encroachments" of Ottawa.

"Two nations," as a phrase, goes back to Lord Durham's 1839 observation that in Canada he found "two nations warring in the bosom of a single state." In the modern period the notion was specifically repudiated by John G. Diefenbaker, Prime Minister from 1957 to 1963, who argued for "one Canada," a phrase that recalls the passage about "one Dominion" in the BNA Act of 1867.

Special status is a theory associated with the administration of Quebec premier Jean Lesage who in 1960–66 demanded that Quebec be treated differently from the other nine provinces because it is different — it has a French specificity. The notion was resisted by federalists, like Pierre Elliott Trudeau, in both private and public life.

Separatism is a theory that recognizes the right of secession. Separatists maintain that Quebec, as a province and a people, has the right to secede from Confederation and form in the process an independent republic. The theory is associated with René Lévesque in the late 1960s and early 1970s. Its implications were steadfastly resisted by Prime Minister Trudeau during his public years (1968–84).

Sovereignty-association is a notion associated with the Parti Québécois, which came to power provincially in 1976 on the separatist ticket. With the defeat of the referendum on independence held in 1980, Péquiste leader René Lévesque opted for a form of limited separatism, called sovereignty-association, which allowed independence but within a monetary union or association with the rest of Canada. The notion was abandoned with the defeat of the P.Q. in 1985.

397. *In which ways do the governments of Canada and the United States differ?*

The governments of the two countries differ in at least four major ways.

1. They differ in regard to head of state and head of government. In the Canadian system, these are two positions; in the American system, one position. In Canada, the Queen acts as head of state, the Prime Minister as head of government. In the United States, the President functions in both capacities.

2. They differ in regard to separation of powers and concentration of powers. In Canada, power is concentrated in the hands of the government, principally cabinet ministers, who are customarily members of the House of Commons. Government bills are introduced by ministers who appear in Parliament. In the United States, there is a separation of powers. Neither the President nor members of his Cabinet sit in either the House of Representatives or the Senate.

3. They differ in regard to parliamentary-cabinet government and presidential-congressional government. In Canada, there is

no fixed term of office. The government must enjoy the confidence of the House of Commons. The system is both responsible and responsive. In the United States, the President and members of both houses are elected for fixed terms — the President for four years, senators for six years, representatives for two years.

4. They differ in regard to written and unwritten constitution. Canada derives its unwritten constitution from Britain and convention, custom, usage, and practice play an important part. The basis of the government in the United States is the U.S. Constitution of 1776. In practice, Canada is centralized, the United States decentralized.

398. *Have any "republics" been proclaimed in Canada?*

At least four "republics" have been proclaimed in Canada. They were unconstitutional and short lived, as Canada has always been a constitutional monarchy.

Navy Island was occupied in December, 1837, by William Lyon Mackenzie and rebel supporters. He proclaimed the island in the Niagara River above the Falls a "republic." It reverted to its former monarchical status in January, 1838, when he sought refuge in the United States.

The Madawaska region of New Brunswick, immediately north of the Maine border, was proclaimed the "Republic of Madawaska" by its inhabitants, who were weary of the boundary dispute of 1837–42. The episode was recalled in 1949 when a "flag" and "coat of arms" were devised, and the mayor of Edmundston was given the honorary title of "President of the Republic."

Fort Garry, Man. was held by Louis Riel and his Métis followers in 1869–70. He proclaimed the fort to be the seat of his provisional government, which was republican in form. Batoche, in Saskatchewan, was Riel's headquarters, and presumably the capital of the "republic" he declared during the North West Rebellion of 1885.

The existence of "The Republic of Manitobah" was proclaimed by a local council, which appointed one Thomas Spence its "President." Its capital was Portage la Prairie. The proclamation was made in 1867 and disclaimed by the Colonial Office in 1868. It collapsed when Spence attempted to tax a local shoemaker. Spence was arrested and the "republic" ended. In 1977, Portage la Prairie recalled the unlikely episode by issuing a souvenir dollar in the name of "The Republic of Manitobah."

399. *Who led his political party to the largest landslide in any general election in Canadian history?*
Brian Mulroney led the Progressive Conservative Party of Canada to victory in the general election held on September 4, 1984. His victory was the largest landslide in any general election in Canadian history. Of the 282 seats in the House of Commons, the PCs took 211, with the Liberals trailing with 40, the NDP with 30, and one independent. The previous record holder was John G. Diefenbaker, who led the PCs to an upset victory on June 10, 1957, when the Conservatives took 111 of the 264 seats.

5. BUSINESS

400. What are the "four pillars" of the Canadian economy?
In the rhetoric of businessmen, the "four pillars" of the Canadian economy are banks, insurance companies, investment dealers, and trust companies.

401. What is the role of the Bank of Canada?
The Bank of Canada is the country's central bank. It began operations on March 11, 1935, charged with regulating "credit and currency in the best interests of the economic life of the nation." It regulates the money supply held by the community in the form of chartered bank deposits and currency. Every Thursday it sets the bank rate, which determines the interest rate. It has the sole right to issue paper money for circulation in Canada. It acts as the fiscal agent for the federal government and manages the public debt. It does not perform any of the commercial services provided by the chartered banks. It is owned by the federal government and is under the management of a board of directors headed by a governor (whose signature appears on the country's bank notes). The directors are appointed by the minister of finance.

402. When was the Canadian dollar allowed to "float"?
The Canadian dollar was allowed to "float" in 1970. The dollar is permitted to establish its own value in terms of world currencies, generally expressed in terms of the American dollar. Earlier it was allowed to "float" between 1950 and 1962. To date, the high-

est the dollar has reached is the equivalent of $1.06 U.S. in August, 1957, and the lowest it has been is the equivalent of $0.69 U.S. in February, 1986.

403. *Is it true some Canadians who earn more than $250,000 a year pay no income tax at all?*

Yes. According to information released by Statistics Canada in March, 1985, there were 140 Canadians who earned $250,000 or more in the year 1982 who paid nothing in income tax. The same year, there were 5,375 Canadians who earned $50,000 or more who paid no income tax. In December, 1985, the Mulroney administration announced they would make changes to the Income Tax Act which would require top earners to pay *some* tax.

404. *What is Canada's national debt?*

The national debt is the amount of money it costs each year to operate the government and supply its services. The national debt by the end of 1985 was close to $200 billion. Here is how each tax dollar is spent: 22¢ for interest on the public debt; 19¢ for old age pensions, family allowance payments, unemployment insurance, etc.; 20¢ to provinces and municipalities for health care, post secondary education, welfare, equalization payments, etc.; 15¢ to Crown corporations, cultural agencies, underdeveloped countries, etc.; 24¢ to cover the cost of the government's own operations. The "national debt" is really the national budget.

405. *What are the "Big Five"?*

The so-called "Big Five" are the five largest chartered banks in Canada. Individually they are big, in comparison with foreign banks, and collectively they are gigantic, controlling a considerable part of the wealth of Canadians. They are, in order of size, Royal Bank of Canada, Bank of Montreal, Canadian Imperial Bank of Commerce, Bank of Nova Scotia, Toronto-Dominion Bank.

Five smaller but nonetheless significant banks are: Banque

Canadienne Nationale, Banque Provinciale du Canada, Mercantile Bank of Canada, Bank of British Columbia, and Unity Bank of Canada. Banks are federally chartered and must meet deposit regulations.

406. *How many chartered banks are there?*
In addition to the so-called Big Five — Bank of Montreal, Bank of Nova Scotia, Toronto-Dominion Bank, Canadian Imperial Bank of Commerce, Royal Bank of Canada — there were seven chartered banks in 1984 (and only five in 1985). The seven institutions are the Mercantile Bank of Canada, Bank of British Columbia, Canadian Commercial Bank, Northland Bank, Continental Bank of Canada, National Bank of Canada, and Western and Pacific Bank of Canada. The two that failed in September, 1985, are the Canadian Commercial Bank, an Edmonton-based institution, and the Calgary-based Northland Bank. (The only previous bank collapse in Canada was in August, 1923, when the Home Bank of Canada closed its doors.)

The twelve (now ten) chartered banks are Schedule A banks, which have no fixed limit on amounts of deposit. In 1984, there were fifty-eight Schedule B banks, all foreign-owned, with fixed limits. They range from the ABN Bank (The Netherlands) to the Wells Fargo Bank Canada (United States).

407. *How many credit unions are there in Canada?*
In the mid-1980s, there are approximately 3,400 credit unions and *caisses populaires* in Canada, with combined memberships of almost 10 million and assets approaching $44 billion.

A *caisse populaire* is a Quebec credit union. The French term means, literally, "people's bank." The first co-operative savings and loan society, or credit union, established in Canada was introduced in Quebec City in 1900 by Alphonse Desjardins, a journalist who noted that bank loans were often not available to those workers who needed them most.

408. *What are trust companies?*

Trust companies have been called "near banks" for they perform some of the services of chartered banks but not others. Banks are federally chartered; trust companies are federally or provincially incorporated. Trust companies do not engage in commercial banking or insurance, but they accept deposits at local branches and offer the public financial services such as the management of estates, trusts, property, and investments. In the mid-1980s there are approximately seventy trust companies in Canada.

409. *What is the oldest life insurance company in Canada?*

The Canada Life Assurance Company is the oldest Canadian company. It was formed in Hamilton, Ont., in 1847 and now has its head office in Toronto. The first life insurance company to set up business in early Canada was The Standard Life Assurance Company, from Edinburgh, Scotland, in 1833. The Standard is in Montreal.

410. *How many Prime Ministers of Canada have been presidents of life insurance companies?*

Five. Sir John A. Macdonald was president of The Manufacturers Life Insurance Company (1887–91). Alexander Mackenzie was president of North American Life Assurance Company (1881–92). Sir Mackenzie Bowell was president of The Imperial Life Assurance Company (1903–12). Sir Charles Tupper was president of the Crown Life Insurance Company (1901–4), as was Sir Robert Borden (1928–37).

411. *What are the ten largest life insurance companies in Canada?*

The ten largest life insurance companies in Canada are listed below (with the location of each head office in parentheses). The companies are ranged by assets held in this country in 1983. The assets of the top ten companies total $39,005 million, almost 65 percent of the total assets of all companies in Canada.

Sun Life Assurance Co. of Canada (Toronto), Mutual Life Assurance Co. of Canada (Waterloo, Ont), London Life Insurance Co. (London, Ont.), Manufacturers Life Insurance Co. (Toronto), Great-West Life Assurance Co. (Winnipeg), Canada Life Assurance Co. (Toronto), Standard Life Assurance Co. (Montreal), Confederation Life Insurance Co. (Toronto), Metropolitan Life Insurance Co. of America (Ottawa), North American Life Assurance Co. (Toronto).

412. *Who is associated with the question, "What's a million?"*
The glib question, which seems to suggest a cavalier attitude towards government revenue and expenditure, is attributed to C. D. Howe, a powerful and outspoken Liberal cabinet minister in the St. Laurent administration. Howe did not use these particular words, when he spoke on financial matters in the House of Commons on November 19, 1945, but the words were pinned on him as they seemed to summarize his lack of accountability in financial matters.

413. *Which country is Canada's largest trading partner?*
Canada's largest trading partner is the United States, and the United States's largest trading partner is Canada. The total annual trade between the two countries exceeded $150 billion in 1985, an amount that surpasses that of any other two countries. Japan is the second-largest trading partner of both Canada and the United States.

414. *What does Canada export?*
Canada's major exports are fabricated materials, raw commodities, and motor vehicles and parts. Fabricated materials include lumber, newsprint, and chemicals. Raw commodities embrace

wheat, metal ores, and crude petroleum. Motor vehicles and parts, which account for one of every four export dollars, have bulked large since the Auto Pact of 1965.

415. *What is free trade?*

Free trade is an economic theory that favours the mutual reduction or abolition of customs duties between countries. It is the opposite of protectionism. A treaty for free trade in natural products between Canada and the United States existed in 1854–56. The issue was raised again in 1911 and yet again in 1947–48. The Conservative administration of Brian Mulroney announced in 1984 that it would seek a comprehensive, free-trade agreement with the United States.

Canada and the United States are each other's leading trading partners. (Japan is the second with both countries.) Three quarters of Canada's exports are shipped to the U.S., and one fifth of U.S. exports are shipped to Canada. In many sectors there are no customs duties, and the automotive sector has been continentalized and rationalized since the Canada–U.S. Automotive Products Agreement (the Auto Pact) of 1965. (It regulates the production of motor vehicles and parts; three quarters of all vehicles sold in Canada must be manufactured here and the Canadian content of all automobiles must be kept at a certain level.)

Whether one country, or both countries, would benefit from restricted or unrestricted free trade is one question. Another question is whether so-called cultural industries — broadcasting, publishing, etc. — should be protected. It is an open question whether sovereignty — political, social, and cultural — can be maintained in a wide-ranging free-trade agreement between two countries, one ten times the size of the other.

416. *Does Canada have "free trade zones"?*

There are no "free trade zones" in Canada but there is a movement to have some approved. A "free trade zone" — called a "foreign trade zone" in the United States — is an industrial area, usually near a port of entry, that is designated to be tax free. No taxes, duties, levies, bonds, or customs are imposed on goods entering the area or products leaving it. Such tax-free trade zones are found in all major countries, excluding Canada, Australia, and the Soviet Union. There were some 425 in the world in 1985, over 100 in the United States.

For a short time — 1860–64 — the Province of Canada authorized tax-free trade zones in the Gaspé and Sault Ste. Marie areas. They were closed when smuggling occurred.

417. What is the Consumer Price Index?

The Consumer Price Index is a measure of changes in the retail prices of goods and services bought by a representative cross-section of the urban population. The CPI, published monthly by Statistics Canada, is a measure of inflation and purchasing power. Some four hundred goods and services are monitored.

418. What is Canada's largest public marketplace for the trading of securities?

The Toronto Stock Exchange meets this description. The securities of more than eight hundred corporations are traded at the TSE, the third-largest stock exchange in North America and the seventh-largest in the world. It deals in the stock market, the options market, and the financial futures market. It was founded in Toronto in 1852 (when each seat was valued at six dollars). From 1937 to 1983, it occupied its distinctive building at 234 Bay Street. It now occupies the Exchange Tower, 2 First Canadian Place, Toronto.

The TSE is one of five stock exchanges in Canada. The others are in Vancouver, Calgary, Montreal, and Winnipeg.

419. What is the TSE 300 Composite Index?

The TSE 300 Composite Index is the Toronto Stock Exchange's

investment performance measurement service. The 300 largest stocks quoted on the Exchange are measured in terms of performance to reflect the overall performance of the TSE market.

Of related interest is the ownership of the corporations rated by the Index. To dispel the myth that the banks dominate the Canadian investment sector, the Canadian Bankers Association released a report on corporate concentration in March, 1985. The report showed that nine families wield financial control over 46 percent of the 300 companies listed in the Index, and that the level of control rises to 53 percent when chartered banks are deleted from the listing. They go unnamed in the report but the financial families are the Black, Bronfman, Desmarais, Jackman, Reichmann, Seagram, Southam, Thomson, and Weston families.

420. *Are many Canadians employed by the manufacturing industry?*

Approximately one out of four Canadian wage earners is employed by the manufacturing industry.

421. *Which company offered the famous guarantee "Goods Satisfactory or Money Refunded"?*

This guarantee was offered by the T. Eaton Co. Limited, which was established by Timothy Eaton in Toronto in 1869. In one form or another, the wording appeared on the Eaton's Catalogue. The jumbo mail-order catalogue was issued annually from 1884 to 1976.

In 1977, the company, with partners, opened the Eaton Centre, a three-level shopping mall with more than 300 stores under one glass roof. In the rotunda is a bronze, seated statue of Timothy Eaton. It is said that the Eaton Centre has eclipsed Niagara Falls as the country's top tourist attraction.

422. *Which forms of fuel or energy are most used?*

Oil accounts for half the energy used in Canada. Here is the breakdown for energy consumption in Canada in the 1980s: 50 percent oil, 21 percent electricity, 21 percent natural gas, 4 percent coal, 4 percent renewable energy (mainly waste wood for heating purposes).

Almost 75 percent of Canada's electrical power is derived from hydro sources; the remainder comes from thermal stations, some of which employ nuclear energy.

423. What is Canada's first publicly owned power corporation?

Ontario Hydro was the country's first publicly owned power corporation. It was established as Ontario Hydro-Electric Power Corporation on June 7, 1906. Its first chairman was Sir Adam Beck, an outspoken proponent of "power for the people," who led the battle for the public ownership of the source of electrical power. One of the world's great energy producers, the corporation has been known as Ontario Hydro since 1974.

424. Which country consumes more energy per person than any other?

Luxembourg, as surprising as it may seem. Its annual consumption is the equivalent of 9 tonnes, or 10 tons, of oil for each man, woman, and child. Canada comes second in per capita energy consumption.

425. What is the name of Canada's only privately owned large confectionery company?

Ganong Bros. Limited, founded in St. Stephen, N.B., in 1872, is Canada's only privately owned large confectionery company. It was a pioneer in the development of the chocolate bar in 1910.

426. Who founded Weston's Biscuits?

Weston's Biscuits was founded by the baker George Weston, who opened a small biscuit-manufacturing firm in Toronto. It was incorporated in 1910. The company expanded into the United States in 1929 and into Great Britain in 1933 under the control of the founder's son, W. Garfield Weston who, in his day, was called "baker to the world." The bakery is now part of a conglomerate with global holdings controlled by Garfield's son Galen Weston.

427. *What cautionary notice appears on every package of cigarettes sold in Canada?*

The following cautionary notice appears in both official languages: "WARNING: Health and Welfare Canada advises that danger to health increases with amount smoked — avoid inhaling."

428. *Is Canada Dry ginger ale really from Canada?*

It used to be. Canada Dry ("the champagne of ginger ales") was developed in Toronto in 1907 by John J. McLaughlin, pharmacist and bottler (and brother of Colonel Sam McLaughlin of McLaughlin-Buick fame). The "dry" in Canada Dry signifies that the ginger ale is nonsweet. The dry taste caught on and was introduced to the United States in 1922. Then the American subsidiary acquired the original Canadian parent company. Canada Dry products are now popular in over sixty countries.

429. *Who is known as "shoemaker to the world"?*

The sobriquet fits Thomas J. Bata, head of Bata Ltd., the world's largest manufacturer of footwear. An eleventh-generation cobbler and the son of a shoemaker in Czechoslovakia, Bata came to Canada in 1939 and founded the company town, Batawa, near Trenton, Ont. He directs the world operations from Bata International Centre, Don Mills, Ont. His company produces 300 million pairs of shoes a year, one third of all the footwear bought in the free world. Bata manufactures shoes in sixty-one countries, supplies shoes in 115 countries, and operates 6,000 retail stores.

430. *Who were the three founders of the Argus Corporation Limited?*

The Argus Corporation Limited was established as an investment company in Toronto to manage a portfolio of securities owned by E. P. Taylor, Wallace McCutcheon, and Eric Phillips, its founders. It was incorporated on September 24, 1945. The company quickly grew and in the 1970s, under the chairmanship of J. A. (Bud) McDougald, controlled six of the country's leading industrial concerns.

Taylor was the best known of the founders. He bred horses and extolled the capitalist ethic. Critics said his initials "E. P." — which stood for Edward Plunkett — should mean "Excess Profits"!

431. *Which corporation has its executive offices at 10 Toronto Street?*

That is the address in downtown Toronto of Argus Corporation Limited, at one time the country's most powerful and best-known investment and management company. It was directed from 1945 to 1969 by E. P. Taylor, who saw the corporation grow at an astronomical rate. It was acquired by the Ravelston Corporation Limited in 1978 and ownership was restructured in 1985.

432. *Who are the principals of the Ravelston Corporation Limited?*

Ravelston, the corporation which acquired control of Argus Corporation Limited in 1978, a move which stunned Bay Street, was controlled by the brothers, Conrad and G. Montegu Black.

Conrad Black rivals E. P. Taylor, the previous head of Argus, as the most conspicuous and controversial capitalist of contemporary Canada. Black came to the attention of London's Fleet Street in 1985, when he acquired majority interest, plus the option to increase his holding, of The Daily Telegraph Group of newspapers.

433. *Who is the richest man in Canada?*
Kenneth R. Thomson is considered the richest man in Canada. According to Peter C. Newman, Thomson is Canada's only billionaire. Thomson is chairman of the International Thomson Organization Ltd., the family holding company, which owns or controls Thomson Newspapers Ltd., Hudson's Bay Company, Scottish and York Holdings Ltd., Thomson Equitable Corporation, and The Woodbridge Company. He resides in Toronto. In the United Kingdom, he is known as Lord Thomson of Fleet.

434. *Where was the first commercial oil well in North America?*
The first commercial oil well in North America was drilled at Oil Springs, a village in Enniskillen Township, south of Sarnia, Ont. It was drilled by James Miller Williams, who put the well into commercial production in the summer of 1857, two years before Edwin L. Drake successfully drilled for oil in Pennsylvania. Up to that time all wells were dug rather than drilled. Williams was the first person to drill. He also established Canada's first oil refinery. The Oil Museum of Canada was opened at Oil Springs in 1959.

435. *What was the Canadian oil industry's most significant discovery?*
The most significant oil discovery in Canadian history was made by Imperial Oil on February 13, 1947, at Leduc No. 1, a site just south of Edmonton. It ushered in Alberta's postwar oil boom. The well produced high-quality crude oil until it went dry in 1974.

The Leduc discovery may be the most significant, but the first was made by Sir Alexander Mackenzie, the explorer, who in 1789 found oil seeping through the ground at Norman Wells, N.W.T. He described it as looking like yellow wax but did not otherwise bother about it. One hundred and thirty years later, Canada's first producing well, Imperial No. 1, gushed forth at the same place.

436. *Where will the world's largest reserve of oil be found?*
The claim is frequently made that the world's largest reserve of oil will be found in the bituminous sands of the Athabasca Tar Sands.

The existence of the oil-rich Athabasca Tar Sands, located along the Athabasca River, near Fort McMurray in northeastern Alberta, was known for almost two centuries before methods of extraction could be devised. Extraction commenced on a minor scale in 1969, and was approved on a major scale by the Alberta government in 1973. It is estimated that the jet-black sands contain 900 billion barrels of oil, more than half the world's proven conventional reserves.

437. *Whatever happened to the Mackenzie Valley Pipeline?*
Plans to lay the Mackenzie Valley Pipeline to carry arctic gas and oil from the Beaufort Sea area to markets in western Canada and the United States were put on hold following the inquiry headed by Thomas R. Berger. In his report released in 1977, Mr. Justice Berger recommended a moratorium on pipeline construction in the Arctic for a period of ten years, stressing the environmental hazards, native land claims, and escalating costs of construction.

438. *What is the name of the publicly owned oil company?*
Petro-Canada is the largest Canadian-owned corporation in the petroleum industry and the only nationally integrated Canadian oil and gas corporation. It was created by an act of Parliament in 1975. Petrocan's head office is in Calgary. In 1983, it had $9.1 billion in assets and employed 6,700 people.

439. *What is Inco Limited?*
Inco Limited, established in 1902, is the world's largest producer of nickel and a substantial producer of copper, cobalt, and pre-

cious metals. It is also the largest producer of metallurgical-based sulphuric acid in Canada.

Inco made what is believed to be the largest single corporate donation in Canadian history when it gave $5 million to Sudbury's Science North. The scientific-educational complex, opened in 1984, concentrates on the Earth sciences and the North. (Inco's contribution was corporate; the contribution of $7 million to the Roy Thomson Hall in Toronto was made by the Thomson family.)

440. *Where is the world's tallest chimney?*
The world's tallest chimney rises 381 m, or 1,250 feet, above Inco's Copper Cliff Smelter at Copper Cliff, west of Sudbury, Ont.

441. *What is Canada's largest gold producer?*
Dome Mines Ltd. is the country's largest gold producer. It began gold production in the Porcupine area of northern Ontario in 1910.

442. *What percentage of the world's uranium comes from Canada?*
About 30 percent of the world's uranium comes from Canada, making this country the world's single largest producer.

443. *What is the difference between aluminum and aluminium?*
There is no difference between aluminum and aluminium aside from the spelling. In North America, the silver-white metal is known as aluminum; the metal's name in other English-speaking countries and in other languages is aluminium. Canada is the world's largest producer of the light-weight metal, and Alcan Aluminium Limited, with its headquarters in Montreal, is one of Canada's largest industrial enterprises.

444. *What company is Canada's biggest exporter?*
Canada's biggest exporter is General Motors of Canada. In 1985, it accounted for more than $9 billion in total Canadian exports.

445. *Which company holds the greatest assets?*
The company with the greatest assets in Canada is Hydro-Québec, with $25.2 billion in 1983. It is followed by Ontario Hydro ($23.1 billion) and Canadian Pacific ($17.6 billion).

446. *What is believed to be the largest privately owned company in Canada?*
Information on privately owned companies, as distinct from publicly owned companies, is hard to find. But it is widely believed that the country's largest privately owned company is Olympia & York Developments Ltd. The Toronto corporation specializes in commercial developments in metropolitan core areas in North America. It has been called the world's largest private landlord.

The Financial Post listed the five largest privately owned Canadian companies in its Summer 1985 issue. Here, in alphabetical order, are the companies: Bata Ltd., T. Eaton Co. Ltd., Irving Oil Ltd., Michelin Tires (Canada) Ltd., Olympia & York Developments Ltd.

447. *Who owns Canada's newspapers?*
The total number of daily newspapers published in Canada (based on total Canadian Press membership on May 1, 1985) is 102. Sixty-six newspapers are members of the following chains: Thomson (39), Southam (14), Sterling (9), and Desmarais (4). The rest — 9 in the Atlantic region, 6 in Quebec, 12 in Ontario, and 9 in the West — are independent newspapers or privately owned (like the Irving family in New Brunswick or Unimedia in Quebec).

Thomson's flagship newspaper is *The Globe and Mail*, which is the only Canadian newspaper to maintain a bureau in China.

Among Southam's leading papers are the *Montreal Gazette*, the *Ottawa Citizen*, and both the *Vancouver Province* and the *Vancouver Sun*. Sterling's papers are concentrated in British Columbia, the Desmarais group in Quebec. Among the leading independent newspapers are the *Montreal Journal* and The *Toronto Star*, the country's leading newspaper in terms of circulation.

448. Articles in newspapers are often accompanied by "(CP)." What do the letters within the parentheses signify?
CP is short for the Canadian Press, the national news co-operative owned by more than one hundred Canadian daily newspapers. An article in a newspaper which begins with a place name and "(CP)" identifies a news or feature story written and supplied by this news agency, the Canadian equivalent of Associated Press, Reuter's, or Agence France-Presse.

CP began service to English-language dailies in 1917 and to French-language dailies in 1951. A wholly owned associate company, Broadcast News Ltd., known as BN, has supplied audio and printer services to more than six hundred radio and television stations and cable systems in English since 1933 and in French since 1945.

The head office is in Toronto but the French service operates out of Montreal. CP has staff in fourteen Canadian cities as well as in New York, Washington, and London, England.

449. Which magazine is bought by more Canadians than any other?
Tricky question. *TV Guide* enjoys the largest sales of any magazine in the country. It reported in 1984 weekly paid sales of 837,256 copies. The key word is "weekly," as it is outstripped in sales by two monthly magazines. *Reader's Digest* reported monthly paid sales of 1,335,988, and *Chatelaine* followed with 1,104,961. More copies of *TV Guide* than of *Reader's Digest* and *Chatelaine* combined are sold each year in Canada.

450. *Are the arts in Canada "big business"?*
Far from being a marginal business activity, the arts in Canada are central to the economy. The arts are one of the twenty largest manufacturing industries, eleventh largest in terms of revenue, sixth largest in terms of salaries and wages, and the largest in terms of employment. The arts-related work force includes 414,000 individuals or 4 percent of the labour force. Arts-related employment is nearly as large as the agricultural labour force. Unlike the overall labour force, which increased between 1971 and 1981 by only 39 percent, the arts labour force increased during the same period by 74 percent.

451. *There is an Intellectual Property Directorate. What is its concern?*
The Intellectual Property Directorate is in the federal Department of Consumer and Corporate Affairs Canada. It deals with patents, trade marks, copyright registration, and industrial design registration.

The Patent Office, in addition to issuing patents, is charged with gathering and disseminating technological information found in the world's patent documents. Information in patents can help Canadian industry stay up to date and can help researchers avoid reinventing the wheel. The seventeen-year protection given to patentees allows them to sell or license their inventions, and prevent other people from making, using, or selling them.

The Trade Mark Office registers trade marks, which are words or designs that serve to distinguish the goods and services of one person from those of others. The trade mark files are searchable by computer, which enables listing of all trade marks associated with given goods or services and their owners as well as listing of trade marks that are similar to ones being considered for adoption. Registering a trade mark allows the owner to license others to use his mark, a very important consideration in a franchising operation.

Copyright is automatic in Canada for literary, dramatic, artistic, or musical works. It exists as soon as the author creates an original work. The Directorate operates a voluntary registration system. Copyright protection usually continues for the life of the author and fifty years thereafter. Canada belongs to the Berne and Universal Copyright conventions. Protection in other countries belonging to the Berne Convention requires no further action on the part of the author or artist. Protection under the Universal Copyright Convention — the United States belongs to this one — requires the inclusion of the letter "c" in a circle, the name of the owner, and the year of publication or production, e.g., © J. R. Colombo 1986. The right to reproduce a work may be assigned by the author or artist.

The original shape, pattern, or ornamentation applied to an article intended to be manufactured in quantity may be protected by an industrial design registration. It allows the owner to prevent others from copying the design for a term of five years, renewable for another five years.

452. *When did the first recorded strike for better wages occur?*
The first recorded strike for better wages in territory now part of Canada occurred in August 1794, when fur trade voyageurs at Rainy River went on strike.

453. *What is the country's major national labour organization?*
The major national labour organization is the Canadian Labour Congress. A kind of union of unions, the CLC was founded in 1956 in a merger of earlier labour groups. It represents the interests of some ninety national and international unions with a combined membership in 1986 of 2 million. (In all, there are 3.6 million members of trade unions in Canada.) Next in size to the CLC is the Confederation of National Trade Unions (CNTU), with some 170,000 members, almost entirely in the Province of Quebec.

454. *Which is the country's largest union?*
The country's largest union is the Canadian Union of Public
Employees, which, in 1986, had 296,000 members. CUPE was
formed in 1924 and took its present form in 1963.

There are sixteen unions with individual memberships in excess
of 50,000. In decreasing order of size the top six are, after CUPE:
National Union of Provincial Government Employees; Public Service Alliance of Canada; United Steelworkers of America; United
Food and Commercial Workers; and the International Unions,
United Automobile, Aerospace and Agricultural Implement Workers of America.

455. *How much of the country's work force is unionized?*
Combined union memberships in 1986 approach 4 million. Of
nonagricultural paid workers, about 40 percent are unionized.
Of the civilian labour force, some 30 percent are unionized.

International unions account for approximately 40 percent of
total union membership in Canada. (An international union is an
American union with locals in Canada.) One of the largest of the
international unions, the United Auto Workers, split in 1985 when
Robert White of the Canadian U.A.W. led his members out of the
international union to form an independent Canadian union.

456. *Who gave the following explanation for his resignation
from the Ontario labour ministry portfolio: "My place is marching with the workers rather than riding with General Motors"?*
At the height of the Oshawa auto workers strike, on April 14,
1937, when he learned that the Hepburn government at Queen's
Park would countenance strike-breaking, labour minister David
A. Croll resigned, including the above explanation in his letter of
resignation. Croll later became a senator.

457. *What is the so-called Rand Formula?*
The Rand Formula, evolved by Mr. Justice Ivan Rand of the

Supreme Court of Canada in a labour dispute involving the Ford Motor Company in 1946, consists in management making deductions equivalent to union dues from wages of nonunion workers, and turning those monies over to the union. It was argued that nonunion workers benefit from the union's bargaining activities.

458. Who called corporations "corporate welfare bums" and why?
The description was first used by NDP leader David Lewis in a speech at New Glasgow, N.S., on August 3, 1972. He was referring to those large corporations that seek government subsidies and find ways to avoid paying business taxes.

459. What are the country's leading industrial corporations?
Every summer *The Financial Post* publishes its listings of "The Top 500" commercial concerns in the country. Here is a list of the twenty-five largest industrial corporations ranked by sales from the Summer 1985 issue. Private companies are excluded from the list. (Location of head office appears in parentheses.)

1. General Motors of Canada Ltd. (Oshawa)
2. Canadian Pacific Ltd. (Montreal)
3. Ford Motor Co. of Canada (Oakville)
4. Bell Canada Enterprises Inc. (Montreal)
5. Imperial Oil Ltd. (Toronto)
6. George Weston Ltd. (Toronto)
7. Alcan Aluminium Ltd. (Montreal)
8. Chrysler Canada Ltd. (Windsor)
9. Texaco Canada Inc. (Toronto)
10. Shell Canada Ltd. (Calgary)
11. Gulf Canada Ltd. (Toronto)
12. Canadian Wheat Board (Winnipeg)
13. Canadian National Railway (Montreal)
14. Petro-Canada (Calgary)
15. Hudson's Bay Co. (Winnipeg)
16. Provigo Inc. (Montreal)
17. TransCanada Pipelines Ltd. (Calgary)
18. Ontario Hydro (Toronto)

19. Brascan Ltd. (Toronto)
20. Canada Development Corp.
    (Vancouver)
21. Hydro-Québec (Montreal)
22. Nova Corp. (Calgary)

23. Hiram Walker Resources
    Ltd. (Toronto)
24. Canada Safeway Ltd.
    (Winnipeg)
25. Steinberg Inc. (Montreal)

460. *What are the largest companies in their fields?*

The editors of *The Financial Post* listed the largest Canadian
companies by their fields and ranked them by sales and operating
revenue. The fields are agriculture, forestry, mining and metals,
manufacturing, energy, transportation, communications, real estate,
and merchandising. Here are ranked lists of the ten largest corporations in each classification from the Summer 1985 issue. Excluded
are private companies, which are not required by law to disclose
earnings.

Agriculture: Canadian Wheat Board, Saskatchewan Wheat Pool,
Cargill Grain Co., Alberta Wheat Pool, James Richardson &
Sons Ltd., United Grain Growers Ltd., Co-operative fédérée de
Québec, Agropur co-operative agro-alimentaire, Manitoba Pool
Elevators, Co-op Atlantic.

Forestry: Abitibi-Price Inc., MacMillan Bloedel Ltd., Domtar
Inc., Consolidated-Bathurst Inc., Canfor Corp., British Columbia Forest Products Ltd., Crown Forest Industries Ltd., Weldwood
of Canada Ltd., Kruper Inc., Boise Cascade Canada Ltd.

Mining and Metals: Alcan Aluminium Ltd., Noranda Inc.,
Inco Ltd., Rio Algom Ltd., Falconbridge Ltd., Denison Mines
Ltd., Sherritt Gordon Mines Ltd., QIT Fer et Titane Inc., Hudson
Bay Mining & Smelting Co., Potash Corp. of Saskatchewan.

Manufacturing: General Motors of Canada Ltd., Ford Motor
Co. of Canada, Chrysler Canada Ltd., Canada Packers Ltd.,
Moore Corp., Seagram Co., Stelco Inc., John Labatt Ltd., Dofasco
Inc., Genstar Corp.

Energy: Imperial Oil Ltd., Texaco Canada Inc., Shell Canada
Ltd., Gulf Canada Ltd., Petro-Canada, TransCanada Pipelines

Ltd., Ontario Hydro, Hydro-Québec, Nova Corp., Total Petroleum (North America) Ltd.

Transportation: Canadian National Railway, Air Canada, Via Rail Canada Inc., CSL Group, Laidlaw Transportation Ltd., Wardair International Ltd., Pacific Western Airlines Ltd., British Columbia Railway Co., Greyhound Lines of Canada Ltd., Algoma Central Railway.

Communications: Bell Canada Enterprises Inc., International Thomson Organisation Ltd., Anglo-Canadian Telephone Co., Southam Inc., Alberta Government Telephones, Maclean Hunter Ltd., Thomson Newspapers Ltd., Torstar Corp., Saskatchewan Telecommunications, Manitoba Telephone System.

Real Estate: Daon Development Corp., Trizec Corp., Bramalea Ltd., Cadillac Fairview Corp., Campeau Corp., Costain Ltd., Bentall Group Inc., Qualico Developments Ltd., Shelter Corp. of Canada, Monarch Investments Ltd.

Merchandising: George Weston Ltd., Hudson's Bay Co., Provigo Inc., Canada Safeway Ltd., Steinberg Inc., Sears Canada Inc., Oshawa Group Ltd., Dominion Stores Ltd., Canadian Tire Corp., Core-Mark International Inc.

461. *What are the largest foreign-owned companies in Canada?*
The largest foreign-owned companies in Canada are listed and ranked in terms of sales by the editors of *The Financial Post*. The list of the top twenty-five comes from the Summer 1985 issue.

General Motors of Canada Ltd., Ford Motor Co. of Canada, Imperial Oil Ltd., Chrysler Canada Ltd., Texaco Canada Inc., Shell Canada Ltd., Gulf Canada Ltd., Canada Safeway Ltd., Sears Canada Inc., IBM Canada Ltd., F. W. Woolworth Co., Mitsui & Co. (Canada), Cargill Grain Co., Amoco Canada Petroleum Co., Suncor Inc., Mobil Oil Canada Ltd., Anglo-Canadian Telephone Co., Alberta & Southern Gas Co., Canadian General Electric Co., Ultramar Canada Inc., Mitsubishi Canada Ltd.,

Dow Chemical Canada Ltd., CIL Inc., Du Pont Canada Inc., Rio Algom Ltd.

462. *What word did a Canadian economist coin in 1958 to describe a large company which operates in two or more countries?*
The word is "multinational," and it is the coinage of Howe Martyn, a Canadian-born economist at the American University, Washington, D.C. Martyn first used the term "multinational firm" in 1958, and although the term "multinational corporation" is more common, the concept of "multinationality" belongs to Martyn.

463. *Are there Canadian-owned multinational corporations?*
Canada has a number of corporations that have "gone global." While Canadians are most aware of foreign-owned multinational corporations that operate in Canada, they should also be aware that there are Canadian-owned multinational corporations that operate in other countries.

The twenty largest Canadian-owned multinational corporations were identified and studied in a report released in 1984 by the Centre for International Studies, Dalhousie University, Halifax. Eighteen of the twenty firms are resource-based; the two manufacturing-based exceptions are Northern Telecom Ltd., a major producer of telephone switching equipment, and Moore Corp. Ltd., a dominant producer of business forms. Foreign sales account for between 30 and 90 percent of total sales. Here is a list of the top corporations in order of size: Alcan Aluminium Ltd., Nova Corp., Hiram Walker Resources Ltd., Northern Telecom Ltd., Noranda Inc., Moore Corp. Ltd., Seagram Co. Ltd., MacMillan Bloedel Ltd., John Labatt Ltd., Massey-Ferguson Ltd., Genstar Corp., Domtar Inc., Abitibi-Price Inc., Amca International Ltd., Molson Co. Ltd., Inco Ltd., Consolidated-Bathurst Inc., Cominco Ltd., Bombardier Inc., National Sea Products Ltd.

6. TECHNOLOGY

464. *What is the cause of the aurora borealis?*

Aurora borealis is the Latin term for the northern lights, the spectacle of multicoloured "curtains" of wavering lights visible in the northern hemisphere. A similar display in the southern hemisphere is called the aurora australis or southern lights. The display is caused by rays from the sun becoming trapped in the earth's Van Allen belts and channelled towards the north and south polar regions by the Earth's magnetic field. The aurorae take place at times of sunspot activity and during magnetic storms.

465. *Who set the world adrift?*

J. Tuzo Wilson is the leading spokesperson for plate tectonics, a theory of continental drift first proposed by Alfred Wegener, who was seeking an explanation for the similarity between the east coastline of South America and the west coastline of Africa. According to plate tectonics, North America broke off from Europe 200 million years ago and has been moving westward at a rate of 2.5 cm, or 1 inch, a year.

Wilson was the first person to graduate in geophysics from a Canadian university. In 1946, he became Professor of Geophysics at the University of Toronto. In 1978 he received the $50,000 Vetlesen Prize, a geology award given by Columbia University. Wilson has served as director of the Ontario Science Centre.

466. *Were there dinosaurs in early Canada?*

Dinosaurs and other prehistoric creatures roamed parts of western

Canada. The word "early" must be taken in an extreme sense, however, for the period of time during which giant reptiles flourished corresponds to the Mesozoic era, when the continent of North America was breaking away from the great landmass of Pangaea. In the late Jurassic period, from 150 to 65 million years ago, prehistoric beasts thrived. Albertosaurus walked the land, the seas were ruled by the giant plesiosaurs, and the great wings of pterodactyls beat the air. All these life forms suddenly expired about 65 million years ago, for reasons scientists still debate.

467. Why is Alberta known as dinosaur country?

More dinosaur bones have been found in the Alberta Badlands than anywhere else in the world. Dinosaur Provincial Park, created in 1955, is a UNESCO World Heritage Site. Three dinosaurs with Canadian names come from the Badlands: the tyrannosaur *Albertosaurus* (Alberta lizard), the duckbill *Edmontosaurus* (Edmonton lizard), and *Lambeosaurus* (Lambe's lizard, after pioneering Canadian paleontologist Lawrence Lambe). All three are on display at the Royal Ontario Museum in Toronto, which houses the world's largest duckbilled dinosaur collection. *Stenonychosaurus* from Alberta is considered the most intelligent dinosaur, with brain power equal to that of an opossum. In 1971, Dale A. Russell of the National Museum of Natural Sciences in Ottawa suggested that a supernova explosion caused the death of the dinosaurs. Since then, many other extraterrestrial killing agents have been proposed.

468. What is Standard Time?

Standard Time is an international system for determining local time. Sir Sandford Fleming (1827–1915) first made the suggestion in Toronto in 1879 that the world should be divided into twenty-four equal time zones to standardize the telling of time. The engineer saw his resolution adopted at a conference in Washington, D.C., in 1884, when Greenwich Mean Time was universally accepted as the foundation of worldwide timekeeping and navigation. In December, 1985, the Greenwich Observatory announced its chronometric service would be terminated and replaced by Coordinated Universal Time, a chronometric service based on atomic clocks and established in Paris in 1972. Standard Time remains in force, but now it is determined by CUT rather than GMT.

469. *How many time zones are there in Canada?*
Canada occupies seven of the world's twenty-four time zones. The only country to occupy more is the Soviet Union, which stretches across nine time zones.

For timekeeping purposes, local time is calculated from noon at Greenwich, England. According to Greenwich Mean Time (or the new Coordinated Universal Time), the time zones are "behind" or "ahead" of Greenwich. Canada's time zones are all "ahead." Newfoundland Standard Time is 3.5 hours ahead; Atlantic Standard Time, 4 hours; Eastern Standard Time, 5 hours; Central Standard Time, 6 hours; Mountain Standard Time, 7 hours; Pacific Standard Time, 8 hours; Yukon Standard Time, 9 hours. In practice, Yukon Standard Time is little used, the Territory having opted for Pacific Standard Time.

470. *What is the point of remembering the mnemonic "Spring forward, fall back"?*
The mnemonic is a reminder to set the clock one hour "forward" in the spring and one hour "back" in the fall. The evenings to adjust the hands of the clock are designated each year, but Daylight-Saving Time usually begins at 2:00 A.M. on the last Sunday in April, and ends at 2:00 A.M. on the last Sunday in October. This departure from Standard Time is a method of adjusting living schedules so as to make maximum use of "daylight." Daylight-Saving Time is thus one hour ahead of Standard Time. It was first introduced in the summer of 1918.

471. *Are there any magnetic hills in Canada?*

Magnetic hills are not magnetized mountains but optical illusions and tourist attractions. There are at least two well-known locations in Canada where the countryside is so tilted that what appears to be an upgrade is really a downgrade. The best-known magnetic hill in Canada is north of Moncton, N.B., where a car driven to the bottom of a hill will appear to coast back up the same hill when the brakes are released. There is another magnetic hill at Dacre, southwest of Renfrew, Ont. The illusion is also sustained at one point on the Chemin de la Côte-des-Neiges in Montreal.

472. *What are some of Canada's worst disasters?*

The first recorded disaster, natural or manmade, is the Great Quebec Earthquake, February 5, 1663, which accounted for the loss of many lives. Forest fires in this century almost destroyed three Ontario towns: Matheson in 1916, Porcupine in 1911, and Haileybury in 1922. The fire that took ninety-nine lives in the Knights of Columbus Hotel, St. John's, Nfld., on December 12, 1942, is attributed to sabotage.

The Frank Slide saw the destruction of the town of Frank, B.C., at 4:10 A.M., April 29, 1903. The Springhill Mine Disaster occurred on November 6, 1958, at Springhill, N.S. The Winnipeg Flood commenced on May 5, 1950. The Regina Tornado hit on July 1, 1912. Hurricane Hazel arrived in Toronto on October 15, 1954.

Over a thousand passengers and crew aboard the *Empress of Ireland* drowned when the ocean liner sank in fourteen minutes on May 29, 1914, after colliding with the *Sorestad* in the Gulf of St. Lawrence. The Halifax Explosion occurred at 9:05 A.M., December 6, 1917.

There have been four notable bridge collapses: Quebec City Bridge, August 28, 1907; Honeymoon Bridge, Niagara Falls, January 27, 1938; Duplessis Bridge, Trois-Rivières, Que., January 31, 1951; and Vancouver's Second Narrows Bridge, June 17, 1958.

The two most disastrous air crashes to occur in Canada involved

DC-8s. The crash of the chartered DC-8 on takeoff from Gander International Airport on December 12, 1985, claimed 258 lives. A TCA (now Air Canada) DC-8 jet airliner crashed at Ste-Thérèse-de-Blainville, Que., four minutes following takeoff from Montreal International Airport on November 28, 1963, with the loss of 118 lives.

Then there was the disaster that might have been — in Mississauga. A CP Rail freight train derailed on November 10, 1979, and chlorine and other highly inflammable and toxic chemicals began to escape. Some 250,000 residents of Mississauga, west of Toronto, were temporarily relocated. There were no deaths or major injuries. This marked the largest peacetime evacuation of any community in North America.

473. When did the Halifax Explosion occur?

The Halifax Explosion occurred in the city's harbour at 9:05 A.M., December 6, 1917, when the Belgian Relief ship *Imo* and the French munitions ship *Mont Blanc* collided. The resulting explosion and its consequence devastated a good part of the city. Several thousand people were injured and 1,630 people died. It was the largest manmade explosion until the detonation of the atom bomb in 1945.

474. Has the camel ever been used as a beast of burden in Canada?

Camels were introduced for use along the Cariboo Trail during the gold rush of the 1860s. They were used in mule trains, but it was found that mules would not follow camels. The camels' soft feet were no match for the rocky trails of British Columbia between Lillooet and Port Douglas. The herd was turned loose in the Thompson Valley, where it terrorized mules and horses until the last camel expired in 1905, thus ending the saga of camel transportation in the Canadian West.

475. *What is the importance of the* Accommodation?

The *Accommodation* was the first steamboat in Canada. It was built by John Molson, founder of Molson's brewery, and was launched on August 19, 1809. The vessel with two paddle wheels transported ten passengers at a time between Montreal and Quebec City.

476. *What was the name of the first vessel to cross the Atlantic under steam?*

The paddle steamer *Royal William*, built in Quebec in 1831, was the first vessel to cross the Atlantic Ocean entirely under steam. It left Quebec on August 4, 1831, and arrived at Gravesend, England, on September 11. The steam crossing may have inspired its part owner, Samuel Cunard, with the notion of establishing a transatlantic steam service in 1839.

477. *When was the first transatlantic cable laid?*

The first successful laying of a transatlantic submarine cable for telegraphic purposes was accomplished in 1858. The cable linked Trinity Bay, Nfld., and Valentia, Ireland. The first message, carried on August 5, 1858, read: "Europe and America are united by telegraphy. Glory to God in the Highest, on earth peace, goodwill toward men."

478. *What was the celebrated accomplishment of Joshua Slocum?*

The Nova Scotian sea captain Joshua Slocum was the first person to complete a solo circumnavigation. He sailed alone around the world in his 11-m, or 36-foot, oyster boat *Spray*, leaving Newport, R.I., on April 25, 1895, and returning 3 years 2 months and 2 days later on June 27, 1898. It was a voyage of 73,600 km, or 46,000 miles. Slocum, a non-swimmer, was fifty-one years old when he set sail.

479. *What were the famous "White Empresses"?*

The famous "White Empresses" were seagoing cruise ships acquired by the Canadian Pacific Railway in 1891 to provide a luxurious service between Vancouver and the Orient. The three best-known were the *Empress of China, Empress of India*, and *Empress of Japan*. World War II ended CP's pre-eminence as a passenger line.

Country cousins of the "White Empresses" were the "Pacific Princesses." These were intercity and coastal steamers, established in 1883 and operated by CPR from 1901 until 1950.

480. *What was the challenge of the* **Manhattan?**

The *Manhattan,* an American-owned supertanker, was refitted to test the feasibility of an oil tanker route through the ice floes of the Northwest Passage. It completed its passage in 1969–70. Although the *Manhattan* required and received the assistance of the Canadian icebreaker *John A. Macdonald*, Canadians felt that its voyage through polar waters constituted a challenge to Canadian sovereignty in the Arctic.

481. *Is it true that a passenger ship completed a transit of the Northwest Passage?*

The passenger ship *Lindblad Explorer* completed a transit of the Northwest Passage on September 11, 1984, taking 23 days to go from St. John's, Nfld., to Point Barrow, Alaska. Aboard were 98 passengers, the first tourists to negotiate the famed Passage.

The *Lindblad Explorer*, a cruise vessel under Captain Hasse Nilsson with Captain Thomas C. Pullen as specialist in ice conditions, was especially reinforced for the ordeal. It became the thirty-third vessel to complete the transit since Amundsen's first voyage aboard the *Gjoa* in 1906. It took the same route as the *Gjoa*, but unlike previous vessels making the voyage, it continued to Yokohama, thus realizing the dream of a safe passage by sea to the Orient.

482. *Who is Canada's "underwater man"?*

The sobriquet fits Joseph B. MacInnis like a cap, or a snorkel. MacInnis is an "underwater man" in the sense that he is a medical doctor, a marine scientist, and an explorer concerned with undersea research. He devised Sublimnos, the country's first underwater habitat, which he tested in Georgian Bay in 1969. After a three-year search he located the wreck of the *Breadalbane*, the world's northernmost shipwreck. It lies beneath 102 m, or 340 feet, of water and 2 m, or 6 feet of ice in the Arctic Ocean, where it sank in 1853. He prepared a television program on the British barque and earned a new sobriquet: "Raider of the Lost Barque."

483. *What is* **Deep Rover***?*

Deep Rover is the most advanced single-person submarine in the world. Built in Dartmouth, N.S., at a cost of $1 million by the Vancouver-based Can-Dive Services Ltd., the first *Deep Rover* was launched in June, 1984. An acrylic sphere, this sub can dive to a depth of 1 km, or 0.6 miles and stay down for a full week. Its pincer-like hands are so sensitive that the operator can make detailed sketches with them. Sea level air pressure is maintained in the sub, so no lengthy decompression procedures are required when surfacing. The original *Deep Rover* has been rented from 1984 to 1986 by Petro-Canada to work at drilling rigs off Newfoundland.

484. *Where was Canada's first railway line?*

The first railway line in early Canada ran between Montreal and the Richelieu River. The track was laid by the Champlain and St. Lawrence Railroad and went from La Prairie, outside Montreal, to Saint-Jean-sur-Richelieu. The company was basically a "portage" railway, transporting freight from the St. Lawrence to the Richelieu River and its connecting waterways, Lake Champlain and the Hudson River. The line was 23.2 kilometres, or 14.5 miles, long. It was opened on July 21, 1836, and the first engine to run along it was the *Dorchester*.

485. *What is the importance of the* **Dorchester** *and the* **Toronto***?*
The *Dorchester* was the first locomotive to operate in Canada. It was purchased from the Robert Stephenson Co. in England in 1836 for use by the Champlain and St. Lawrence Railroad. The wood-burner weighed 4,950 kg, or 11,000 pounds, and was 6.4 m, or 21 feet, long. The *Toronto* was the first Canadian-made locomotive. It was built in Toronto in April, 1853, by James Goode for the Ontario, Simcoe and Huron Railway.

486. *Who was largely responsible for the construction of the CPR?*
Sir William Van Horne (1843–1915) was the first general manager and later president of the Canadian Pacific Railway. He oversaw the expeditious completion of the railway over difficult terrain in 1885. He lived to see the CPR become a giant transportation system with ships as well as trains.

487. *How did the CPR mark the passing of Sir William Van Horne?*
Sir William Van Horne was the general manager of the Canadian Pacific Railway and the man chiefly responsible for its construction. The CPR marked his passing on September 11, 1915, by briefly suspending all vehicle traffic in its vast transportation network. The President of Cuba declared a day of national mourning, as Van Horne was largely responsible for Cuba's national rail operation, too.

488. *What is the Crows Nest Pass Agreement?*
The agreement goes back to 1897 when the federal government granted a subsidy to the Canadian Pacific Railway. In return, the CPR agreed to construct a branch line through the Crows Nest Pass in the Rocky Mountains and to reduce freight rates on cargoes destined for the prairies and on grain destined for world

markets. The agreement, modified over the years, remains in
effect to this day.

489. *What was the* Newfie Bullet*?*

The *Newfie Bullet* was the nickname of the narrow-gauge Newfoundland Railway. Finished in 1898, it went across the interior
of the island from St. John's to Port-aux-Basques. It was taken
over by the CNR in 1949 and replaced two decades later by a
standard-gauge line. In its day it was known as "the slowest train
in North America."

490. *What is Canada's largest railway system?*

The largest railway system is Canadian National Railways, created as a Crown corporation in 1919 to acquire the assets and
provide the services of five bankrupt or near-bankrupt systems
(Canadian Northern Railway, Grand Trunk Pacific, Grand Trunk
Railway, Intercolonial Railway, and National Transcontinental).
In 1960, to stress the company's involvement in communications,
it unveiled its now-familiar CN logo, designed by Allan Fleming.
Today, CN operates the longest trackage and controls 54 percent
of all rail in Canada.

491. *What is VIA Rail?*

VIA Rail Canada Inc. is the federally owned corporation that
manages Canada's passenger rail service. VIA offers intercity,
transcontinental, regional, and remote rail services from coast to
coast on a network of over 20,975 km, or 13,033 miles. Originally a subsidiary of Canadian National Railways, VIA was given
separate Crown corporation status on April 1, 1978. It assumed
the passenger rail services formerly offered by Canadian National
(CN) and Canadian Pacific (CP).

492. *How does one travel across the country by rail?*

VIA Rail offers a near-national passenger rail service in the *Supercontinental*, which runs from Montreal through Winnipeg to Vancouver in five days. VIA Rail also offers the *Continental* service from Toronto through Winnipeg to Vancouver in four days.

493. *How long does it take to go by train from Toronto to Montreal?*

The fastest trip available is on VIA Rail's *Rapido* service, which takes four and a half hours to complete the 530-km, or 330-mile, trip. The *Rapido*'s average speed is 117 km/h, or 73 mph.

494. *What canal circumvents Niagara Falls?*

Niagara Falls is circumvented by the Welland Canal. The waterway connects Lake Erie and Lake Ontario, has seven locks, and is 42 km, or 26 miles, in length. The canal was first cut in 1829, and significant improvements were made in 1932 and 1973. The number of transits in 1983 was 1,240 ocean-going vessels and 3,449 lakers. It takes about twelve hours for a vessel to pass through the Welland Canal.

495. *When was the St. Lawrence Seaway officially opened?*

The St. Lawrence Seaway, a network of navigable waters made up of a river and the five Great Lakes, was officially opened by Queen Elizabeth II and U.S. President Dwight D. Eisenhower at St. Lambert, Que., on April 26, 1959. The need for a deep waterway to open the midcontinent's inland lakes to ocean traffic was appreciated more than three centuries ago. The Seaway route stretches 3,862 km, or 2,400 miles, from the Atlantic Ocean to the westernmost point of Lake Superior. Because of the winter freeze-up, it is used only from April 1 to December 18 of each year.

496. *How long is the world's longest covered bridge?*
The world's longest covered bridge spans the Saint John River at Hartland, northwest of Fredericton, N.B. Built in 1897 and rebuilt in 1920, the wooden structure is 390.8 m, or 1,282 feet, in length.

497. *What is the longest bridge in Canada? The longest tunnel?*
The longest bridge in the country, and the longest cantilever span in the world, is the Pierre Laporte Suspension Bridge. Located outside Quebec City, it is 668 m, or 2,192 feet, long.

The longest tunnel is the Connaught Railway Tunnel, Rogers Pass, B.C. It is 8.08 km, or 5 miles, long.

498. *Where is the world's highest multiple-arch dam?*
The world's highest multiple-arch dam is officially known as the Daniel Johnson Dam, originally named Manic 5, and it is part of the Manicouagan-Outardes hydroelectric power project in northern Quebec. The centre arch is 214 m, or 702 feet, high, and in length it is 1,315 m, or 4,310 feet. It was opened on September 26, 1968. Quebec Premier Daniel Johnson would have officiated, but he died at the site the day before the official ceremonies. The monument became his memorial.

499. *What is the new name of Labrador's Grand Falls?*
Newfoundland Premier Joey Smallwood renamed Labrador's mighty Grand Falls Churchill Falls, after World War II leader Winston Churchill. Churchill Falls Power Project is the largest single-site power station in the Western world. Waters of the Churchill River in central Labrador were diverted to generate electrical power. The giant power project was completed in September, 1974.

500. *What is the "Project of the Century"?*
This was Quebec Premier Robert Bourassa's description of the James Bay Power Project announced by his administration in April, 1971. The mammoth hydroelectric power development requires the reversing and damming of the La Grande Rivière in northern Quebec. The entire undertaking, which involves the settlement of native land claims, will be completed in the late 1980s. Hailed as essential to the Quebec economy, it has also been criticized as too costly to the environment.

501. *What was the first car imported into Canada and when?*
The first automobile imported into Canada was a Winton, brought into the country from Cleveland, Ohio, by a wealthy Canadian industrialist, John Moodie of Hamilton, Ont., in 1898. The Winton was steered by a tiller and had 1-m, or 36-inch spoke wheels and a leather dashboard. Moodie paid a thousand dollars for the car, and got it through customs with a 10 percent duty reduction by declaring it "a locomotive." On April 12, 1898, he took it on his first spin through the streets of Hamilton. A few months later, on a visit to Toronto, he caused Canada's first traffic jam involving an automobile; people lined up for three blocks at Yonge and Melinda streets to view the new contraption. In 1899, he taught his wife to drive it, and she became Canada's first woman car driver.

502. *What Canadian car was named after the French sovereign?*
The automobile was the LeRoy (from the French *le roi*, "the king"), built by Nelson and Milton Good of Berlin (Kitchener), Ont., beginning in 1901. The Good brothers experimented with mechanical devices for two years before they built their first car with the help of a blacksmith. They test drove it to Michigan and back and cleared customs by calling it "farm machinery." Thirty-two LeRoys were built before U.S. competition forced the Good brothers out of business for good. The very first LeRoy survives, proudly displayed in the Doon Pioneer Village, Doon, Ont.

503. *What high-quality Canadian car was built by CCM prior to World War I?*

The automobile was the Russell, built in Toronto by Canadian Cycle and Motor Company (subsequently better known for their CCM bicycles) and named after the company vice president Tommy Russell. As early as 1906, the Russell had its gearshift mounted on the steering column, with three speeds forward and one reverse. Sales were brisk (even with prices as high as three thousand dollars apiece) until the outbreak of the World War I, when the company switched to munitions manufacture. The company never resumed automobile production.

504. *What steam-powered car was built in the 1920s in Stratford, Ont.?*

The Brooks steamer was manufactured by U.S. financier Oland J. Brooks, who bought an empty thresher plant in industry-hungry Stratford and began building cars in 1924. He had over a hundred men manufacturing them and another twenty in service stations and showrooms across the country. Brooks planned to sell his car in the U.S. as well as in Canada. However, with only one unattractive body style and a price tag of $3,885, the product fizzled in 1927 and the company was dissolved in 1931, laying to rest the country's last steam-powered production automobile.

505. *The U.S. automotive industry made many men extremely wealthy, but the Canadian industry produced only one automotive tycoon. Who was he?*

He was Colonel R. S. (Sam) McLaughlin, the Oshawa, Ont., carriage maker who helped create General Motors of Canada in 1918 and who died a multimillionaire at the age of one hundred. His fifty-five-room mansion in downtown Oshawa is open to the public, as is the McLaughlin Planetarium in Toronto, both paid for by profits earned by building cars. He had wisely decided not to build an all-Canadian car but rather to cash in on the technical know-how of Americans. The result was the McLaughlin Buick, which, by an interesting coincidence, appeared in 1908, the same year as Henry Ford introduced the Model T.

506. *What was the Bricklin?*
The Bricklin was a short-lived, two-seater sports car built by Arizona-based entrepreneur Malcolm Bricklin with the financial assistance of the New Brunswick government. The first of the Bricklins rolled off the assembly line at Saint John in 1973; the last, in 1975. The company was plagued with financial difficulties, producing a high-priced luxury car at a time when the public was becoming cost-conscious and ecologically minded.

507. *Why was the Alaska Highway constructed?*
The Alaska Highway was constructed as an all-weather, gravel road from Dawson Creek, B.C., to Fairbanks, Alaska. It was built by the U.S. Army in 1942 for military supply purposes during World War II. It became part of Canada's highway system on April 1, 1946. Its length is 2,451 km, or 1,523 miles.

508. *When was the Trans-Canada Highway opened?*
The Trans-Canada Highway is a modern highway system that links all ten provinces. It was officially declared open on September 3, 1962, at a ceremony at Rogers Pass, Glacier National Park, Alta. The roadway, which extends 7,777 km, or 4,860 miles, from St. John's, Nfld., to Victoria, B.C., is the longest paved road in the world.

509. *Which Canadian cities have subway systems?*
The two largest cities in Canada have subway systems. Toronto opened the first system in the country in 1954. Montreal opened its Métro in 1966. Both systems have been extended over the years.

510. *Who invented the Ski-doo?*

The Ski-doo, the world's first snowmobile, was invented by Joseph-Armand Bombardier in 1922. The Quebec manufacturer reasoned that a little tractor which was driven like a tank would run on snow and ice and thus meet Canada's winter needs. It was not until November 9, 1959, that the first 250 Ski-doos rolled off the assembly line of Bombardier's plant at Valcourt, near Sherbrooke, Que. The vehicle was an immediate success for both recreation and service.

511. *Where is the world's tallest, free-standing structure?*

The tallest, free-standing structure in the world is the CN Tower, which rises 553 m, or 1,815 feet, above Toronto's harbourfront. The soaring landmark, with its restaurant, three observation decks, and radio and television transmission facilities, was erected by the Canadian National Railway and opened in 1976. The principal designer was the engineer Malachy Grant.

512. *How tall is the tallest building in the country?*

The tallest building in the country is First Canadian Place in Toronto. The office tower is 284 m, or 935 feet, high. The seventy-two-storey skyscraper was erected by Olympia & York Developments Ltd. for its principal tenant, the Bank of Montreal, which took occupancy in April 1975.

513. *Is Toronto's Yonge Street really the longest street in the world?*

The claim was first recorded almost a century ago by George Augustus Sala, an English journalist and world traveller. The claim was accepted by Norris McWhirter, who wrote in the *Guinness Book of Records* (1978): "The longest designated street in the world is Yonge Street, which runs north and west from Toronto, Canada."

There are various estimates of its length. The actual driving distance, from 1 Yonge Street, the address of the Toronto Star building at the shore of Lake Ontario, to Rainy River, the community near the Ontario–Manitoba border, is 1,885.3 km or 1,171.5 miles. The road was opened by Lord Simcoe in 1794 and named in honour of Sir George Yonge, British minister of war. As Yonge Street, it is Toronto's principal north-south thoroughfare. As Highway 11, it proceeds north and then west, over the top of the Great Lakes, passing through communities like North Bay and Thunder Bay. It crosses the 49th parallel, one time zone, and the Atlantic watershed. The final stretch, between Atikokan and Fort Francis, was paved only in 1965.

514. *Did Alexander Graham Bell invent the telephone in Canada?*
There is no question that the telephone is the invention of the Scottish-American scientist Alexander Graham Bell (1847–1922). But there is some question about which country, Canada or the United States, can claim to be the "home" of the invention. Bell himself made a distinction between conception and construction. "The telephone was conceived in Brantford in 1874, and born in Boston in 1875," he explained. When the principle of the telephone occurred to him, he was living in the family home at Tutela Heights, outside Brantford, Ont. But it was not until he returned to his laboratory in Boston, Mass., that he was able to construct the device and test it. So the telephone has two "homes." The Bell Homestead at Tutela Heights is now a National Historic Site.

515. *Who placed the world's first long distance telephone call?*
The first long distance telephone call was placed by Alexander Graham Bell to his father, Melville Bell, on August 10, 1876. The inventor installed his primitive telephone in a shoe store in Paris, Ont., and spoke with his father at the telegraph office in Brantford. The two communities are 13 km, or 8 miles, apart. The telephone message was carried over the telegraph lines which

connected the two places via Toronto. The opening words were Melville Bell's. He said, "Yes, Alec, it is I, your father, speaking." The first long distance telephone call was three hours in duration.

516. Did Alexander Graham Bell undertake any other scientific work in Canada?

Alexander Graham Bell had a summer home at Baddeck, N.S., and, ever the scientist, he combined his vacations with scientific and technological experimentation. He founded the Aerial Experiment Association (1907–9) with F. W. (Casey) Baldwin, Glen Curtiss, J. A. D. McCurdy, and Thomas Selfridge. The group experimented with tetrahedral kites and hydrofoils, but its most famous craft was the *Silver Dart*, the biplane that transported McCurdy a kilometre, or half a mile, at an elevation of 9 m, or 30 feet, on February 23, 1909, marking the first flight of a heavier-than-air machine in the British Empire. (This was six years after the Wright Brothers first flew at Kitty Hawk.) There is a replica of the *Silver Dart* at the National Aviation Museum, in Ottawa, and there is a Bell Museum at Baddeck, N.S.

All railway and telephone service throughout North America was suspended for one minute to mark Bell's passing. He died at Baddeck on August 2, 1922. The tribute was held at 6:25 P.M., two days later.

517. Are Canadians the world's greatest telephone users?

No, but they once were. "The largest telephone users in the world are the people of Canada," reported the *Guinness Book of World Records* (1968), "with 664.1 calls per person in 1966." Canadians are no longer the most "telephone-conscious" people in the world. Since then they have been overtaken by Americans as the people who most use the instrument.

As well, Canadians follow Americans in the number of telephones in use in recent years on a per capita basis. For every 100

Americans, there are 78.7 telephones; for every 100 Canadians there are 64.7 telephones. Canada is one of seven countries reporting over 1 million telephones, the other six being the United States, Japan, the United Kingdom, France, West Germany, and Italy.

518. *Which province has the greatest number of area codes?*
The decision to replace the letter-number system with the all-number system for long distance dialling throughout North America was made in 1959. The area code, which is part of this system, precedes the seven-digit telephone number and indicates a specific area. A characteristic of the area code is that the second digit is always 0 or 1. For instance, the number of the Governor General's residence is: 1 (for long distance), then 613 (the area code for Ottawa), followed by 749-5933 (the telephone number for Government House). The area code for Alberta is 403; British Columbia, 604; Manitoba, 204; New Brunswick, 506; Newfoundland, 709; Saskatchewan, 306; Nova Scotia and Prince Edward Island are both 902; the Northwest Territories and Yukon Territory are both 403, the same as Alberta. Ontario has five area codes: 416, 519, 613, 705, 807; Quebec has three: 418, 514, 819. Thus Ontario has the greatest number of area codes.

519. *What is the Postal Code?*
The Postal Code is the name of Canada Post's automated mail system, the equivalent of the Zip Code used in the United States and the British Postcode. The system, in place in 1973, requires the use, in addition to the regular postal address, of six alpha-numeric characters to facilitate speedy delivery.

The Postal Code of Government House, the residence of the Governor General, is K1A 0A1. The first three characters (K1A) identify the geographical area for sorting purposes, and the last three characters (0A1) identify the specific locality for delivery purposes. The code identifies eighteen geographical divisions, each with its initial identifying letter: A, Newfoundland; B, Nova Scotia; C, Prince Edward Island; E, New Brunswick; G, Quebec east; H, Montreal metropolitan; J, Quebec West; K, Eastern Ontario; L, Central Ontario; M, Metropolitan Toronto; N, South-Western Ontario; P, Northern Ontario; R, Manitoba; S, Saskatchewan; T, Alberta; V, British Columbia; X, Northwest Territories; Y, Yukon Territory.

520. What was Marconi's connection with Newfoundland?

The Italian inventor Guglielmo Marconi received the Nobel Prize in physics for the development of wireless telegraphy. The most dramatic demonstration of his invention was arranged in St. John's, Nfld. The night of December 11–12, 1901, Marconi attached an aerial to a kite, flew it from Cabot Memorial Tower on Signal Hill, and received the world's first transatlantic wireless message. The message was sent from Marconi's installation at Poldhu on the western coast of Cornwall. The message consisted of a repetition of three dots, the Morse Code signal for the letter *e*.

521. What historic research was undertaken at McGill's Macdonald Physics Laboratory?

Research in theoretical physics undertaken at the Macdonald Physics Laboratory, McGill University, Montreal, resulted in the awarding of Nobel Prizes in chemistry to Ernest Rutherford in 1908 and Frederick Soddy in 1921. Their work conducted at McGill in 1900–5 on the structure of the atom and the principles of radioactivity clearly anticipated the immense energy potential of atomic fission. Rutherford's original equipment is on display in the Rutherford Collection at McGill.

522. Who is Canada's leading physicist?

Gerhard Herzberg, born in Hamburg, Germany, in 1904, moved to Canada in 1935 and became a Canadian citizen in 1945. In 1948 he was appointed director of the National Research Council of Canada. Herzberg is a spectroscopist, a scientist who studies the emission and absorption of light by matter. He performed a series of ground-breaking experiments with free radicals, fragments of molecules that appear during chemical reactions but last for just millionths of a second. Herzberg found a way to get radiation from these radicals by flashing a bright light at them. He was able to determine the atomic structure of two free radicals, methyl (CH_3) and methylene (CH_2). In 1971, he received the Nobel Prize in chemistry for this work. The National Research Council named the Herzberg Institute of Astrophysics in his honour and the Canadian Association of Physicists annually presents the Herzberg Awards.

523. *Who developed the electron microscope?*

The electron microscope, responsible for much of man's understanding of the minute structure of all things, was developed at the Physics Department of the University of Toronto. Electron microscopes use electrons instead of light, focussing them with magnetic fields instead of glass lenses. The object is then reviewed when the electrons hit a fluorescent screen. James Hillier from Brantford and Albert Prebus, who came to Toronto from Alberta on a National Research Council scholarship, developed and constructed the world's first working model in April, 1938. Their original microscope is on display in the Ontario Science Centre's Hall of Life.

A new kind of microscope using ultrasound waves is being pioneered in Canada today. The acoustic microscope is a joint project of the National Research Council, McGill University, and the University of Sherbrooke.

524. *Does Canada make "designer genes"?*

Twenty-seven Canadian universities and fifty Canadian companies are involved in biotechnology research — the creation of new life forms through genetic engineering. In the summer of 1983, the federal government pledged $22 million to help develop this country's biotechnology industry. Previously, $60 million had been spent to construct the Montreal Biotechnology Institute and $6 million donated to expand the Saskatoon Plant Biotechnology Institute. The Ministry of State for Science and Technology maintains a twenty-five-member National Biotechnology Advisory Committee, directed by microbiologist David Shindler. Canada's largest biotechnology company is Allelix, Inc., of Mississauga, funded 50 percent by the Canada Development Corporation, 30 percent by John Labatt Ltd., and 20 percent by the government of Ontario.

In a related field of biotechnology Canada's greatest achievement to date is the Moo-Young Process, developed by University of Waterloo chemical engineering professor Murray Moo-Young. Microbes are used to convert wood-pulp sludge into an edible fungus that contains as much protein as soybeans and can be used as animal feed. The University of Waterloo expects to make $1 million in royalties from the process.

525. Who are two of Canada's most outstanding portrait photographers?

The most outstanding portrait photographers who have opened studios in Canada are the Scottish-born William Notman (1826–1891) and the Armenian–born Yousuf Karsh (b. 1908). Notman opened the first of his numerous studios in Montreal in 1856, and Karsh established his studio in Ottawa in 1933. Both are known for their formal portraits of notables and celebrities. The Notman Archives in McGill's McCord Museum preserves almost 400,000 prints and negatives. Karsh is renowned for his interpretive portraits of artists and statesmen such as Sir Winston Churchill, whom he caught with a characteristic "bulldog" expression in 1941.

526. What is the significance of "Wait for Me, Daddy"?

This is the title of the most famous Canadian photograph of World

War II. It was taken in New Westminster, B.C., in 1940, by C. P. Detloff, staff photographer for the *Vancouver Province*. It catches a poignant moment: a young boy is trying to catch up to his father, who is marching away with the British Columbia Regiment. The photograph appears in *Canada: A History in Photographs* (1981) by Roger Hall and Gordon Dodds.

527. *What is the Ouimetoscope?*

The Ouimetoscope was the world's first luxury movie theatre. It was designed, built, and opened in Montreal on August 31, 1907, by pioneer film exhibitor Léo-Ernest Ouimet. It had 1200 seats, a seven-piece orchestra, and a liquor licence. The movie house operated until 1926.

528. *Who makes the biggest motion pictures?*

IMAX Systems Corporation of Toronto produces IMAX motion pictures, the largest film format in the world. Invented by Grahame Ferguson and Roman Kroitor in 1968 for Canada's pavilion at Expo 70 in Osaka, Japan, IMAX uses 70 mm film turned sideways, producing six-storey-high projected images. The special projectors are built in Oakville, Ont. The lenses have to be water cooled to keep them from incinerating the film. The first permanent IMAX theatre opened in 1971 as Cinesphere, part of Ontario Place on Toronto's waterfront. The Cinesphere screen covers 1,000 square metres, or 10,760 square feet. There are also IMAX theatres at the Edmonton Space Sciences Centre, at Pyramid Place in Niagara Falls, Ont., and at ten locations in the United States, including Disney's Epcot Center in Florida. IMAX cameras captured the launch of a NASA Space Shuttle in two documentaries, *Hail Columbia* and *The Dream Is Alive*.

529. *What was the cause of the Great Blackout?*

The world's most impressive power failure was the Great Blackout, which occurred the evening of November 9–10, 1965. It plunged into darkness northeastern Canada and the eastern seaboard of the United States. For some hours the entire area was totally without electrical power. The cause was traced to the overloading of a breaker-tripping device at Sir Adam Beck Power Station No. 1, Niagara Falls, Ont. It backed up and short-circuited other breaker devices, cutting the flow of all electricity through the world's most extensive power grid.

530. *What was the source of the uranium used in the atomic bomb exploded over Hiroshima?*

A portion of the uranium used in the atomic bomb exploded over Hiroshima on August 6, 1945, came from Eldorado Nuclear Limited's mine at Great Bear Lake, N.W.T. Pitchblende was discovered there by Gilbert A. Labine on May 16, 1930. Eldorado was expropriated by the Canadian Government on January 28, 1944. Its fissionable materials fuelled about half of the U.S. nuclear weapons manufactured in the late 1950s and early 1960s.

531. *What nuclear reactor has been designated an historic site?*

The ZEEP reactor at Chalk River Nuclear Laboratories — named the Zero Energy Experimental Pile — went into operation on September 5, 1945, and was the first functioning reactor in the world outside the United States. An historic plaque erected by the Archaeological and Historic Sites Board of Ontario marks the site of the reactor, which still stands at Chalk River, Ont., although it is no longer in use.

532. *What is CANDU?*

CANDU is the world's most successful nuclear power reactor system. The name is an acronym of Canadian Deuterium Uranium. It is a system developed in Canada using as a fuel natural uranium — a plentiful Canadian resource — and deuterium oxide, otherwise known as heavy water, as the agent which enhances fission in the uranium atoms. This reaction creates heat which is converted to electricity. In 1985, CANDU reactors provided more than one third of Ontario's electricity. Among the more than two hundred large reactors in the world, five CANDUs are in the top ten in lifetime efficiency rating.

533. *What continuing experiment in radioactive waste burial has attracted international attention?*

In 1960, Chalk River Nuclear Laboratories began an experiment to test the durability of nepheline syenite glass blocks containing high levels of waste fission products, in the soil at the site of the laboratories. Tests have shown that the small amount of radioactive material that has leaked from the glass in a quarter of a century has moved only a few metres, or yards, through the soil, and presents no danger to humans, even though the glass blocks were deliberately buried in sand above groundwater to simulate less than ideal conditions for disposal.

534. *What is the Whiteshell Nuclear Research Establishment?*

The Whiteshell Nuclear Research Establishment is a research and development laboratory about 100 km, or 60 miles, northeast of Winnipeg at Pinawa, Man. It pioneered the successful development of a reactor cooled by a light oil but moderated by heavy water. While recognized for fundamental research in areas varying from medical biophysics to materials development, it has more recently come to prominence as the leading agency in research and development of a Canadian nuclear fuel waste management program. This program is aimed at demonstrating the safe disposal of used fuel or radioactive fuel wastes in deep geologic formations. Whiteshell is also leading in the development of small nuclear energy systems that can be used in locations where more conventional energy sources are expensive or where long-time reliability is important.

535. *Which Canadian may claim to be the father of radio broadcasting?*

The Quebec-born inventor Reginald A. Fessenden (1866–1932) may claim to be the neglected father of radio broadcasting. After working with Thomas A. Edison in New Jersey, he devoted himself to work on radio broadcasting. On December 23, 1900, he successfully transmitted the sound of a human voice on Cobb Island, Potomac River, near Washington, D.C. On December 25, 1906, he beamed the first radio broadcast to the astonished crews of ships in the Atlantic and the Caribbean — a mixed broadcast of carol singing, Bible reading, and violin playing, all performed by Fessenden.

536. *What is "batteryless" radio?*

Until 1925, radio receivers were operated by bulky, expensive batteries (which provide direct current) instead of household electricity (which provides alternating current) because the latter produced a deafening hum when used to heat the cathodes inside radio tubes. Ted Rogers, Sr. (1900–1939), of Toronto, found a way around this, and in 1925 was granted a patent for his "batteryless" radio. From then on radio production and reception raced ahead.

Rogers believed in the future of radio. Realizing that people would need something to listen to on his new, convenient radio receivers, Rogers founded the Toronto radio station CFRB in 1927. It quickly established itself as the country's most popular radio station. The call letters are instructive. *CF* stands for Canada; *RB*, for "Rogers Batteryless."

537. *Is it true that the Canadian Broadcasting Corporation is the world's largest broadcasting system?*

The Canadian Broadcasting Corporation offers more services to more people over a larger area than any other broadcasting system in the world. Among its many operations are four national radio networks (AM and FM in both English and French) and two national television networks (in English and French), in addition to the Northern Service (radio and television in the Yukon and Northwest Territories) and Radio Canada International (short-wave radio service abroad).

The Corporation is a Crown corporation created in 1936 to offer listeners a public — as distinct from a private — radio service. Its French name is Société Radio-Canada. The CBC commenced its television service in 1952 and its colour television service in 1966.

538. What is the significance of the quotation, ''The question is, the State or the United States?''
The well-known remark was made by Graham Spry, an enthusiast for national broadcasting, during his appearance before the Parliamentary Committee on Broadcasting, April 18, 1932. Spry was rhetorically stating that if Canadians wished to preserve their economic, social, political, and cultural autonomy alongside the United States, Canadians would have to insist on state intervention in the form of national goals and objectives and federal funding.

539. What is the CRTC?
The Canadian Radio-Television and Telecommunications Commission (the CRTC) was established in 1969 to regulate and supervise all aspects of private and public broadcasting and communications — radio, television, cable, and pay TV. The CRTC consists of a five-member executive and ten part-time members chosen on a regional basis. One function of the Commission is to ensure that broadcast schedules meet the Canadian content regulations.

540. What is ''Canadian content''?
The term ''Canadian content'' was introduced by the Broadcasting Act of 1958 and over the years has been defined and redefined by

the CRTC, the federal broadcasting regulatory agency. The term defines the ratio of prime-time Canadian programming to imported (usually American) programming content on a radio or television station's schedule. The CBC has managed to meet the Canadian content regulations, and then some, but the private broadcasters have always regarded them as an imposition and have made only token gestures towards meeting them.

In the early years of regulation, programming had to be "Canadian in content and character." In 1983, the CRTC introduced Canadian-content certification based on a point system that considers how many key members of the cast and production team are Canadian citizens.

541. Why is CTV sometimes called "the second network"?
The Canadian Television Network, whose call letters are CTV, is occasionally called "the second network" because it was the second network to be authorized in Canada. Strictly speaking, it should be called "the third network," as the French and English CBC-TV networks were authorized in 1952. CTV is "the second English network." Unlike the CBC, which is publicly owned, CTV is privately owned. It went on the air on October 1, 1961, with eight newly licensed, individually owned television stations in Vancouver, Edmonton, Calgary, Winnipeg, Toronto, Ottawa, Montreal, and Halifax. The head office and main production studio, CFTO-TV, are located in Toronto. The CTV Network now has sixteen affiliate stations and four supplementary stations.

542. Who said, "A TV franchise is a licence to print money"?
The aphorism came from the lips of Roy Thomson, later Lord Thomson of Fleet, after the Toronto-born media magnate acquired the licence to operate the first television station in Edinburgh, Scotland, in the fall of 1957.

543. *How wired is Canada?*

Canada is per capita the most wired country on Earth. Five million homes — 62 percent of the population — receive television by cable. Cable, begun in London, Ont., in 1952, was authorized as a means of signal carriage by the CRTC in 1968. There are currently 610 cable systems across Canada. In March, 1982, the CRTC awarded five organizations licences to operate subscription or pay TV services. In 1984, First Choice and Superchannel, competing pay TV services, merged to form a single national pay movie channel. The CRTC is now licensing specialty services like sports and pop music channels.

544. *What happened at Grassy Narrows in 1970 that attracted considerable national attention?*

In the spring of 1970 it was learned that the rivers on the Indian reserves of Grassy Narrows and Whitedog, near Kenora, Ont., were contaminated with mercury from nearby chemical and pulp and paper plants. Ojibwa who fished in the rivers and ate the catch were found to be suffering from Minamata disease, named after the Japanese town where mercury poisoning was first detected in 1956. Many other harmful side effects were noted. A ban on commercial fishing along the English-Wabigoon river system was imposed. The native population was relocated and eventually offered monetary compensation.

545. *What is acid rain?*

Acid rain occurs when sulphur dioxide and nitrogen oxides oxidize and then combine with cloud moisture to form mild solutions of sulphuric and nitric acids. The sulphur dioxide comes from the smokestacks of utility plants or smelters, the nitrogen oxides primarily from smokestacks and automobile and truck exhausts. Sulphur oxides are currently the main cause of acid rain. Utility and industrial plants in the United States produce about 30 million tons annually. Canada's smelters and plants contribute another

5.5 million tons. The Mulroney administration, in an attempt to reduce emissions in both Canada and the United States, took the initiative to establish a binational committee to explore ways and means to reduce if not eliminate acid rain.

546. *Who wrote the Ritual of the Calling of an Engineer?*
Members of the Engineering Institute of Canada invited Rudyard Kipling to draw up the Ritual of the Calling of an Engineer. The English author agreed and in 1922 contributed an unpublished and still secret text which binds the young engineer "upon my Honour and Cold Iron" — a reference to the iron ring worn by Canadian engineers — to maintain professional and personal standards. The Ritual will probably remain the last unpublished writing of Kipling's.

547. *Who discovered insulin?*
The isolation of insulin for the treatment of diabetes was announced by "the Toronto Group" at a medical conference on May 3, 1922. The group consisted of four medical researchers at the University of Toronto — Frederick G. Banting, Charles H. Best, J. B. Collip, and J. J. R. Macleod. The 1923 Nobel Prize for chemistry was awarded to Banting and Macleod, Banting sharing his monetary reward with Best, and Macleod sharing his with Collip. The isolation of insulin was a milestone in the treatment of diabetes and a landmark in the history of medical research in Canada.

548. *What is the Gallie Living Suture?*
The use of human tissue in surgical repair work was pioneered by Edward A. Gallie (1882–1959), a prominent Toronto surgeon, who performed the graft-like operation in the 1920s, fashioning the suture from a strip of fascia usually removed from the patient's thigh. The procedure is called the Gallie Living Suture.

549. *Was "baby food" invented in Canada?*
The first food manufactured specifically for infants and babies was prepared in Toronto. The precooked, vitamin-enriched cereal was devised by three doctors — Frederick Tisdall, T. G. H. Drake, and Alan Brown — at the Hospital for Sick Children, Toronto. It was marketed internationally by Mead Johnson in 1930 as Pablum, a word derived from the Greek word for food, *pabulum*. Royalties from the sale of Pablum are donated to the hospital's Pediatric Research Foundation.

550. *Who developed the anticoagulant Heparin and pioneered the corrective surgery for blue babies?*
Dr. Gordon Murray (1897–1976) of the Toronto General Hospital developed the anticoagulant Heparin from the livers and lungs of domestic animals. The substance, introduced into the human bloodstream, prevents thrombosis. Heparin was first described clinically in 1936. Dr. Murray is also credited with performing the first blue baby operation in the British Empire and one of the world's first, in 1947. He devised the surgical technique to correct the congenital heart defect of a baby or child whose features have a bluish tinge owing to the poor circulation of blood.

551. *What is the so-called Barr Body and who discovered it?*
The Barr Body is the name sometimes given the sex nucleus of a cell, after the medical researcher, Dr. Murray Barr of the University of Western Ontario, who first recognized it in 1949. Working with the nerve cells of female (but not male) cats, Dr. Barr noted the presence of a small mass of chromatin (the bearer of the hereditary qualities of an organism). The discovery was subsequently confirmed in the cells of human females.

552. *Who undertook the first systematic mapping of the human brain?*
The first systematic mapping of the human brain was undertaken

by Dr. Wilder Penfield (1891–1976), the world-famous neurosurgeon. In 1934, he established the Montreal Neurological Institute at McGill University for the purpose of determining the relationship between human functions and areas of the brain.

553. *What are brain banks?*
Research into neurological and psychological disorders requires the careful study of human brains. There is a Canadian Brain Tissue Bank at the Clarke Institute of Psychiatry, Toronto, which stores brains that have been willed to science. There are only three other brain banks in the world, one in Los Angeles, one in Boston, and one in Cambridge, England.

The Canadian Brain Bank opened in September, 1981, under the direction of Dr. Oleh Hornykiewicz. Half of each donated brain is examined to double-check the cause of death. The other half is wrapped in plastic and aluminum foil and frozen at –80° C, or –112° F, in one of five freezers. Canadian researchers who require brains from either a normal person or one with a specific mental disorder can order them from the Bank.

554. *Whose life's work was the study of stress?*
The study of stress and distress occupied the professional life of Dr. Hans Selye (1907–1982), a Viennese-born biochemist on the faculty of the Université de Montréal. He began to study stress in 1936, and in 1944 his observations of the response of rats to stressful situations led him to formulate his general theory about stress as a nonspecific factor in human health. According to Dr. Selye, everyone suffers some degree of stress but no one should suffer distress.

555. *What is the L'Arche movement?*
L'Arche is a movement to care for mentally handicapped people in small homes as opposed to large institutions. It was founded by

Dr. Jean Vanier (son of the late Governor General Georges Vanier), who opened the first home for the mentally handicapped at Trosly-Breuil, a French village north of Paris, in 1964. Since then, hundreds of homes for the handicapped have been opened in many parts of the world. *Arche* is French for "ark," an allusion to Noah's refuge.

556. *What were* 5BX *and* 10BX?

These were exercise programs developed by the RCAF in the late 1950s and early 1960s to encourage fitness. *5BX* was a series of "Five Basic Exercises for Men" which took eleven minutes a day to perform; *10BX* was a series of "Ten Basic Exercises for Women" which took twelve minutes a day to perform.

557. *What is Canada's largest airline?*

The country's largest airline is Air Canada. A Crown corporation, it was established in 1937 as Trans-Canada Air Lines (TCA). It acquired its present name in 1965. Air Canada flies to fifty-seven destinations around the world. In 1985, it ranked as the world's eighth-largest commercial carrier, with a fleet of 104 aircraft.

The country's second-largest airline is Canadian Pacific Air Lines. This privately owned company, established in 1942, was known until 1986 as CP Air. It flies to fewer than half Air Canada's destinations and has about a quarter the number of aircraft.

Regional carriers include Air B.C., Eastern Provincial Airways, Nordair, Pacific Western Airlines Ltd., Quebecair, and Wardair International Ltd. The territories are served by Northwest Territorial Airways Ltd. from Yellowknife, and Trans North Air from Whitehorse.

558. *What was the importance of the British Commonwealth Air Training Plan?*

The British Commonwealth Air Training Plan was a training program for pilots from Australia, Canada, New Zealand, and the United Kingdom operated by the RCAF from 1939 to 1945. There were more than a hundred schools and depots across the country. Franklin Delano Roosevelt called the BCATP "the aerodrome of democracy."

559. *What does the Great Circle have to do with Goose Bay and Gander?*

The Great Circle is any line which when continued completely around the globe divides the globe into two equal parts. The shortest distance between any two points on the globe lies along a Great Circle. Aviators, flying between eastern North America and Europe by the Great Circle route, found Goose Bay, Labrador, and Gander, Nfld., to be convenient refuelling stops. The need for refuelling declined with the modern jet engine, but older planes and flights between western North America and Europe continue to refuel at Goose Bay or Gander.

560. *What was the* Avro Arrow *and why was its cancellation so controversial?*

The *Avro Arrow* was the popular name of the CF-105, a highly advanced, delta-wing supersonic interceptor aircraft, designed and built under government contract in 1953–59 by A. V. Roe Canada Ltd. at Malton, near Toronto. It was Canada's foothold in aviation technology and the country's contribution to Western defence. The program was summarily cancelled by the new Diefenbaker administration on February 20, 1959, and all prototypes were ordered destroyed. Reasons given for the cancellation were high development and production costs and the belief that bomber threats would in the future best be met by guided missiles rather than jet planes. With the cancellation of the *Avro Arrow*, the production team dispersed, and henceforth Ottawa would buy American planes rather than build Canadian ones.

561. *What are the Y prefixes?*

The three-letter codes employed by the International Air Transport Association are called Y prefixes because they all begin with the letter *Y*. They designate over two hundred Canadian cities for flight destination purposes. They are most commonly encountered on airline tickets and luggage claim checks. The international airports at Gander, Montreal, Ottawa, Toronto, and Vancouver are, respectively, YOX, YUL, YOW, YYZ, and YVR.

562. *Where is the world's largest airport?*

The world's largest airport in terms of area is Mirabel International Airport. It is not, however, one of the world's busiest; it is not even Montreal's busiest airport. Mirabel was opened northwest of Montreal in 1975 and is now considered a "white elephant" on account of its immense size and unrequired capacity. It handles less traffic than Montreal International Airport, at Dorval, Que.

The most important airport in the country in terms of total air traffic is Lester B. Pearson International Airport, the name since 1984 of Toronto International Airport. It ranks eighteenth in the world in traffic volume and is located at Malton, Ont.

Gander International Airport, in the interior of Newfoundland, is used as a refuelling stop by transatlantic carriers, many of them Eastern European. Gander has the distinction of being the "defection capital" of Canada. There are more defections at Gander International Airport than anywhere else in the country. There are about fifty defections each year, largely from flights that originate in Eastern Europe.

563. *What is the International Civil Aviation Organization and where is it?*

The International Civil Aviation Organization, a specialized agency of the United Nations, is the single UN agency located in Canada.

Its headquarters is in Montreal. It is concerned with regulating international air travel and transport.

564. *When and why did Canada decide to "go metric"?*
In 1871, the administration of Sir John A. Macdonald legalized the use of the metric system for all purposes in Canada. The Trudeau administration, in 1970, released a White Paper announcing the government's intention to move from the imperial system to the metric system "for all measurement purposes." The White Paper received all-party approval. The reasons for the change are to facilitate world trade and to simplify measurement procedures. Canada is one of the few countries of the world not yet fully metric. The policy of the Mulroney administration has been to "go slow" on metrication.

565. *How does one convert units from one system to the other?*
The advice of specialists concerned with measurement is: Don't convert. However, if you wish to convert, here are some approximate conversion factors.

IMPERIAL TO METRIC

Multiply **inches** by 2.54 to get **centimetres** exactly
Multiply **feet** by 0.305 to get **metres**
Divide **yards** by 1.1 to get **metres**
Multiply **miles** by 1.6 to get **kilometres**
Divide **pounds** by 2.2 to get **kilograms**
Multiply **ounces** by 28 to get **grams**
Multiply **fluid ounces** by 28 to get **millilitres**
Multiply **gallons** by 4.5 to get **litres**

METRIC TO IMPERIAL

Divide **centimetres** by 2.54 to get **inches** exactly

Divide **metres** by 0.305 to get **feet**
Multiply **metres** by 1.1 to get **yards**
Multiply **kilometres** by 0.62 to get **miles**
Multiply **kilograms** by 2.2 to get **pounds**
Divide **grams** by 28 to get **ounces**
Divide **millilitres** by 28 to get **fluid ounces**
Divide **litres** by 4.5 to get **gallons**

566. *What is Canada's leading research centre?*

The National Research Council of Canada, with headquarters in Ottawa, specializes in scientific research in areas not being pursued by industrial scientists. The NRC was established by an act of Parliament in 1916. The act was amended in 1924 to allow the council to run research laboratories. The NRC is not part of the civil service. Rather, it is run completely by scientists. This turned out to be a most effective method, and the NRC Act has been copied by many other countries as the basis for their national laboratories. Dr. E. W. R. Steacie of Montreal was director of the NRC in 1952–62. He raised it to one of the leading scientific establishments in the world. Among the NRC's many accomplishments are a pocket calculator for the blind, the world's most precise atomic clock (accurate to within three seconds per million years), and extensive exploration of the ionosphere, which extends from 50 to 650 kilometres, or 30 to 390 miles, above the Earth's surface, using Black Brant rockets, mostly launched from the Churchill Research Range in Manitoba.

The NRC originates the National Research Council Official Time Signal, which gives the precise time with a thirty-second sounding at 1:00 P.M. over the CBC Radio Network.

567. *Where is Kanata and for what is it most known?*

Kanata is a municipality west of Ottawa. It was planned in 1961 and incorporated as a city in 1978. Much of the country's high technology is concentrated here — some three hundred corporations concerned with telecommunications, computers, and micro-technology. Journalists have described Kanata as Canada's Silicon Valley, or Silicon Valley North. The name of the community recalls Jacques Cartier's use of the Iroquois word for "clusters of dwellings." Kanata, a planned community, was laid out in "clusters of dwellings." Thus the earliest word used to describe Canada is the word increasingly identified with its technological future.

568. What is the country's best-known videotext system?

Telidon is the country's best-known videotext system. The advanced interactive television system permitting exchanges of information between home TV sets and data banks was announced in August, 1978, by the Department of Communications after nine years of research into European videotext systems. The driving force behind Telidon was Douglas Parkhill, assistant deputy minister of research, Department of Communications.

569. What was detected by LANDSAT in 1976?

LANDSAT is the name used since 1976 for a series of unmanned satellites that orbit the earth, monitoring its resources from an altitude of 910 km, or 560 miles. Routine examination of images from LANDSAT in 1976 revealed a hitherto uncharted island off the coast of Labrador. The small island — 225 square metres, or 2,475 square feet, 6 m, or 20 feet, above sea level — was officially named Canadian Landsat Island.

570. Which university is computerizing the entire Oxford English Dictionary?

The University of Waterloo, in Waterloo, Ont., will become the repository of 60 million words when the University's computer science faculty completes the computerization of the *Oxford English Dictionary*. The undertaking was announced in 1984 and is expected to take up to ten years. It will make available, on an on-line basis, the contents of what is being called the "Super OED."

571. Which Crown corporation is concerned with Canada's international telecommunications service by cable and satellite?

Teleglobe Canada is the Crown corporation, established in 1950, responsible for international telecommunications by cable and satellite, including telephone, television, telex, telegraph, and computer communications.

572. Why do stargazers turn to Canada?

The annual *Observer's Handbook* of the Royal Astronomical Society of Canada is used throughout the world as the standard reference for observational astronomy. Published since 1907 and currently edited by Roy L. Bishop of Acadia University, N.S., the *Handbook* gives night-by-night positions for the moon, the planets, their moons, and information about both the brightest and nearest stars.

The RASC was incorporated in Ontario in 1890, received its Royal Charter in 1903, and was incorporated federally in 1968. Its 3,000 members are divided into twenty centres from Victoria to St. John's. The Toronto centre, with eight hundred members, is the largest local astronomy club in the world.

573. Is there a Canadian telescope in Hawaii?

Counting the 6 km, or 3.6 miles of it below sea level, the extinct volcano Mauna Kea in Hawaii is the world's tallest mountain, rising 4,300 m, or 14,190 feet, above the ocean. Since 1979, the Canada-France-Hawaii Telescope has been operating on its summit. Scientists from Canada and France, who co-operated in the search for an observatory site, are each allotted 42.5 percent of the observing time. Hawaii is entitled to the remaining 15 percent in return for providing the land. The observatory, which took eight years to build, has a 32-metre, or 106-foot, dome housing a telescope with a 366-centimetre-, or 144-inch-wide primary mirror. That mirror, the other optics, the primary mirror support, the telescope's computerized drive and control system, and the covering dome were all built in Canada. The telescope is so high up that clouds form beneath it. The air above the CFHT is so clear and steady that excellent views of very faint and distant objects are obtained there. Because it is near the equator, CFHT can examine both the northern and southern skies.

574. *Where are the biggest "ears" in Canada?*

The Algonquin Radio Observatory at Lake Traverse in Ontario's Algonquin Provincial Park is a 46-metre, or 150-foot, radio telescope operated by the National Research Council. Though its resolution is 200 times poorer than that of the Canada-France-Hawaii Telescope, it is able to probe the universe in invisible radio wavelengths — and it can operate twenty-four hours a day. Since 1974, NRC astronomer Paul A. Feldman has used the telescope to examine the radio emissions of several nearby stars at frequencies of 22.2 gigahertz in hopes of detecting signals from extraterrestrial civilizations.

Canada is a pioneering nation in radio astronomy. The next step forward will be the Canadian Long Baseline Array, a network of new radio telescopes in British Columbia, Alberta, Saskatchewan, Ontario, and Newfoundland. If funding permits, additional telescopes may be added in Manitoba and Quebec. The Long Baseline Array will be used to examine quasars and other cosmic radio sources at very high resolution through the process of interferometry, in effect turning all of Canada into one giant radio telescope.

575. *Neil Armstrong left a message from Canada on the surface of the moon. What was it?*

Neil Armstrong, commander of the *Apollo 11* mission to the

moon, deposited on the lunar surface on July 20, 1969, a disc the size of a fifty-cent piece with miniaturized messages from seventy-three world leaders. Prime Minister Trudeau drafted Canada's message using both official languages. Here is what it says: "Man has reached out and touched the tranquil moon. Puisse ce haut fait permettre à l'homme de redécouvrir la terre et d'y trouver la paix. [May that high accomplishment allow man to rediscover the earth and there find peace.]"

576. *Has Canada launched any satellites into orbit?*
There are no facilities in Canada for the launching of satellites, but satellites designed and built in Canada are in orbit around the Earth. The *Alouette, ISIS, Anik,* and *CTS* satellites were all launched by NASA, mainly from Cape Canaveral, Florida.

Telesat Canada, a partnership between the federal government and the commercial carriers, was established in 1969 to supply satellite-based telecommunications services. *Alouette,* launched September 29, 1962, was the first satellite produced by a country other than the U.S. or the USSR. Three *Anik* satellites were launched in 1972, 1973, and 1975 for television and telephone communication. The *Aniks,* in orbit 35,680 km, or 22,300 miles, above the Earth, are the world's first geostationary satellites designed for domestic commercial use. The *ISIS* and *CTS* satellites are experimental and exploratory objects.

577. *What was code-named Operation Morning Light?*
Operation Morning Light was the Canadian code-name for the most massive search for nuclear debris ever undertaken. In January, 1978, the Soviet spy satellite *Cosmos 954,* carrying 45 kg, or 100 pounds, of enriched uranium 235, malfunctioned and plunged into the atmosphere. It fell to Earth and scattered debris across 46,000 square kilometres, or 18,000 square miles, north of Great Slave Lake in the Barren Lands of the Northwest Territories. There was widespread contamination from particles ranging from

under 2.5 cm, or 1 inch, to over 1.5 m, or 5 feet, in size. The search for debris took more than a year.

578. Was the astronaut's "space suit" developed in Canada?

The "space suit" worn by the American astronauts was devised by NASA in the United States. But its ancestor, the pressurized suit designed to minimize the effects of acceleration and deceleration on the human body, was developed in Toronto in 1940. The prototype of the space suit was named the "Franks Flying Suit" after its inventor, Dr. Wilbur R. Franks (1901–1986), who has been called "the Father of Aviation Medicine." The original suit was a rubber garment with water pads laced onto the legs. It was worn by Allied pilots during World War II as a protection against the ill effects of gravity during high-speed flight. Although the water pads are gone, many of Dr. Franks's innovations influenced the NASA-designed space suit of the Apollo and other space missions.

579. What is the Canadarm?

Canadarm is the name given to the Remote Manipulator System designed by the National Research Council of Canada and built by Spar Aerospace Limited of Toronto for the American space shuttles. Costing $100 million, the first Canadarm was donated to the American space agency NASA for use on its space shuttle *Columbia*, on condition that, if it worked, NASA would then buy three more for its other shuttles, *Discovery, Challenger*, and *Atlantis*. The prototype was a success and the additional arms were sold in 1984.

The 15-metre, or 50-foot, arm is used to transfer satellites and other objects to and from the shuttle's cargo bay. The first space repair mission, in April, 1984, was performed by *Challenger* using its Canadarm to pluck the malfunctioning Solar Maximum Mission (Solar Max) satellite out of orbit. The satellite was repaired by the shuttle crew, then repositioned by the Canadarm. The movements of the shoulder, elbow, and wrist joints, as well as operation of the cylindrical "end effector" hand, can be controlled by a single person inside the shuttle. Cameras on the end effector and just below the elbow allow the operator to see what he or she is doing. In space, the arm can lift up to 30,000 kg, or 66,000 pounds, even though on Earth it cannot lift its own weight off the ground. Both the arm and its control panel inside the shuttle's cockpit are clearly labelled with the word "Canada" and the Canadian flag. An engineering prototype of Canadarm is on display at the Ontario Science Centre in Toronto.

580. *Who is the "highest" Canadian?*

On October 5, 1984, Marc Garneau became the first Canadian in space when he flew on NASA Flight 41-G, the sixth mission of the U.S. Space Shuttle *Challenger,* the same shuttle which was to come to a tragic end in 1986. Commander Garneau, a Canadian Armed Forces engineering specialist, was born in Quebec City in 1949. He made 132 orbits, ranging from 230 to 350 kilometres, or 138 to 210 miles, in altitude, at a speed of 29,000 km/h, or 17,400 mph, during the eight-day mission, which was the thirteenth shuttle flight.

Garneau performed ten Canadian-designed experiments dealing with the effects of space travel on humans. The shuttle crew presented him with a prepackaged turkey meal on October 8, Canadian Thanksgiving. In honour of his homeland, Garneau carried a hockey puck with him on the flight. In a phone conversation with the shuttle crew, U.S. President Ronald Reagan said he knew that the mission commander "appreciates having three strong Canadian arms" on board, referring to Garneau and the remote manipulator Canadarm.

Canada's other astronauts are Dr. Robert Thrisk of Montreal (who was Garneau's backup on 41-G); Dr. Roberta Bondar of Sault Ste. Marie, Ont.; Steven Maclean of Ottawa; Kenneth Money of Toronto; and Bjarni V. Tryggvason, who was born in Reykjavik, Iceland. Two of them are scheduled to fly on future shuttles.

581. *Does Canada have a UFO landing pad?*

Yes. The country's sole UFO landing pad was erected by the citizens of St. Paul, a town in Alberta northeast of Edmonton. The platform, 12 m, or 40 feet, long, decorated with provincial and territorial flags, was built as a Centennial project in 1967. It includes a time capsule to be opened on June 3, 2067. The pad has yet to be employed by aliens.

A sign at the foot of the stairs reads: "The area under the world's first UFO Landing Pad was designated international by the town of St. Paul as a symbol of our faith that mankind will maintain the outer universe free from national wars and strife. That future travel in space will be safe for all intergalactic beings. All visitors from Earth or otherwise are welcome to this territory and to the town of St. Paul."

582. *Is anything Canadian "immortal"?*

Toronto artist Jon Lomberg codesigned the visual portions of the twin Voyager Interstellar Records. These aluminum-plated copper discs contain the sights and sounds of planet Earth. They were launched on the U.S. space probes *Voyager 1* and *Voyager 2* in 1977. Both Voyagers will eventually leave our solar system and travel into interstellar space. The records should last at least a billion years. Two Canadian voices are preserved on the records. One is that of Robert B. Edmonds, Canadian delegate to the United Nations, saying, "I should like to extend the greetings of the government and people of Canada to the extraterrestrial inhabitants of outer space." The other is University of Toronto professor Richard Lee offering greetings in the !Kung language of the Kalahari Bushmen of southwest Africa. Also included in the audio portion is pianist Glenn Gould's rendition of Johann Sebastian Bach's *The Well-Tempered Clavier*, Book 1, Prelude and Fugue in C Major, No. 1, lasting four minutes and forty-eight seconds. Besides many original diagrams by Lomberg, the only Canadian image is an aerial photograph of what was then known as Toronto International Airport. One cannot help but wonder what, if anything, extraterrestrial civilizations will make of these sights and sounds.

7. SOCIETY

583. *What is the difference between a British subject and a Canadian citizen?*

A Canadian citizen is a British subject, but a British subject is not necessarily a Canadian citizen. Before the passage of the Canadian Citizenship Act, which came into force on January 1, 1947, a Canadian was a British subject, the official designation for a person born or naturalized within the British Commonwealth. The Canadian Citizenship Act created the distinct nationality of a Canadian citizen. Specifically, a Canadian citizen is someone born in Canada or born of a Canadian parent outside of Canada or a British subject or other foreigner who has become naturalized in accordance with the provisions of the Act. A Canadian citizen retains the status of a British subject.

584. *How does a foreigner go about acquiring Canadian citizenship?*

For a foreigner to acquire Canadian citizenship, he or she must gain admission to the country as a landed immigrant for permanent residence, meet the residence requirement of five years, speak at least one of the two official languages, be of good character, possess a knowledge of the responsibilities and privileges of citizenship, and be ready to take the Oath of Citizenship.

585. *What is the text of the Oath of Citizenship?*

The official text of the Oath of Citizenship is the following:

"I swear [affirm] that I will be faithful and bear true allegiance to her Majesty Queen Elizabeth the Second, Queen of Canada, Her Heirs and Successors, according to law and that I will faithfully observe the laws of Canada and fulfil my duties as a Canadian citizen.''

586. *What is Canada's immigration Point System?*
Employment and Immigration Canada has evolved immigration selection criteria, called the "Point System," to determine the eligibility and desirability of prospective immigrants, who are allowed 100 "points" in 10 categories. The categories (with total points as of 1985 allowed in parentheses) are the following: education (12), specific vocational preparation (15), experience (8), occupational demand (15), arranged employment or designated occupation (10), location (5), age (10), knowledge of English and French (10), personal suitability (10), relative (5).

General categories of admission are the following: family class; Convention refugee; and independent and other immigrants.

587. *Do Canadians display too much "deference to authority"?*
Edgar Z. Friedenberg, a social scientist at Dalhousie University, maintains that Canadian society is deficient not in respect to law but in respect for liberty. Canadians place too much trust in their government and not enough in their fellow man. The argument is presented in his book *Deference to Authority: The Case of Canada* (1980).

588. *What is the ethnic composition of the population?*
The Census of 1981 gives the composition of the population of Canada in terms of "ethnic origins." Statistics Canada's categories are reproduced below, along with Statscan figures and subtotals for subsections. Excluded are "other categories" and their

figures. This explains why the figures do not equal the 1981 population of 24,083,495.

EUROPEAN

British	20,762,025
English	9,574,250
Irish	6,109,295
Scottish	1,151,955
Welsh	697,460
French	6,439,100
Western European	451,240
Belgian	42,270
Dutch	410,885
Luxembourger	730
Northern European	335,110
Finnish	52,315
Scandinavian	282,795
Danish	57,940
Icelandic	22,755
Norwegian	102,735
Swedish	78,360
Central European	1,651,375
Austrian	40,630
Czech & Slovak	67,700
Czech	24,625
Slovak	18,710
German	1,142,365
Polish	254,485
Magyar (Hungarian)	116,385
Swiss	28,805
East European	652,960
Baltic	50,300
Estonian	15,915
Lettish (Latvian)	16,145
Lithuanian	18,240
Byelorussian	1,125
Romanian	22,485

Russian	48,430
Ukrainian	529,615
South European	1,288,495
Balkan	129,075
Albanian	1,265
Bulgarian	2,935
Croatian, Serbian	114,595
Macedonian	10,045
Greek	154,350
Italian	747,970
Maltese	15,440
Portuguese	188,105
Spanish	53,540
Other European	259,500
Jewish	254,020
WEST ASIAN AND NORTH AFRICAN	101,895
Armenian	21,155
Asian Arab	50,140
Lebanese	27,320
Palestinian	1,005
Syrian	3,455
Asian Arab	28,365
North African Arab	10,545
Egyptian	9,140
North African Arab	1,410
West Asian	10,055
Iranian	5,600
Israeli	305
Turk	4,155
Indian-Pakistani	196,390
Bengali	795
Gujarati	1,530
Punjabi	11,005
Singhalese	795
Tamil	530
Bangladeshi	425

Indian	60,705
Pakistani	13,400
Sri Lankan	2,400
FAR EAST ASIAN	407,085
Chinese	289,245
Indo-Chinese	43,725
Burmese	400
Cambodian	4,310
Laotian	7,145
Thai	505
Vietnamese	31,360
Japanese	40,995
Malay	1,860
Korean	22,095
Pacific Islands	80,340
Fijian	5,545
Indonesian	1,555
Philippino	72,530
Polynesian	515
African	45,215
African Black	5,890
Canadian Black	635
NORTH AND SOUTH AMERICAN ORIGINS	530,930
Native Peoples	413,380
Inuit	23,200
Métis	76,520
Status or Registered Indian	266,450
Non-Status Indian	47,235
LATIN AMERICAN	117,555
Argentinian	1,190
Brazilian	1,150
Caribbean	81,505
Chilean	5,710
Cuban	350
Ecuadorian	1,055

Haitian	15,295
Mexican	3,125
Peruvian	1,220

589. *Who are the Doukhobors?*

The Doukhobors are a sect of fundamentalist Christians whose ancestors emigrated as a group from Russia to Saskatchewan in 1899. Their passage was paid by Leo Tolstoy, who earmarked the royalties of his novel *Resurrection* for this purpose. About 1910, most of them moved farther west to British Columbia, where they established farming communities in the Kootenay and Kettle Valley areas.

The Doukhobors are pacifists who live in isolated communities which remain untouched by twentieth-century values. There are in Canada today about 12,000 Doukhobors. Some 1,250 are members of the Sons of Freedom group who protest such matters as compulsory education and make headlines burning and bombing buildings (usually their own) and staging nude protest.

590. *What is a remittance man?*

A remittance man was a person, usually an Englishman, given a remittance or legacy by his family on the condition that he live abroad. The remittance man was a familiar but unpopular figure, especially in the West, around the turn of the century.

591. *Do Japanese Canadians use special words for children and grandchildren of immigrants?*

Indeed they do. Japanese has a number of words for which precise English equivalents are lacking. A *nikkei* is a Japanese-born person who lives outside Japan. An *imin* is an emigrant. An *issei* is a first-generation person born outside Japan. A *nisei* is second-generation, and a *sansei* is third-generation.

592. *How many Japanese were evacuated during World War II?*
About 22,000 Japanese were evacuated from the coast of British
Columbia in 1942. It did not matter whether they were native-
born or naturalized Canadians or foreigners, they were resettled
in internment camps in the B.C. interior and elsewhere in Canada.
They were allowed to take only one suitcase per person. The
rest of their property was confiscated and sold at distress prices.
The Canadian public seemed to favour such a move because of
racism and fear of fifth column activities. Yet the Japanese in
Canada were loyal to Canada. The Japanese community — and in
particular the 11,000 or so who were evacuated who are alive in
1986 — await a formal government apology and the offer of
reparations.

593. *Who were the Home Children?*
The Home Children were British children, either homeless or
from indigent homes, who were sent to Canada to join farm
families. Between 1870 and the 1930s, over 80,000 children were
resettled from the streets and slums of the British Isles to rural
Canada. Included among the Home Children are the "Barnardo
Boys," 30,000 male youths who came to Canada under the direction of the humanitarian Dr. Thomas Barnardo (who called the
youngsters "nobody's children").

594. *Who were the Redeemed Children and the Deemed Suspect?*
The Redeemed Children were displaced youngsters from Europe
who were given new homes in Canada after World War II. About
1,100 Jewish war orphans were settled by the Canadian Jewish
Congress in 1947–52.

The Deemed Suspect were refugees from Germany and Austria
deported from England to Canada and treated and interned as
"enemy aliens" rather than "friendly aliens." Almost 2,300 were
interned in 1940–43 in eight camps. A list of these refugees reads
like a who's who of Canadian achievers and includes theologians

(Gregory Baum), philosophers (Emil Fachenheim), musicologists (Helmut Blume), and writers (Eric Koch).

595. *How many Jewish refugees were admitted to Canada between 1933 and 1945?*

Canada admitted fewer than 5,000 Jewish refugees between 1933 and 1945, despite the fact that the Jews were a stateless people and victims of persecution and that there were Canadian agencies willing to sponsor them. During the same period, the United States admitted 200,000 Jewish refugees. Canada's record for providing sanctuary was the worst in the world, in the opinion of Irving Abella and Harold Troper, authors of *None Is Too Many: Canada and the Jews of Europe 1933–1948* (1982). They found this country's restrictive immigration policy of the time to be anti-Semitic and racist.

596. *How has Canada treated postwar refugees?*

Canada has proved to be a world leader in the settlement of refugees in the postwar years. It opened its doors to immigration based on the Point System in 1962, but of equal importance it has offered refuge to political refugees, including large groups from Hungary, Czechoslovakia, Hong Kong, Tibet, Uganda, Pakistan, Vietnam, Chile, El Salvador, etc. Canada admitted more than 3.6 million immigrants, including a great many refugees, between 1945 and 1983.

597. *Why is there no federal ministry of education?*

By the terms of the BNA Act, education is a provincial and not a federal responsibility. Hence, in the absence of a federal ministry of education, there are provincial and territorial ministries or their equivalents.

Yet the federal government is deeply involved in education, for it is charged with maintaining schools for the native people and for children of service personnel overseas. In addition, it maintains the three service colleges, and it oversees education in federal penitentiaries. It finances a program of adult occupational training and retraining as well as a program of postsecondary education. Since 1970, it has materially supported bilingual education across the country.

In light of this activity, it seems surprising there is not yet a national secretariat, if not a ministry for education, to establish national guidelines and an international presence or at least minimum standards.

598. What are public schools, separate schools, and private schools?
Education is a provincial matter and there is surprising diversity across the country within the primary and secondary school system. Canadians enjoy free public education with a public school system that is nondenominational and publicly supported. Public schools are open to all. Separate schools are denominational schools operated for and by the Roman Catholic Church. They are publicly supported in Alberta, Ontario, Saskatchewan, and the two territories; they are privately funded elsewhere. Private schools are operated for and by private bodies for specific religious, educational, or social purposes; they may or may not be denominational, but they are all privately funded.

599. Do all the provinces have separate schools?
No. Only three provinces — Ontario, Saskatchewan, and Alberta — have separate or sectarian schools as well as public schools. The term ''separate schools'' is not used at all in Newfoundland and Quebec, for they enjoy a system of parallel ''denominational schools.'' There are no separate schools whatsoever in the remaining provinces — Nova Scotia, New Brunswick, Prince Edward Island, Manitoba, and British Columbia — although at one time Manitoba had Roman Catholic, French-language schools.

600. *Which are the best known private schools for boys and girls?*
The best known private school for boys is Upper Canada College, established in Toronto in 1829. The best known private school for girls is Bishop Strachan School, established in Toronto in 1867. Upper Canada College has an enrolment of about nine hundred primary and secondary students, Bishop Strachan about seven hundred.

601. *What are CAATs and CEGEPs?*
These acronyms identify community colleges, that is, postsecondary institutions for vocational and technical education. CAATs are Colleges of Applied Arts and Technology. CEGEPs are Collèges d'Enseignement Général et Professionnel. Both appeared on the educational scene in the mid-1960s. There are approximately two hundred community colleges in all the provinces. They are to be distinguished from the sixty-six or so public, degree-granting colleges and universities for the professions and the humanities.

602. *Which are the best known universities in Canada?*
The fame of McGill University has spread far and wide for many years. Chartered in Montreal in 1821, it specializes in the humanities and medicine. It is probably Canada's best known university. Canada's largest university, and McGill's chief rival, is the University of Toronto. It was founded in Toronto in 1827 and consists of a loose federation of colleges and faculties, many of them quite distinguished.

The oldest university in Canada, and indeed the oldest in the British Commonwealth outside the British Isles, is the University of King's College. Founded in 1789 at Windsor, N.S., King's College is now part of Dalhousie University, Halifax.

Two Francophone universities in Quebec are particularly notable. Université Laval, founded in Quebec City in 1852, is North America's oldest French-language institution of higher learning.

Université de Montréal, established in Montreal in 1870, is the largest French-language educational institution in the world outside France.

603. *What was Rochdale College?*
Rochdale College was a "free university" named after the birthplace in England of the co-operative movement. It was established in a new eighteen-storey co-operative apartment building in Toronto in 1968 and closed in 1975. The building is now the Senator David A. Croll Apartments for Senior Citizens. Some seven thousand students and others resided at Rochdale, in the heady atmosphere of alternate culture, informal education, and drugs.

604. *Is there a United World College located in Canada?*
There are United World Colleges in various parts of the world. They are secondary schools designed to promote international understanding and fellowship. Students are selected on the basis of merit and are supported by scholarships. Canada's United World College is located near Victoria, B.C. In 1974, it was named Pearson College of the Pacific, in honour of the late statesman Lester B. Pearson. Approximately half the students are Canadian; the balance come from many countries of the world.

605. *Are there "think tanks" in Canada?*
Independent institutes for the analysis of social issues, commonly called "think tanks," began to influence public policy in the postwar United States. They were a longer time coming to this country, although the Conference Board of Canada and the Science Council of Canada could be considered semi-autonomous "think tanks." For some years the Hudson Institute, founded in Upper New York State by Herman Kahn, has operated in Canada. But it was not until the 1970s that indigenous independent institutions proliferated: Canada West Foundation, the Fraser Institute, C. D.

Howe Research Institute, the Niagara Institute, North-South Institute. All are independent but most are conservative in orientation.

606. *If you are entitled to use the letters F.R.S.C. after your name, what does it signify?*

What is signifies is that you are a Fellow of the Royal Society of Canada, a national academy whose aim is the promotion of learning and research in the arts and sciences. It was founded in Ottawa in 1882, and it awards an array of distinctions to bring recognition to outstanding achievement among its members. The French initials are *s.r.c.* Some seven hundred Canadians are entitled to use these letters after their names. The Society meets each spring in conjunction with other learned societies.

607. *Who was the first Canadian to be awarded the Victoria Cross?*

The Victoria Cross, the British Empire and Commonwealth's highest military decoration, was established by Queen Victoria to reward outstanding gallantry in the Crimean War. The first Canadian to be awarded the V.C. was Alexander Roberts, a native of York, U.C., who received the honour in 1857 for "outstanding Gallantry" during the Charge of the Light Brigade at Balaclava. To quote the citation, "Having emptied his revolver at the Russians he flung it at them and resorted to his sabre, which he used to such good effect . . . that he saved Sergeant Bentley's life by cutting down several Russians who were attacking him."

Out of the 1,351 individuals who hold the award, ninety-three Canadians or foreign nationals serving in Canadian units received the Victoria Cross, from its establishment in 1856 to 1972, when the Order of Canada instituted its own awards for military and civilian bravery — the Cross of Valour, the Star of Courage, and the Medal of Bravery.

608. *What is the Order of Canada?*
The Order of Canada was established on July 1, 1967, to honour
Canadians for outstanding achievement and service to their coun-
try or to humanity. There are three levels of membership. Com-
panions of the Order, limited to 150 at one time, are entitled to use
the initials C.C. after their names. Officers may use O.C., and
Members C.M. In addition, there are three awards for bravery:
the Cross of Valour, the Star of Courage, and the Medal of Bravery.
The motto of the Order of Canada is *Desiderantes Meliorem
Patriam* (They Desire a Better Country).

609. *How many Canadians have received Nobel prizes?*
Four Canadians have been recipients of the international awards
established in 1901 and named after Alfred Nobel, the Swedish
munitions manufacturer.

Frederick Banting and Scots-born **J. J. R. MacLeod** shared
the prize for medicine in 1923 for their work in the isolation of
insulin. **Lester B. Pearson** was awarded the prize for peace in
1957 for his work at the UN in regard to the Suez Crisis. **Gerhard
Herzberg**, a German-born scientist associated with the National
Research Council, received the 1971 chemistry prize for studies
in spectroscopy.

As well, at least five Canadian-born scientists working in the
United States as naturalized citizens became Nobel laureates. They
are **William F. Giauque** (chemistry, 1949), **Charles B. Huggins**
(medicine, 1966), **David H. Hubel** (medicine, 1981), **Arthur
Schlawlow** (physics, 1981), and **Henry Taube** (chemistry, 1983).

At least four foreign-born scientists have received the coveted
prize for work conducted in part in Canadian laboratories. They
are **Ernest Rutherford** (chemistry, 1908), **Guglielmo Marconi**
(physics, 1909), **Frederick Soddy** (chemistry, 1921), and **Har
Gobind Khorana** (medicine, 1968).

Saul Bellow, a naturalized American but a native of Lachine,
Que., was named laureate in literature in 1976.

610. *What are the Gairdner Foundation International Awards?*
The Gairdner Foundation International Awards are the most prestigious awards given in the field of medicine by a Canadian body. Awarded annually for medical research since 1959, they are sponsored by the Gairdner Foundation, established in Toronto in 1957 with funds provided by James Arthur Gairdner, a Toronto underwriter, and his family. In a typical year, one Award of Merit and four Annual Awards are made to scientists, irrespective of country, "who have made contributions in the conquest of disease and the relief of human suffering" in order "to assist in focussing public, professional and scientific attention upon significant achievement in the medical field." The Award of Merit is $25,000; the Annual Awards are each worth $10,000.

611. *What are the most substantial Canadian awards and prizes?*
Short of winning a lottery or the Nobel Prize, the best a Canadian can do is to be offered the Royal Bank of Canada Award. The award has been made annually since 1967 "to Canadians whose achievements contribute substantially to human welfare." The amount is $100,000.

Next in size is the Ernest C. Manning Award of $75,000 to a Canadian "who has shown outstanding talent in conceiving and developing new concepts, processes, or products of potential widespread benefit to Canada." It was established in 1982 as an annual award by the Manning Foundation, named in memory of the late premier of Alberta.

The Molson Award, established by the Molson Foundation and awarded annually by the Canada Council since 1963, is now worth $50,000. Each year three prizes are awarded for outstanding contributions in the arts, humanities, and social sciences.

Also worth $50,000 is the McLuhan Teleglobe Canada Award "for outstanding contribution to the field of communications." The biennial award was established in 1983 in memory of the late Marshall McLuhan.

Seal Book's First Novel Competition has been held annually

since 1977. The prize consists of a $50,000 nonreturnable advance against royalties for a first novel.

A newly established award is the Glenn Gould Prize for Distinguished Contribution to Music and Communications. The prize of $50,000 will be awarded triennially beginning in October, 1987, by the Glenn Gould Foundation.

612. *What are the Juno, Genie, Actra and Gemini awards?*
These annual awards honour excellence in Canadian recordings, motion pictures, and radio and television productions. The Juno Awards were instituted by the Canadian Academy of Recording Arts and Sciences in 1969. The Genie Awards, nicknamed the Etrogs, were first given in 1968 by the Academy of Canadian Cinema. The Alliance of Canadian Cinema, Television and Radio Artists (ACTRA) has sponsored the Actra Awards since 1963. In 1986, it was announced that the Actra Awards would be given by the newly enlarged Academy of Canadian Cinema and Television and would be called the Gemini Awards

613. *Who has won the Governor General's Award for Literature more often than anyone else?*
The Governor General's Award for Literature was established by the Canadian Authors' Association in 1936 to honour the authors of the year's best books in various categories. Since then the Canada Council has taken over the administration of the awards, and each award is now worth $5,000. There have been a number of multiple winners, but no one has yet equalled Hugh MacLennan's feat of winning five awards. He received them for novels published in 1945, 1948, 1949, 1954, and 1959.

614. *Which two national institutions share quarters at 395 Wellington Street, Ottawa?*
The National Library of Canada and the Public Archives of Can-

ada have shared quarters at 395 Wellington Street, Ottawa, since 1967. The National Library, formally established in 1953, requires that two copies of every book (and that includes maps, periodicals, pamphlets, records, audio tapes, etc.) be deposited with the collection for copyright purposes. The Public Archives of Canada, the national collection of documents relating to the history of Canada, goes back to 1872. It is charged with preserving federal government records as well as historical documents. Some two million separate items of concern to Canada's culture and history are preserved at 395 Wellington Street.

615. *What are the names of the four National Museums of Canada?*

The four National Museums of Canada are in Ottawa. They are the National Gallery of Canada (devoted to art), the National Museum of Man (including the Canadian War Museum, the Archaeological Survey of Canada, and the Canadian Centre for Folk Culture Studies), the National Museum of Natural Sciences (which supports polar and other research), and the National Museum of Science and Technology (which administers the National Aeronautical Collection).

616. *What is Canada's largest public museum?*

The Royal Ontario Museum, in Toronto, is the country's largest public museum. It was established in 1912, and became a world class institution through the efforts of Charles T. Currelly, its first curator. The Sigmund Samuel Collection of Canadiana was acquired in 1951, and in 1968 the McLaughlin Planetarium opened.

617. *Where is the Glenbow Centre?*

The Glenbow Centre is a major social, educational, cultural, and artistic resource, founded in 1954 to collect western Canadiana in order to tell the story of the West from prehistoric to modern times. The Centre is in Calgary and operates a major museum and library and archives. It was originally established by the oil magnate Eric L. Harvie.

618. *What is the Banff Centre?*

The Banff Centre for Continuing Education, founded at Banff in 1933, began as an extension of the University of Alberta. It now offers both year-round and summer courses in the arts, crafts, business administration, French, etc.

619. *Who sponsors the annual Couchiching Conferences and what purposes do they serve?*

The Couchiching Conferences are a series of summer and winter conferences held at Geneva Park, on the shore of Lake Couchiching, north of Orillia, Ont. They are sponsored by the Canadian Institute on Public Affairs and they "provide an open forum for discussion of Canadian social and economic problems in an international setting." Summer conferences have been convened since 1932, winter since 1954. The proceedings, which involve well-known speakers from many countries, are usually newsworthy.

620. *What is the Antigonish Movement and why is it known around the world?*

The Antigonish Movement is a co-operative, self-help movement with worldwide influence but with particular relevance to developing and Third World countries. It grew out of the extension program at St. Francis Xavier University, Antigonish, N.S., where James J. Tompkins, a Roman Catholic priest, began a course in group action in 1921. It expanded eight years later through the efforts of Father M. M. Coady and others to assist fishermen and farmers in the maritimes to establish co-operatives, credit unions, etc. The Coady International Institute, established in 1960, trains students from foreign lands in social leadership so that all men and women may be "masters of their own destiny."

621. *What is Frontier College?*

Frontier College is a volunteer organization founded in Toronto in 1899 to bring education to those who need it and would not otherwise receive it. Participating individuals work as labourer-teachers in rural communities, as full-time field workers, and as literacy tutors for adults throughout the country. In recent years it has focussed on adult literacy.

622. *What are some organizations which help to place students, seniors, and others overseas for developmental work?*

There are numerous organizations devoted to international development. They include Canada World Youth, Canadian Crossroads International, Canadian International Development Agency (CIDA), Canadian University Students Overseas (CUSO), Canadian Executive Service Overseas (CESO), Inter Pares, OXFAM Canada, and World University Service of Canada (WUSC). Katimavik, until discontinued in 1986, placed volunteers in communities in Canada.

623. *What was the earliest recorded church service in what is now Canada?*

The earliest recorded church service was an Anglican Eucharist celebrated aboard Martin Frobisher's ship off Baffin Island, N.W.T., in the summer of 1578. The earliest recorded Roman Catholic Mass was celebrated in New France on the Island of Montreal on June 24, 1615. Earlier than either of these are ceremonial events held by the native peoples.

624. *What are the two largest religious denominations in the country?*

The largest religious denomination in the country is the Roman Catholic Church, which had almost eleven million adherents in 1985. The second-largest religious denomination is the United

Church of Canada, which had close to five million adherents in the same year.

625. What is the largest Protestant religious denomination in Canada?

The largest Protestant religious denomination in the country is the United Church of Canada. It was formed through a union of Methodists, Presbyterians, and Congregationalists in 1924–25. The first United Church service was celebrated in Toronto on June 10, 1925.

626. Who is the patron saint of Quebec?

The patron saint of Quebec, according to the canon of the Catholic Church, is St. John the Baptist. It was on this saint's feast day, June 24, that John Cabot made his historic landfall in eastern Canada in 1497. There are two Sociétés Saint-Jean-Baptiste in Quebec, and his feast day in that province is a provincial holiday. The patron saint of Canada is St. Joseph.

627. What is the principal Roman Catholic shrine in Canada?

The principal Roman Catholic shrine is Sainte-Anne-de-Beaupré, a basilica dedicated to the Virgin Mary, northeast of Quebec City. The present Romanesque basilica is the eighth place of worship to occupy this site. The church has been called "the Lourdes of North America," as miraculous cures have been claimed by pilgrims.

628. Why is St. Joseph's Oratory in Montreal known as "Brother André's Shrine"?

St. Joseph's Oratory is an imposing, domed Renaissance-style basilica perched on Montreal's Mount Royal. The Oratory was the dream of Brother André (1845–1937), a Roman Catholic lay brother with a reputation for piety and miracle-working. He inspired its construction, which was commenced in 1924 but completed in 1967, long after his death. The Oratory can hold 16,000 persons.

629. *When was the Pope in Canada?*
Pope John Paul II made an official visit to Canada in September, 1984. Between his arrival on September 12 and his departure on September 21, he visited a total of sixteen cities in eight provinces, including Quebec's Sainte-Anne-de-Beaupré and Ontario's Huronia, shrines especially important to Canada's eleven million Roman Catholics. Weather conditions forced the last-minute cancellation of a scheduled three-hour visit to Fort Simpson, N.W.T., where, in anticipation of the papal visit, the village of 975 residents mushroomed to some 4,000 Indians, Inuit, and Métis. The 1984 visit was the first by a Pope. It cost federal and church groups an estimated $50 million.

630. *What are the names of the most important private clubs in the country and why are they important?*
Private clubs for business executives and others continue to play an important role in Canadian life. Many important business and corporate decisions are made within the walls of private clubs, which offer their select members dining and other facilities. According to the writer Peter C. Newman, only seven private clubs rank as "national institutions." These are the Mount Royal Club and the St. James Club, both of Montreal; the National Club, the Toronto Club, and the York Club, all of Toronto; the Rideau Club, Ottawa; and the Vancouver Club, Vancouver.

631. *What is the name of the world's largest annual exhibition?*
The Canadian National Exhibition is often described as the world's largest annual exhibition. As an agricultural fair held each fall in Toronto, it dates back to 1846. It became the Canadian National

Exhibition — the CNE, the "Ex" — in 1878. It has a permanent site of 152 ha, or 380 acres, at the CNE grounds. Average annual attendance is about three million. The CNE Grandstand Show and the Midway are prime attractions.

632. *Which annual event advertises itself as "the greatest outdoor show on earth"?*
Such hyperbole and advertising are characteristic of and appropriate to the Calgary Stampede, the internationally famous annual exhibition of rodeo events, amusements, and livestock shows. It is held for ten days each July in Stampede Park, Calgary, Alta. It was founded in 1912 by Guy Weadick, an American promoter and showman, and it came into its own in 1923, when it was amalgamated with the old Calgary Industrial Exhibition. It features the famous chuckwagon race.

633. *In which city was Expo 67 held?*
Expo 67 was a world exposition held in Montreal in 1967. Over 50 million visitors viewed pavilions and exhibits from over seventy countries from April 28 to October 27. Expo 67 proved to be a way for the *Québécois* to celebrate the Centennial of Confederation, and for other Canadians to take pride in their technical and social expertise. The theme of Expo 67 was "Man and His World/ Terre des Hommes." This is now the name of the annual exhibition held on Ile Sainte-Hélène, one of Expo's sites, open from mid-June to Labour Day.

634. *Which city agreed to host Expo 86?*
The 1986 World Exposition (Expo 86) took place in Vancouver, B.C., from May 2 to October 13, 1986. The actual site of 70 ha, or 173 acres, was on Vancouver's waterfront at False Creek and Burrard Inlet. The centrepiece was Expo Centre, a seventeen-storey geodesic pavilion. There were more than eighty pavilions

and theme plazas. It was described as a worthy successor to Expo 67, which was held in Montreal in the Centennial year, and as "an event of historic significance and universal interest." The theme of Expo 86 was "World in Motion — World in Touch."

635. *What are Tents 28, 47, 58, 61, and 63?*

These are the names of local Canadian chapters of Variety International, the entertainment industry's service club devoted to assisting disabled and needy children. Variety takes its terminology from the world of the circus. Chapters are called Tents, members are known as Barkers, the board of directors is a Crew, etc. The Canadian Tents are located in the following cities (corresponding to the order above): Toronto, Vancouver, Winnipeg, Calgary, and Edmonton. Variety Club of Ontario, the earliest and second-largest of Variety's forty-eight chapters in twelve countries, was chartered on July 11, 1945. One of its many charities is Variety Village in Toronto.

636. *What holidays do Canadians observe?*

Holidays are days set aside each year by law or custom to mark specific events or occasions. Statutory holidays are established by the federal government, the provincial legislatures, or municipalities. Nonstatutory holidays, observed by custom among certain groups, have no official standing.

There are sixty-one federal holidays each year, plus those established by the provincial legislatures and municipalities. Here is a list of the federal holidays:

Sunday: The first day of the week, 52 in number

New Year's Day: January 1, which marks the beginning of the new year

Good Friday: Commemoration of the crucifixion of Jesus, observed on the Friday immediately preceding Easter, which never occurs before March 22 or after April 25

Easter Monday: Observed on the Monday following Easter Day (Easter, which celebrates the resurrection of Jesus, falls on the first Sunday following the full moon that occurs on or after the vernal equinox — March 21)

Victoria Day: May 24, anniversary of the birth of Queen Victoria, observed on the first Monday before May 25

Canada Day: July 1, anniversary of Confederation in 1867

Labour Day: September 1, observed on the first Monday in September, to recognize organized labour

Thanksgiving Day: Second Monday in October; a day of thanksgiving for the bountiful harvest

Remembrance Day: November 11, to commemorate the dead of the two world wars

Christmas Day: December 25, traditional birthday of Jesus

As for holidays legislated or proclaimed by the provinces or municipalities, Boxing Day (the day after Christmas) and Civic Day (the first Monday in August) are observed in the majority of the provinces. Quebeckers enjoy St. John the Baptist's Day (June 24). Newfoundlanders have a slew of holidays, among them (observed on the nearest Monday to the anniversary date): St. Patrick's Day (March 17), St. George's Day (April 24), Commonwealth Day (May 24), Discovery Day (June 26), Memorial Day (July 1), and Orangemen's Day (July 10).

637. *What ever happened to Dominion Day?*

It was renamed. The statutory holiday that marks the anniversary of Confederation, the creation of the Dominion of Canada on July 1, 1867, was called Dominion Day until 1982, when it was renamed Canada Day. The bill responsible for this change received royal assent on October 27, 1982.

638. *Is National Heritage Day an official holiday?*

It is not a holiday, official or otherwise. But there is the possibility that it will become a statutory holiday. At present it is an idea whose time has not yet come. Since 1978, the Heritage Canada Foundation has promoted the idea of a statutory holiday to fall on the third Monday in February. It would celebrate the social past, the same way Canada Day celebrates the political past, and it would give Canadians some relief from the blahs of February.

639. *How old is the Canadian Army?*
The Canadian Army is one of the oldest institutions in the country. It has a long and honourable history, but it was known as the Canadian Army for a period of only twenty-eight years — from 1940 to 1968. Before 1940, it was known as the Canadian Militia; since 1968, it has been part of the Canadian Armed Forces.

The Canadian Militia consisted originally of volunteers and conscripts who fought alongside the British regulars in the War of 1812 and the Rebellion of 1837. The Militia Act of 1846 recognized the volunteer principle. The first permanent active units date from 1871. The Canadian Militia served during the Fenian Raids (1866–70), in the Red River Rebellion of 1870, and the North West Rebellion of 1885–86. Over 7,000 members served in the South African War (1899–1901). The Canadian Expeditionary Force fought in World War I, and the Canadian Army fought in World War II. An infantry brigade group saw service in Korea in 1950–53. The Canadian Army has provided personnel for UN peacekeeping tasks since 1954.

640. *Who were the Dumbells?*
The Dumbells was a popular vaudeville group that entertained the troops of World War I and was such a success it toured Great Britain, the United States, and Canada until 1929, when it was disbanded. It was formed from the Canadian Corps's 3rd Division Concert Party by Captain Merton Plunket near Vimy Ridge in August, 1917. The original eight members and their replacements played, sang, danced, and juggled their way into the hearts of a generation of military and civilian audiences.

641. *Who were the Canadian "Air Aces"?*
"Air Aces," also called "Fighter Aces," were Allied pilots who during World War I destroyed ten or more enemy fighter planes. They were a brave and daring lot. Any mention of the Canadian Air Aces must include George (Billy) Barker, George (Buzz) Beurling, William (Billy) Bishop, C. H. (Punch) Dickens, and Wilfrid (Wop) May, a Canadian who flew with the Royal Flying Corps.

642. *Did a Canadian pilot shoot down the Red Baron?*
Credit for shooting down Captain Manfred von Richthofen, the German Air Ace known as the Red Baron, has traditionally gone to A. Roy Brown (1893–1944), a Canadian pilot who flew with the Royal Air Force. Brown downed eleven enemy planes plus, it is maintained, the Fokker triplane piloted by Richthofen on April 21, 1918. Military historians now believe that although bullets from Brown's guns hit the triplane, credit for the "kill" should be given to antiaircraft fire from the ground. Brown himself took no pleasure in his fame and went into a profound depression soon after the dogfight.

643. *Did Billy Bishop deserve the Victoria Cross?*
The Victoria Cross, the highest Commonwealth military decoration, was awarded to William (Billy) Bishop (1894–1956), the Canadian flier and Air Ace with the Royal Flying Corps. Billy Bishop was officially credited with destroying seventy-two enemy aircraft during the Great War. On June 2, 1917, he staged a single-handed dawn raid against a German airfield near Cambrai, France, and destroyed three enemy aircraft. It was for this daring raid that he was awarded the Victoria Cross. The award was a coveted one, and during World War II Bishop served as Canada's Air Marshal.

The question of whether or not Bishop deserved the Victoria Cross was raised in passing by the producers of the NFB film *The*

Kid Who Couldn't Miss, a revisionist look at Bishop and his flying legend. The film pointed out that there is no proof that Bishop ever made the solo, predawn raid for which he was awarded the V.C., only Bishop's word for it. It is the opinion of retired Air Marshal C. R. Dunlap that there is no reason to doubt Bishop's word, considering his record. Dunlap thinks it surprising that Bishop was not recommended for a second V.C. The NFB agreed to call the film a "docu-drama" rather than a "documentary."

644. *Who were the "bush pilots"?*

The "bush pilots" were those commercial aviators, many of them trained in World War I, who flew freight and passengers into and out of the northern bush and barrens after the first northern flight in 1920. Early bush pilots like C. H. (Punch) Dickens, Wilfrid (Wop) May, and Grant McConachie were figures of daring and resourcefulness. They did much to open up the country in the 1920s and 1930s. The era of the bush pilot ended in 1939, with the outbreak of World War II, when new flying techniques were evolved.

645. *Who were the "war artists"?*

Lord Beaverbrook established the Canadian War Memorials Fund in late 1916. It engaged artists to portray the Canadian war effort from first-hand experience for documentary, historical, patriotic, and artistic purposes. In all, 100 artists produced 800 paintings, drawings, and sculptures. Among the British artists were Augustus John, Paul Nash, and Wyndham Lewis; among the Canadians were David Milne and A. Y. Jackson. Their art is now in the National Gallery of Canada.

646. *What happened at "the eleventh hour of the eleventh day of the eleventh month"?*

The reference is to the armistice which officially ended World War

I. It was signed on November 11, 1918, at 11:00 A.M. Since then November 11 has been set aside as a statutory holiday to honour the war dead. Now known as Remembrance Day, it honours the dead of both world wars. Ceremonies of a patriotic and memorial nature, with the traditional two-minute silence, take place at cenotaphs and other war monuments across the land. In Ottawa, the Remembrance Day service is conducted before the National War Memorial in Confederation Square and broadcast nationally by radio and television networks.

647. *What is the Last Post Fund?*

The Last Post Fund is a voluntary organization which provides an honourable funeral, burial, and grave marker for any veteran of the Commonwealth or Allied forces who dies without means, relatives, or friends to do so. It was established in 1908 when Arthur H. D. Hair, a Montreal hospital orderly, realized no provision existed for a burial at public expense for indigent veterans. Through his efforts the Last Post Fund was founded. Interments are arranged across the country. The Fund also operates the Field of Honour, Pointe Claire, Que., where Hair himself lies buried. Markers are inscribed ''Lest We Forget.''

648. *What is a Legion Hall?*

A Legion Hall is a building in which a branch of the Royal Canadian Legion is housed. There are some eighteen hundred branches across the country, ranging in size from small halls to community centres. A club for ex-service people, the Royal Canadian Legion dates back to 1925. It organizes the annual poppy campaign on Remembrance Day. Its motto is *Memoriam forum retinebimus* (''We Will Remember Them'').

649. *What is* **The Brooding Soldier***?*

The Brooding Soldier is the name of the Canadian War Memorial at St. Julien, northeast of the Belgian city of Ypres. It marks the battlefield where 2,000 Canadians fell and now lie following the first German gas attacks on April 22–4, 1915. Rising some 11 m, or 35 feet, from a stone-flagged court, a single shaft of granite is surmounted by *The Brooding Soldier*, the bowed head and shoulders of a Canadian soldier. It was the work of the Regina architect Frederick Chapman Clemesha, who was wounded while serving with the Canadian Corps. It was unveiled on July 8, 1923.

650. *Was there a "Crucified Canadian"?*

The usual version of this World War I rumour has it that the Germans captured a young Canadian soldier and, across no man's land, in full view of his comrades, exhibited him in the open, spread-eagle on a makeshift cross, his hands and feet pierced by bayonets. He is said to have died slowly. According to Paul Fussell in *The Great War and Modern Memory* (1975), the favoured setting was Maple Copse, near Sanctuary Wood in the Ypres sector of Belgium. Fussell suggested that the powerful image of the "Crucified Canadian" was prompted by roadside calvaries and the crucifixion as "the pattern of all suffering."

651. *Where is the Vimy Memorial and what does it commemorate?*

The Vimy memorial is Canada's most impressive tribute overseas to the fallen of World War I. The memorial is imposingly situated on the crest of a chalk ridge overlooking the village of Vimy, near Arras, in northern France. The soaring twin pylons, designed by Walter S. Allward, have been likened to "a gate leading to a better world." Vimy was captured by the four divisions of the Canadian Corps fighting together for the first time on Easter Monday, April 9, 1917. Three thousand Canadians died taking the chalk ridge. More than ten thousand Canadians attended the dedication service held on July 26, 1936, under the auspices of the Canadian Legion.

652. Who wrote the famous war poem "In Flanders Fields"?

"In Flanders Fields," the most famous poem of the Great War and one of the most moving of all war poems, was written by John McCrae (1872–1918), a medical officer with the First Canadian Contingent. Mourning the death of a friend, he wrote the fifteen-line poem in twenty minutes on May 5, 1915, during the Second Battle of Ypres, Belgium. The poem begins, "In Flanders fields the poppies blow / Between the crosses, row on row," and urges the living not to "break faith with us who die" or else "We shall not sleep, though poppies grow / In Flanders fields."

The poem appeared anonymously in *Punch*, December 8, 1915. Its fame stems from its recital at the first Armistice Day service on November 11, 1918. The red poppy, an ancient symbol of sleep, has been synonymous with the supreme sacrifice and military mourning since then. The birthplace of John McCrae in Guelph, Ont., is now a national historic site.

653. Where is the grave of John McCrae?

John McCrae, the author of "In Flanders Fields," died without the knowledge that the poem he had so hastily composed would be committed to memory by millions of people throughout the English-speaking world. At the time of his death from pneumonia, he was in charge of medicine at No. 3 General Hospital at Boulogne, France. He is buried at Wimereux Communal Cemetery, near Boulogne, France. The regulation granite marker is engraved with a cross, the maple-leaf badge, and the words: "Lieutenant Colonel / J. McCrae / Can. Army Medical Corps / 28th January 1918." Behind the granite marker was erected a stone bench with a plaque suitably inscribed. It is Canada's custom to inter military personnel in the countries in which they fall. The graves of 218 Canadian soldiers and one nurse will be found at Wimereux.

654. What is the story behind the poem "High Flight"?

John Gillespie Magee, Jr., was an eighteen-year-old American student at Yale when he enlisted with the Royal Canadian Air Force in Montreal in October, 1940. He trained with the Royal Air Force in England and was killed in action on December 11, 1941. On the back of a letter addressed to his mother three months before his death, he wrote the sonnet "High Flight." It was chosen as the official poem of the RAF and the RCAF and posted in pilot training centres throughout the Commonwealth. The sonnet catches the sense of excitement and danger in the air. It begins: "Oh, I have slipped the surly bonds of earth / And danced the skies on laughter-silvered wings." It ends with he "touched the face of God." U.S. President Ronald Reagan recited part of the poem on TV following the explosion of the Space Shuttle in March, 1986.

655. *What is conscription and why has it been such a divisive element in Canadian life?*

Conscription is another name for compulsory military service. It was a major issue in both world wars, for it divided the English and the French as well as the volunteers and the conscientious objectors. In Quebec it seemed that "French-Canadian boys are being drafted to fight overseas in Britain's wars." In the rest of Canada it appeared that French Canadians were cowardly, unpatriotic, and unwilling to fight for their freedom.

656. *What was a zombie?*

A zombie was the derogatory term applied to any able-bodied man who, failing to volunteer for service overseas during World War II, was conscripted for home defence. The West Indian word for a supernaturally animated corpse was indiscriminately applied to pacifists, conscientious objectors, shirkers, malingerers, and others.

657. *Where and what was "Camp X"?*

"Camp X," Canada's best-kept World War II secret, was an important Allied training camp and communications centre for guerilla warfare and intelligence operations. Run by Sir William Stephenson, using the CBC as "cover," it was in operation between August, 1941, and May, 1945, on 80 ha, or 200 acres, of farmland on the north shore of Lake Ontario near Oshawa.

658. *Who was code-named "Intrepid" and sometimes called "the Quiet Canadian"?*

"Intrepid" was the World War II code name of Sir William Stephenson (b. 1896), Canadian inventor, businessman, and chief of British espionage in North America in 1940–45. For his secrecy about his military work he was dubbed "the Quiet Canadian." But he broke cover in two bestselling biographies by a journalist with a confusingly similar name, William Stevenson.

659. *What are some Canadian World War II rumours?*

Rumours were rife during World War II. These made the rounds. King George VI will move from Buckingham Palace to Toronto's Casa Loma. Pope Pius XII will reestablish the Vatican in the Château Frontenac, Quebec City. And Winston Churchill will move Nazi captive Rudolf Hess to Fort Henry in Kingston.

660. *Was Canada a founding member nation of NATO?*

Canada was one of the dozen founding member nations of NATO. The other member nations were Belgium, Denmark, France, Iceland, Italy, Luxembourg, the Netherlands, Norway, Portugal, the United Kingdom, and the United States. Nations that later joined are Greece, Spain, Turkey, and West Germany.

NATO is the acronym for the North Atlantic Treaty Organization, a military alliance concerned with collective security and mutual defence against aggression in Europe and North America.

The treaty establishing NATO was signed at Washington, D.C., on April 4, 1949. A Canadian is credited with first proposing the formation of the military alliance (whose "opposite number" is the Warsaw Pact). Louis St. Laurent, then secretary of state, speaking in the House of Commons on April 29, 1948, noted that "the formation of such a defensive group of free states would not be a counsel of despair but a message of hope." NATO's headquarters is in Brussels.

661. *What is the name of the joint Canadian–American air defence alliance?*
The North American Aerospace Defence Command (NORAD) was formed on September 12, 1957, to integrate air reconnaissance and defence systems for the United States and Canada. NORAD's Combat Operations Centre is inside Cheyenne Mountain in Colorado. Its Canadian command centre is at North Bay, Ont.

662. *What is the North Warning System?*
The North Warning System is a system of North American air defence, the agreement for which was signed in Quebec City on March 18, 1985, by Prime Minister Brian Mulroney and U.S. President Ronald Reagan. The new system gives a new look to the various "lines" of continental defence: the Pine Tree Line (along the 49th parallel), the Mid-Canada Line (generally along the 55th parallel), and the DEW Line (Distant Early Warning, roughly along the 70th parallel). The Mid-Canada Line was discontinued in 1965. The "lines" consist of manned and unmanned tracking, warning, and interceptor or control stations largely built by Americans and manned by Canadians.

663. *Is Canada a member of the OAS?*
A place on the Permanent Council of the Organization of Ameri-

can States has been reserved for Canada but the country has never joined. The OAS was founded in 1948 in Bogotá, Columbia, and has about thirty members, from Argentina to Venezuela, including Mexico and the United States. The headquarters is in Washington, D.C.

664. How many Canadian military colleges are there, and where are they?

There are three Canadian military colleges. The Royal Military College of Canada, the oldest of the three, was established in 1876 in Kingston, Ont. The Royal Roads Military College, founded in 1941, originally as a naval training establishment, is outside Victoria, B.C. Le Collège Militaire Royal de Saint-Jean was opened, originally for French-speaking cadets, in 1952 at Saint-Jean, Que. All three colleges educate and train officer cadets and commissioned officers for careers in the Canadian Armed Forces. They offer scientific and military training and baccalaureate degrees. They accept Canadian citizens who are single and between the ages of sixteen and twenty-one.

665. In what sense is there "unification" of the Canadian Armed Forces?

Canada is the first — and only — country to unify its fighting forces. The unification order became effective on February 1, 1968, bringing the three services — the Royal Canadian Navy, the Canadian Army, and the Royal Canadian Air Force — under a single civilian Chief of Defence Staff. The order sought to streamline the services by eliminating service differences and adopting a common uniform. It was (and remains) a controversial piece of legislation introduced in the interests of efficiency and economy. Individual uniforms for the services were reintroduced in 1985.

The Canadian Armed Forces has five functional commands. These are Maritime, Mobile, Air, Communications, and Canadian Forces Europe. The CAF has a common nomenclature for officers and other ranks.

OFFICERS: General Officers: General, Lieutenant-General, Major General, Brigadier General. **Senior Officers:** Colonel, Lieutenant-Colonel, Major. **Junior Officers:** Captain, Lieutenant, 2nd Lieutenant. **Subordinate Officers:** Officer Cadet.

OTHER RANKS: Chief Warrant Officer, Master Warrant Officer, Warrant Officer, Sergeant, Master Corporal, Corporal, Private.

666. *What symbolic elements appear on the Canadian Forces Badge?*

The Canadian Forces Badge is worn by servicemen and servicewomen in the Canadian Armed Forces. The gold crown is emblematic of the CAF's relationship to the sovereign as Queen of Canada. The wreath of red maple leaves symbolizes the ten provinces. The anchor, swords, and eagle represent the three elements in which the CAF carry out their missions. The blue of the oval shield suggests loyalty and devotion.

667. *Who may join the Canadian Armed Forces Cadets?*

The Canadian Armed Forces sponsors a program of training in the fundamentals of citizenship and leadership called the Canadian Armed Forces Cadets. The three leagues — Army Cadets, Air Cadets, and Navy Cadets — maintain summer camps where young Canadian men and women between the ages of thirteen and eighteen can become familiar with the elements of the Armed Forces and pursue a program of physical fitness. Some 70,000 cadets are enrolled in approximately a thousand corps across the country.

668. *How does one enlist in the Canadian Armed Forces?*

The nearest Canadian Armed Forces recruiting centre may be found by looking in the Yellow Pages of the telephone directory under "Recruiting." An applicant must apply at a recruiting centre in person. An applicant must be a Canadian citizen between the ages of seventeen and twenty-five, have a good education, be able to meet physical and mental standards, be of good moral character, be in possession of a birth certificate and a Social Insurance Card, both of which bear the same name.

If selected for enrolment, the applicant will be issued joining instructions and arrangements will be made for him or her to proceed to the Canadian Forces Recruit School at Cornwallis, N.S., or to L'Ecole des recrues des Forces canadiennes at Saint-Jean, Que., for basic training. The usual initial engagement period is three years.

669. *What are the various entry plans of the Canadian Armed Forces?*

The various entry plans open to civilian applicants may be grouped in three broad categories: Officer Entry Plans; Subsidized University Entry Plans; and Other Ranks Entry Plans. The Officer Entry Plans provide for training for high-school graduates or for direct entry for university graduates and technologists. Subsidized University Entry Plans provide for candidates who wish to pursue a university degree with a subsidy from the Canadian Forces at either a military college or a Canadian university, with special attention to medical and dental officer training. Other Ranks Entry Plans provide for either skilled or unskilled candidates, with special attention to marine engineering technician training.

670. *In which countries have Canadians served as "peacekeepers"?*

Canada has taken part in every United Nations peacekeeping operation since the role was defined in 1949. Canadians have served as "observers" or as part of the UN Emergency Force, an international police force created to separate rival forces and to patrol border points, in Palestine, Egypt, Kashmir, Lebanon, Congo,

West New Guinea, Indonesia, Yemen, and Cyprus. Canada has also been represented on non-UN international commissions, such as the one in Indochina following the Vietnam war.

671. *How many U.S. war resisters emigrated to Canada rather than condone the war in Vietnam?*

It has been estimated that as many as 25,000 American citizens emigrated from the United States and settled in Canada to protest the American involvement in the war in Vietnam. The majority of immigrants were young men of draft age. Some Canadians regarded them as "draft dodgers," others as "war resisters." They began to arrive in 1965. Many returned with the first limited amnesty granted in 1975. Others remained to enrich Canadian life.

672. *When was the RCMP established?*

The Royal Canadian Mounted Police was established in 1873 as the North West Mounted Police. It was granted the "Royal" prefix in 1904. In 1920, the headquarters was moved from Regina to Ottawa, and the Force acquired its present name. The French name of the Force is *Gendarmerie royale du Canada* (GRC). The Force is headed by a commissioner who holds the rank of deputy minister.

Established for service in the Northwest, the Force evolved into a federal civilian police force. It also acts as the provincial police force in eight of the ten provinces — Ontario and Quebec have their own provincial police — and as municipal police forces in some hundred and sixty municipalities. As well, it acts as the territorial police force in the North.

673. *What are the official — and unofficial — mottoes of the Royal Canadian Mounted Police?*

The official motto of the RCMP, established in 1873, is the French phrase "Maintiens le droit," which is officially translated "Uphold the Right.'' The unofficial motto of the force, which goes back to the words of J. J. Healy, a whisky trader in 1877, is ''They always get their man.''

674. *Did Charles Dickens's son serve with the Mounted Police?*
Indeed. Francis Jeffrey Dickens (1844–1886), third son of the novelist Charles Dickens, served as an inspector with the North West Mounted Police. He led the defence of Fort Pitt against Big Bear in April 1885 but was not judged an outstanding officer.

Here are some more quasi-literary associations. Lord Byron's father led the demolition of Louisbourg. Lord Tennyson's nephew Bertram wrote verse in Moosomin, Sask. Sir Walter Scott's favourite brother is buried in Quebec City. Thomas Carlyle's sweetheart was a Charlottetown-born lady who later married the lieutenant-governor of Prince Edward Island. Victor Hugo's daughter once stayed in Halifax. Oscar Wilde's lover Robert Ross was a Canadian. Sigmund Freud's brother worked as a furrier in Toronto. And Walt Disney's father was born in Fort Erie, Ont.

675. *What is the name of the operetta about the Mounties?*
The operetta about the Mounties is *Rose-Marie*, the hit of the 1924 Broadway season. The music was written by Rudolf Friml, the lyrics by Otto Harbach and Oscar Hammerstein II. It was filmed three times. The second version, produced by MGM in 1936, starred Jeanette MacDonald and Nelson Eddy as the singing lovers. ''Rose-Marie, I love you . . . '' has become a stock phrase. In the RCMP, a soft assignment is known as ''a Rose-Marie posting.''

676. *Did a little girl ever "join" the Mounties?*
This happened only on the page and on the screen. Among the hundreds of books about the Mounted Police, none is more appealing than *Susannah, A Little Girl with the Mounties* (1936), about a

nine-year-old girl who "joins" the North West Mounted Police in Regina in 1896. It was written by the Winnipeg-born author Muriel Denison, who added three sequels to the saga. It was filmed in 1936 as *Susanna of the Mounties* with the part of the plucky little girl played by Shirley Temple.

677. Who was "King of the Royal Mounted"?

The Western novelist Zane Grey created the newspaper comic strip called "King of the Royal Mounted" in 1935, supposedly modelling his RCMP Constable King on Constable Alfred King, who hunted down the Mad Trapper of Rat River. The strip was actually written by Grey's son and drawn by artist Allen Dean.

678. Who was "Sergeant Preston of the Yukon"?

"Sergeant Preston of the Yukon" was a popular children's radio series heard five afternoons a week throughout North America from 1947 to 1955. That year it went from radio to television for a few years. Sergeant Preston was the Force's snowshoe-shod constable on the trail of criminals in the Yukon Territory. The TV series was sponsored by the Quaker Oats Company, which launched a big promotion when it offered faithful viewers a "Big Inch" of land from Sergeant Preston's country — a square inch, or 6.5 square centimetres, in a tract of land near Dawson, Y.T.

679. Who is Sergeant Renfrew?

Sergeant Renfrew and his dog Cuddles are creations of the comedian Dave Broadfoot and a mainstay of "The Royal Canadian Air Farce," the popular weekly CBC Radio program. According to Broadfoot, Renfrew, the Mountie "who never gets his man," lives in "a lonely log cabin on the fourteenth floor of Mountie headquarters."

680. *What is the RCMP's ceremonial cavalry drill called?*
Members of the Royal Canadian Mounted Police have performed
their ceremonial cavalry drill, the Musical Ride, throughout Canada and in many countries of the world. It was first performed as
drill in 1876 by new members of the North West Mounted Police.
The full troop of the Ride is composed of 32 uniformed men
riding black horses specially trained to walk, trot, and canter in
intricate patterns. The highlight and finale of the Musical Ride is
the charge, a thrilling display of wheeling and turning performed
at the gallop.

681. *Where is the RCMP's museum?*
The Centennial Museum of the RCMP Depot Division is located
at Regina. Here there are displays devoted to the historical, social,
and cultural aspects of the country's federal and civilian police
force.

**682. *Why are members of the RCMP sometimes called
"barnburners"?***
Members of the RCMP have been called "barnburners" in reference to a covert action to contain subversion. It seems that in May,
1972, zealous members burnt down a barn at Ste. Anne de la
Rochelle, near Montreal, that was used as a meeting place for the
FLQ and the American Black Panthers.

683. *What are the levels of security classification for documents?*
According to a Privy Council document dating from 1956, official documents may be classified Top Secret, Secret, Confiden-
tial, or Restricted.

684. *What is the work of CSIS?*
The initials stand for the Canadian Security Intelligence Service,
the agency of the federal government concerned with security and

intelligence work. The Canadian Security Intelligence Service Act was proclaimed on July 16, 1984. This marked the first time that the mandate for conducting security intelligence activity in Canada was legislatively defined. Until that time such work was undertaken by the RCMP.

The primary duties and functions of the CSIS are to collect and analyze information, produce intelligence assessments, and keep the government informed of activities which may threaten the security of Canada. These activities are defined in Section 2 of the Act as espionage or sabotage, foreign-influenced activities, political violence and terrorism, and subversion.

The CSIS headquarters is in Ottawa, with regional and district offices throughout the country. There are also liaison officers stationed in a number of Canadian missions around the world. The director is appointed by the governor in council for a term of five years.

The CSIS is not the sole branch of the federal government concerned with espionage and related matters. There is an Interdepartmental Committee on Security and Intelligence, sometimes called the Security Panel, concerned with the co-ordination of security and intelligence activities. There is also the Communications Security Establishment, a branch of the Department of National Defence, which maintains an information data bank, protects federal communications from interception, and gathers foreign intelligence.

685. *What is Pierre Elliott Trudeau's celebrated quip about privacy?*
Pierre Elliott Trudeau was Minister of Justice when, in Ottawa on December 22, 1967, he said: "There's no place for the state in the bedrooms of the nation." It has been widely quoted ever since.

686. *Does James Bond have a Canadian connection?*
James Bond may lack a Canadian connection, but the same cannot be said of the creator of Secret Agent 007. During World War II,

Ian Fleming, the British author who wrote the Bond novels, was trained in espionage procedures at Camp X, the centre for guerilla warfare and intelligence operations near Oshawa, Ont. Fleming, ordered to "murder" an operative in a Toronto hotel, disobeyed orders. Some of Camp X's tricks and devices turn up in the Bond novels. In the Bond movies, Miss Moneypenny is played by the Ontario-born actress Lois Maxwell.

687. Does Sherlock Holmes have a Canadian connection?

Not really. However, the boot worn by Lord Baskerville in Sir Arthur Conan Doyle's *The Hound of the Baskervilles* (1902) bears the manufacturer's mark "Meyers, Toronto." This led to the formation in 1970 of the Bootmakers of Toronto to study the Holmes books. The group occasionally meets in the Conan Doyle Room, a re-creation of Holmes's study at 221B Baker Street, in the Metropolitan Toronto Library. Also, the 1944 Hollywood film *The Scarlet Claw*, with Basil Rathbone as Holmes and Nigel Bruce as Dr. Watson, is set in an imaginary Quebec village called La Morte Rouge. Finally, two writers, Jack Batten and Michael Bliss, wrote a brand-new Holmes-in-Canada story called "The Adventure of the Annexationist Conspiracy," in which the great detective meets Sir John A. Macdonald.

688. What are Superman's Canadian connections?

Superman, the world's first caped superhero, was created in 1938 by Toronto-born writer Joe Shuster and Cleveland-born artist Jerry Siegel. Clark Kent, Superman's other identity, worked for the *Daily Planet*, said to be modelled on *The Toronto Star*, a paper known to Shuster. Superman's redoubt, his Fortress of Solitude, is at the North Pole. The small-town sequences of *Superman: The Movie* and its sequels were shot in High River, Alta., where the skid marks of his starship are pointed out to tourists. In the movies, Quebec-born Glenn Ford played Superman's adoptive father, and Regina-born Margot Kidder played Clark Kent's girlfriend, Lois Lane.

689. *What is the International Pugwash Movement?*

The International Pugwash Movement is a loosely knit group of scientists from around the world who hold international meetings and national workshops to discuss the prevention of nuclear war and the responsibilities of scientists in a nuclear age. The director-general resides in Geneva, the international secretary in London. It has been estimated that one thousand scientists have taken part in Pugwash conferences.

The movement takes its name from the tiny community of Pugwash, N.S., birthplace of industrialist Cyrus Eaton, who offered accommodation and expenses to twenty-three distinguished scientists from ten nations, including the United States and the Soviet Union, for an inaugural meeting at his Thinker's Lodge. The meeting was held in July, 1957, under the sponsorship of Bertrand Russell and Sir Julian Huxley.

Canada has made two outstanding contributions to world peace. One is the country's contribution to UN peacekeeping missions; the other is its connection with the International Pugwash Movement. For many years the Canadian Pugwash Group was headed by the distinguished physicist John Polanyi.

690. *What does the Voice of Women do?*

The Voice of Women is a national organization whose purposes are to "unite women in concern for the future of the world" and to "crusade against the possibility of nuclear war." Founded in Toronto in 1960 by Kay Macpherson, Thérèse F. Casgrain, and other committed women, it is a nonpartisan group that speaks out on such social and international issues as the proliferation of atomic arms, Canada's participation in the "nuclear club," and abortion reform.

691. *What became of the "Don't Make a Wave Committee"?*

The Don't Make a Wave Committee was formed in Vancouver in 1970 to protest U.S. nuclear tests at Amchitka. The following year, the concerned Vancouverites formed the Greenpeace

Foundation and chartered a 24-m, or 80-foot, trawler boat, christened *Greenpeace*, which established a beachhead on the island off the tip of Alaska. In 1972 and 1973, Greenpeace mounted expeditions to Mururoa to protest French nuclear testing in the South Pacific. Over the years Greenpeace evolved from a national protest group to an international preservationist movement. Expeditions were mounted to save the great whales in 1975 and to ban the seal hunt in 1976. In the words of its Declaration of Independence, "The Greenpeace Foundation hopes to stimulate practical, intelligent actions to stem the tide of planetary destruction. We are 'rainbow people' representing every race, every nation, every living creature. We are patriots, not of any one nation, state, or military alliance, but of the entire earth."

The Greenpeace Foundation had 1.5 million members internationally in 1985. On July 10 of that year, its flagship, the *Rainbow Warrior* (a converted, 48-m, or 160-foot, trawler formerly named *Phyllis Cormack*) was bombed and sank in the harbour at Auckland, N.Z., where it was set to sail to protest French nuclear tests in Polynesia. Two members of the French security service were caught, convicted of the bombing, and imprisoned.

The *Rainbow Warrior* was named in honour of the Declaration and a native North American prophecy which runs: "Learn to be a Warrior of the Rainbow, for it is only by spreading love and joy to others that hate in the world can be changed to understanding and kindness, and war and destruction shall end!"

692. *What is the Canadian Institute for International Peace and Security?*

The Institute was established by an Act of Parliament on August 15, 1984. The purpose of the Institute is to increase knowledge and understanding of issues relating to international peace and security from a Canadian perspective, with particular emphasis on arms control, disarmament, defence, and conflict resolution. The Institute has a seventeen-member board of directors. The first executive director is Geoffrey Pearson.

693. *Why is there a statue of Sir Galahad on Parliament Hill?*
The statue of Sir Galahad, the brave knight of the Round Table, was erected at the foot of Parliament Hill in Ottawa to commemorate the sacrifice of Henry Albert Harper, a young friend of W. L. Mackenzie King, who drowned in 1901 in a vain attempt to rescue a little girl from drowning. The romantic-looking memorial, unveiled in 1905, was close to the heart of Prime Minister Mackenzie King, who found in the life of self-sacrifice "the secret of heroism."

694. *What did Lester B. Pearson say that is so quotable in his Nobel Prize acceptance speech?*
Accepting the Nobel Prize for peace on December 10, 1957, in Oslo, Norway, Lester B. Pearson noted ruefully: "The grim fact is that we prepare for war like precocious giants and for peace like retarded pygmies."

695. *Is there a park or a garden dedicated to peace on the 49th parallel?*
Both a park and a garden are dedicated to peace and located on land divided by the 49th parallel, the international boundary between Canada and the United States.

Peace Arch Park, located near White Rock, B.C., was dedicated in 1921 to peace between the two countries. Its centrepiece is a Peace Arch 30 m, or 100 feet, in height.

The International Peace Garden, located near Boissevain, Man., is the world's largest such area dedicated to world peace. The garden was opened in 1938, and its centrepiece is the Chapel of Peace.

The 49th parallel has been described as "the longest undefended border in the world." The park and the garden seem to prove it.

8. PEOPLE

696. *Who are the native peoples of Canada?*
The native peoples of Canada are the Inuit, the Indians, and the Métis. The term "native peoples" is sometimes used in the singular — "native people" — but is more properly employed in the plural. The term "aboriginal peoples of Canada" is used in the Constitution Act, 1981.

697. *How numerous are the native peoples?*
According to the census of 1981, the native peoples number 413,380. The breakdown runs like this: Indian, 291,920; Métis, 98,260; Inuit, 23,200.

698. *What is the origin of the Inuit and Indian peoples?*
It is maintained by scientists that the modern-day Inuit and Indians are an Asiatic people whose ancestors migrated from northwestern Siberia, across the Bering Strait, to North America. The migration is believed to have occurred from 10,000 to 30,000 years ago.

699. *Who are the Eskimos and why do they wish to be called the Inuit?*
The Eskimos are the original inhabitants of the polar region. They live on the arctic shores of Canada, Greenland, Alaska, and Siberia. There are approximately 100,000 Eskimos today, about 23,000 of

whom live in Canada in settlements in the Yukon Territory, the Northwest Territories, northern Ontario, northern Quebec, and northern Labrador.

The word "Eskimo" is a misnomer, being the Algonkian word for "eaters of raw flesh." The word is considered derogatory, for they cook their fish and game. They refer to themselves as the Inuit, which in their own language means "the people." Archaeologists have determined the existence of two Eskimo cultures prior to the present one. These are the Dorset and Thule cultures. The present culture, which merges traditional and contemporary North American life-styles, is called the Inuit culture.

700. *What is Inuktitut?*

Inuktitut is what the Inuit call their language. The word means "like a man." Today, more than half of the country's Inuit are able to converse in the language, and with it speak with Inuit in the other circumpolar nations — the United States, the Soviet Union, and Denmark. The language sounds throaty to non-Inuit listeners. The structure is agglutinative — long words are the norm.

701. *If the Inuit speak Inuktitut, what language do the Indians speak?*

The Indians of Canada do not share a single language. All the Inuit once spoke Inuktitut, but the Indians of Canada have more than fifty indigenous languages. These languages are usually grouped into one dozen linguistic families. The families are: Algonkian, Athapascan, Beothukan, Chinookan, Haidan, Iroquoian, Kootenayan, Salishan, Siouan, Koluschan, Tsimshian, and Wakashan. Two of these families — Beothukan (which may have been a variety of Algonkian) and Chinookan — are extinct. In 1982, one linguist estimated the total number of native speakers in all of Canada to be 154,000. Linguists consider a language spoken by fewer than 5,000 speakers to be endangered. On that basis, only five languages spoken by native Canadians today have assured futures, and these are Algonkian, Athapascan, Salishan, Siouan, and Inuktitut.

702. *What is the name of the system of writing used by many Indians and Inuit?*
The system of writing used by some Cree Indians and many of the Inuit is known as the syllabic system. This wholly new alphabet was derived from shorthand notation by James Evans in 1840 for use among the Cree at Norway House, and adapted for use among the Eskimo on Baffin Island by E. J. Peck in 1894. The Inuktitut syllabary used today has eleven symbols for different consonants which may be rotated into four different patterns to represent the forty-four possible vowel combinations.

703. *What were Chinook Jargon and Bungee?*
Chinook Jargon and Bungee were *linguae francae* used in the nineteenth century by Indian and white traders. Chinook Jargon combined English, French, and Indian words. It was employed by the Chinook Indians on the West Coast and had a colourful vocabulary. At least one expression—*hyiu muckamuck*—has been embedded in the English language. It means ''big shot'' (though the literal meaning is ''plenty to eat''). Bungee incorporated words from the Algonkian language of the Cree, French, and Scots English into a common tongue spoken in the Red River Settlement area. The word Bungee is said to mean ''few,'' perhaps a reference to the few traders who mastered it.

704. *What is an inukshuk?*
An inukshuk is a cairn constructed of rocks in the shape of a man. Inukshuks were built by the Inuit as landmarks. The word itself means ''man-like.'' They are found in the Arctic, and some have been erected in public places in the south.

705. *What is the difference between an* umiak *and a* kayak?
Both are boats built by the Inuit, the difference being that an
umiak is a multi-passenger vessel whereas a *kayak* is a single-
passenger vessel.

706. *Is there any difference between a* mukluk *and a* kamik?
The two Eskimo words refer to the same thing, an ankle-length
boot made of deerskin. *Mukluk* is used in the western Arctic,
kamik in the eastern Arctic.

**707. *Is it true that in the Eskimo language there are twenty-
three words for kinds of snow but no single word for "snow"?***
This statement is generally true. One dictionary of Inuktitut lists
ten different terms for spreading snow, beating snow, building
snow, drifting snow, first snow, potable snow, salty snow, watery
snow, newly drifted snow, soft snow — ten snows in all but no
generic term for "snow." The Department of Indian and Northern Affairs once compiled from various sources a list of twenty-
six different types of ice and snow. So the point is more or less
true. It is frequently said that Arabic has ninety-nine words for
kinds of camels but not one single word for the concept of "camel."
It is certainly true that the Eskimos have a great many words for
"snow" but no word for "camel."

708. *Who is the most widely known Eskimo of all time?*
That distinction belongs to an Eskimo from Inukjuak named
Alakarialak. He is not known under that name, however, but by
his "professional name" — Nanook. This Eskimo hunter of the
Belcher Islands and the Ungava Peninsula starred in the feature
film *Nanook of the North*, which, since its release in 1922, has
been seen by millions of movie-goers around the world.

Nanook of the North was the world's first feature-length
documentary film. It was directed by Robert J. Flaherty, who

depicted in the film the everyday experiences of Nanook and his family. The name Nanook means "bear" and is certainly easier for most people to remember than Alakarialak. Sadly, the year after the release of the film made him a "star," Nanook died of starvation in the North.

709. *Whose photographs helped to save a people?*

Richard Harrington, a still photographer with a special interest in the North, had his toughest human experience with the Inuit in 1952. On his fourth photographic trip in the North, he decided to visit the isolated Padleimiuts, Eskimos who live on the barrens of the Northwest Territories. When he reached their settlement, he found a gaunt people who were starving to death. He immediately distributed his own supply of food and conducted a search for caribou. The band's starvation temporarily alleviated, he left for Toronto. His photographs and account of the starving people appeared on the front page of *The Toronto Star* and many of the world's leading newspapers. The federal government dropped in emergency food supplies and ultimately airlifted the entire population to a region well supplied with caribou. The photographs appear in Harrington's *The Inuit: Life as It Was* (1981).

710. *Do Eskimos live in igloos?*

No, but they once did. An igloo is a domed structure made entirely of blocks of hard snow. During the winter months, the Eskimos inhabited igloos. During the summer months, they lived in tupeks — tents made of animal skins.

Such structures belong to the past. In fact, in a survey conducted in the 1920s and reported by Vilhjalmur Stefansson in *The Standardization of Error* (1928), fewer than three hundred of over 14,000 Eskimos in Greenland had ever seen an igloo!

One historian of architecture maintained that Canada's contribution to the history of human dwellings consisted of the igloo and the teepee or wigwam.

711. *What is an Eskimo co-operative?*
An Eskimo co-operative is a centre in the North owned and operated by the Inuit to arrange the manufacture and sale of the native
arts and crafts produced by its members. Every authentic piece of
Eskimo sculpture or print has a tag with registration number and
co-op name. The art of Pitseolak and Kenojuak, for instance,
comes from the West Baffin Eskimo Co-operative at Cape Dorset,
N.W.T., the first of the co-ops, established in 1959 with the
assistance of arts administrator James Houston. There are almost
sixty Eskimo co-operatives in the Northwest Territories and northern Quebec.

712. *What is the Inuit Tapirisat of Canada?*
The Inuit Tapirisat of Canada is an organization dedicated to the
needs and aspirations of Canada's Inuit. The name of the organization, founded in 1971, means "Eskimo Brotherhood." The
head office is in Ottawa.

713. *Eskimo carvings are made of steatite. What is it?*
Steatite is a soft stone, grey in colour, the use of which is limited
to Eskimo craftsmen who employ it for "soapstone" carvings and
engraving plates for prints. The stone has a smooth "soapy" feel
and, indeed, softer varieties have been used for cleansing.

714. *Haida carvings are made of argillite. What is it?*
Argillite is a dull grey, slate-like sedimentary rock found near
Skidegate in the Queen Charlotte Islands, B.C. It is quite scarce
and the quarry is the exclusive property of Haida carvers who
work the rock into sculptures and pendants. When polished, argillite shines with a bright black sheen. Powdered argillite is moulded
into souvenirs such as miniature figurines and totem poles.

715. What "tags" guarantee the authenticity of the arts and crafts produced by the Indians and Inuit of Canada?

The "tags" are called the Beaver Pelt and the Igloo Tag. The former, a brown oval tag, depicts a beaver pelt enclosed within a black border (symbolic of the brotherhood of all Indians). The latter, a black and white tag, includes, within a cartouche, the schematic representation of an igloo. Attached to a pair of moccasins or a piece of Eskimo sculpture, the pelt or tag attests to the authenticity and the individuality of the work.

716. Who are the outstanding Inuit carvers of the past and present?

James Houston, who introduced the modern crafts movement to the Inuit world, named ten outstanding Inuit carvers in his article "Inuit Sculpture," *Town and Country*, November 1983. Here is his list.

> Akeeaktashuk (1898–1954) of Inukjuak and Ellesmere Island
> Karoo Ashevak (1940–1974) of Spence Bay
> Henry Evaluarjuk (b. 1923) of Igloolik and Frobisher Bay
> Kiugak (Kiawak) Ashoona (b. 1933) of Cape Dorset
> Vital (Makpa) Makpaaq (1922–1978) of Baker Lake
> Davidee (Munamee) Mannumi (1919–1976) of Cape Dorset
> Ipeelee (Oshaweetok) Osuitok (b. 1923) of Cape Dorset
> John Pangnark (1920–1980) of Eskimo Point
> Joe Talirunili (1899-1976) of Povungnituk
> John Tiktak (1916–1981) of Rankin Inlet

Added Houston, "Many highly regarded carvers do not appear on this limited list. A surprisingly large number of sculptors create noteworthy pieces but then, in a way typical of folk artists, return to their traditional hunting life and create few more."

717. What is the name of the most famous Eskimo print?

The most famous (and most valuable) of all the fine prints produced by the Eskimo people is *The Enchanted Owl*. It was drawn by Kenojuak, an artist at Cape Dorset known for her fantastic owls, and engraved by Eegyvadluk, a Cape Dorset stone-cutter and printmaker. Fifty prints were pulled, twenty-five in black and red, twenty-five in black and green. The proud owl, a symbol of wisdom, with spreading plumage and tail, appeared on a six-cent stamp issued in 1970 to mark the Centennial of the Northwest Territories. That same year one print of *The Enchanted Owl* sold for $10,000.

718. *What is "throat-singing"?*

The Inuit tradition of "throat-singing" was revived at Povungnituk, Que., in the 1970s. In its usual form, two Inuit women face each other and produce vocal sounds by the manipulation of their breathing. Their sounds blend and the "music" seems to emerge from one person rather than two. Everyday rather than musical sounds are made, and the effect is sometimes arresting, sometimes comic, even for the Inuit, who may break into giggles.

719. *Who is the greatly feared Sedna?*

Among the central Eskimos, Sedna is the ruler of the lower depths. She is a malicious and impulsive being who lives in a bubble at the bottom of the sea. Her fingertips, cut off by her father, turned into seals, walruses, and the other sea mammals.

720. *What is the difference between a status and a non-status Indian?*

A status Indian is one whose name appears on the Indian Register maintained by the Department of Indian and Northern Affairs pursuant to the Indian Act. A non-status Indian is one whose name does not appear on the Indian Register. The Indian Register is principally a collection of Band Lists compiled by the councils of bands or bodies of Indians.

According to the Census of 1981, 276,436 status Indians are

members of 565 bands with access to 2,274 Indian reserves. Estimates of the number of Métis and non-status Indians go as high as
750,000. Métis and non-status Indians may regard themselves as
Indians but they are not so recognized in law. They or their
predecessors may have lost or never gained such status.

A status Indian who lives on an Indian reserve pays no federal
income tax. A status Indian woman who marries a non-status
person loses her own status and in some instances that of any
offspring of the union.

721. *What is the name of the most famous Indian of all time?*
People of all ages and of many cultures are familiar with the name
Hiawatha, the most famous Indian of all time. Hiawatha is the
hero of *The Song of Hiawatha* (1855), a book-length epic poem by
the American poet Henry Wadsworth Longfellow. In Longfellow's narrative, Hiawatha is an Ojibwa reared by Nokomis, daughter of the moon, on the south shore of Lake Superior, in present-day
Wisconsin. He marries Minnehaha and brings civilization to his
people before departing for the Isles of the Blest in Keewaydin,
present-day Northwest Territories, where he rules over the kingdom of the Northwest wind.

That is Longfellow's version of the story. There is another
Hiawatha, a figure not of myth but of legend. According to Indian
tradition, Hiawatha was an Iroquois hero who was born an
Onondagan, near present-day Kingston, Ont., raised a Huron,
and adopted by Mohawks. His name is said to mean ''he who
combs,'' that is, unties knots or knotty problems. Hiawatha is
credited with the invention of *wampum*, a form of money, and
with assisting Dekanahwideh in the creation of the Iroquois
Confederacy.

**722. *What was the Great Peace and why does it remain of con-
tinuing interest?***
The Great Peace is another name for the Iroquois League or

Confederacy, which united the Five Nations. No one knows when the Mohawk, Oneida, Onondaga, Cayuga, and Seneca united, but in 1720 the Five Nations became the Six Nations with the inclusion of the Tuscarora. The Great Peace was implemented by the semi-legendary leader Dekanahwideh with the assistance of Hiawatha. Dekanahwideh uprooted a great fir tree and had the formerly warring tribes bury their weapons before the tree was replanted. He promised to return in time of need. "If the Great Peace should fail," he said, "call on my name in the bushes, and I will return."

The Great Peace has been called the longest honoured covenant in the world. The Nations chose the eagle, an ever-watchful bird, as a symbol, which is said to have inspired its use by the American colonists in 1776. Observers as dissimilar as Friedrich Engels and Edmund Wilson admired the constitution of the Great Peace, and the poet Duncan Campbell Scott respected the poetic power of its ceremonies and rituals.

723. *Which province has no Indian reserves?*
Newfoundland is the only province with no Indian reserves. (The native Beothuk Indians have been extinct for more than a century and a half.) In all, there are 2,274 Indian reserves in Canada.

724. *Which is the largest Indian reserve in the country?*
The Blood Reserve is the largest Indian reserve in the country, being 139,850 ha, or 349,618 acres, in area. It is near Stand Off, southwest of Lethbridge. The traditional Sun Dance is held here for two weeks each summer.

725. *What is the Kainai Chieftainship?*
The Blood Reserve, near Stand Off, Alta., maintains the tradition of the Kainai Chieftainship of the Blood Indian Tribe (Blackfoot Confederacy). There may be no more than forty living members

with honorary chieftainships. Some members of the past and present, with English names and years, are the following: The Prince of Wales (Red Crow, 1919, 1977), Lord Tweedsmuir (Eagle Head, 1936), Vincent Massey (Running Antelope, 1952), J. W. Grant MacEwan (Owns Many Horses, 1967), and Pierre Berton (Big Plume, 1973).

726. What are some Indian "firsts"?

Here are some Indian "firsts" in public life.

Frank A. Calder, a Nishga, became the first Indian elected to a provincial legislature. This occurred in British Columbia on June 15, 1949.

James Gladstone, a Blood, was the first Indian to be summoned to the Senate. This occurred on February 1, 1958.

Len Marchand, a status Indian, was the first to be elected to the House of Commons. This came about on June 25, 1968.

Ralph G. Steinhauer, a Cree, was the first Indian to be sworn in as lieutenant-governor. This occurred in Alberta on June 2, 1974.

727. What is a totem pole?

A totem pole is the name given by Europeans to the carved wooden pillars made by Indian peoples of the northwest coast. Figures carved into the poles are primarily visual statements about the group membership and identity of those who erected them. In this way the totemic images resemble crests.

Totem poles were usually erected at potlatches and may be distinguished according to use. There are house posts, house frontal poles, memorial or commemorative poles, mortuary poles, grave markers, and welcome figures. Some remain standing in west coast villages but the majority have fallen and rotted. A few dozen have been preserved in museums.

728. Who was Mungo Martin?

The traditional arts and crafts of the peoples of the northwest coast have undergone a revival in the postwar period. Leadership was shown by Mungo Martin (1881–1962), a master Kwakiutl carver who designed and executed poles for the University of British Columbia and the Provincial Museum in Victoria. He carved the world's tallest cedar pole, which stands 38.25 m, or 127 feet 6 inches, in height in Victoria's Beacon Hill Park.

Martin's work has continued in the hands of a younger generation of native artists. Among the new carvers are Tony Hunt and Douglas Cranmer, both Kwakiutl; Bill Reid, Robert Davidson, Gary Edenshaw, and Jim Hart, all Haida; Nishga artist Norman Tait; and the Gitksan artists of the 'Ksan movement.

These artists and craftsmen adapt the traditional forms to modern means and materials. Some of them work on totem poles. In fact, more totem poles are being carved today than were at any point in the past. They are acquired by museums and by the Department of External Affairs for donation or use abroad as hallmarks of native Canadiana.

729. *What is* The Raven and the First Men?

The Raven and the First Men is a massive cedarwood sculpture that depicts the culture hero and trickster, Raven, discovering the first Haida men in a giant clamshell. It was conceived by the Haida sculptor Bill Reid and carved by Reid and four traditional carvers — George Norris, George Rammell, Gary Edenshaw, and Jim Hart. Architect Arthur Erickson designed a special rotunda to receive it at the Museum of Anthropology, Vancouver. The powerful and dramatic work, unveiled by Prince Charles on April 1, 1980, was later dedicated by representatives of the Haida villages of Massett and Skidegate, Queen Charlotte Islands, with a great feast.

730. *Which native artist defied tribal taboos by painting traditional legends and myths?*

The Ojibwa artist Norval Morrisseau (b. 1931) was living near Beardmore, Ont., when he defied tribal taboos and began to depict traditional legendary and mythical figures in a personal, semi-abstract "X-ray" style in acrylic. His first exhibition in Toronto in 1962 was an outstanding artistic and commercial success. He won the approval of the tribal elders and inspired a generation of native artists of the Eastern Woodlands. Among the new generation were such talented artists as Daphne Odjig, Carl Ray, Joshim Kakegamic, Roy Thomas, Saul Williams, and Blake Debassige. Other talented native painters include Jackson Beardy and Alex Janvier.

731. *Who played Tonto to the Lone Ranger?*
The role of Tonto, the faithful Indian companion of the Lone Ranger, the Masked Rider of the Plains, was played in the 1950s in Hollywood Westerns and on radio and television by Jay Silverheels. The Mohawk actor was born Harry Jay Smith at the Six Nations Reserve, Brantford, Ont.

732. *Was Chief Dan George an actual Indian chief?*
He was. A spokesman for the native people of North America, Chief Dan George (1899–1982), was chief of the Squamish people of Burrard Reserve, near Vancouver, B.C. His chieftainship was of the elected rather than the hereditary variety. He was a magnificent orator with a message of toleration for man and nature, a fine lyric poet, and in later years an actor. He was nominated for an Academy Award for his performance as an elderly chief in the 1970 Hollywood film *Little Big Man*.

733. *The words* orenda, manitou, *and* wakanda *signify the same concept. What is it?*
The three words mean "spirit" (or "god" or "mystery") in the languages spoken by the Iroquoian, Algonkian, and Siouan Indians. *Manitou* is probably the most familiar term to whites. *Gitchi-manitou* means "great spirit," *Mitchi-manitou* means "evil spirit."

734. *What is* wampum*? What was its use?*
Wampum, the Algonkian word for "white string," refers to a string or belt of white and purple beads made of shells, used by the Indians of the Eastern Woodlands. *Wampum* was traded for goods, used for decoration, and employed as a memory aid. Significant events of the tribe's past could be recalled through stylized motifs expressed in the arrangement of beads. Today the word is used in the sense of "money."

735. *What is a conical structure of poles covered with buffalo hide, bark, or canvas and used as a dwelling?*
The Indians of the prairies called such a dwelling in the Siouan language a *teepee*. The Algonkian-speaking Indians referred to it as a *wigwam*. The northern equivalent of such a dwelling was the *tupek*, inhabited by Eskimos during summer months. In winter months the Eskimos lived in igloos.

736. *What is the Shaking Tent?*
The Shaking Tent is a rite of the Algonkian Indians, especially the Cree of the plains in the nineteenth century. As witnessed and described by European fur traders, a naked medicine man, bound and wrapped in a robe, left on the floor of a teepee, would cause the tent to shake as if rocked by winds. When unbound, the medicine man would expound on the message he had received from the spirits.

737. *Who or what is the Windigo?*
The Windigo (or Wendigo) is the spirit of cannibalism among the Algonkian-speaking Indians. The word may mean "evil spirit" or "cannibal." The Windigo may be a gigantic spectre or an Indian "turned Windigo" through an act of cannibalism. Indian tales of the evil spirit are legion.

738. *Who or what is the Thunderbird?*

The Thunderbird is a mythic bird of great power, the subject of stories told by the Ojibwa and other Algonkian-speaking Indians. Thunderbirds are gigantic creatures that are either a curse or a blessing to the Indian people. When angry, bolts of lightning flash from their eyes; thunder crashes from the flapping of their wings. They personify power that must be appeased.

739. *What was the practice of potlatch?*

Potlatch was the practice of the Kwakiutl and other Pacific coast Indians. On ceremonial occasions, chiefs gave gifts to their guests to demonstrate their social position and power. As the giving was reciprocated on later occasions, the custom did not lead to the progressive impoverishment of the Indian people. On the mistaken belief that it did impoverish the tribes, as well as a general mistreatment of native peoples, the custom was prohibited from 1884 to 1951, when the ban was lifted.

740. *With which region of the Maritimes is the Micmac culture hero Glooscap associated?*

By tradition, Glooscap resides at Cape Blomidon, a rocky promontory on the shore of Minas Basin north of the village of Blomidon, N.S. The Micmac culture hero arrived from across the sea in a great stone canoe. He created the Indians, the first of men, and all the animals. He seized the queen Summer from the south and married her to the giant Winter. After many more exploits and deeds, he sang a strange sad song, then sailed away again in his great stone boat.

741. *Who or what is the Gougou?*

The Gougou is a fabulous female giant, twice the height of a sailing vessel, who catches sailors and stores them in her huge pocket before devouring them. Champlain in 1603 described the Gougou and said that according to Micmac legend she lives on an island near the Baie de Chaleur in the Gulf of St. Lawrence. The lawyer Lescarbot dismissed the Micmac belief and Champlain's incredulity, maintaining that the Gougou expresses the terror of those who "see and hear things which are not."

742. *What is the name of the fabulous sea serpent said to inhabit the waters of Okanagan Lake?*

Okanagan Lake, in the interior of British Columbia, is said to be the home of Ogopogo, a variously described sea serpent. The creature was known to the Salish and Chinook Indians long before it was named Ogopogo after an English musical hall song in 1926. Sightings have been reported on many occasions but, like Scotland's Loch Ness Monster, there is scant evidence of the lake monster's existence.

743. *What is the legend of Qu'Appelle Valley?*

The verdant valley in southeastern Saskatchewan takes its name from the Qu'Appelle River, which is French for "who calls" and derived from the Cree *Kah-tep-was*, "the river which calls." At Lebret, near Fort Qu'Appelle, there is a marker which tells the legend of the valley. An Indian brave, returning by canoe, hears his name. He shouts, "Who calls?" The only reply is the echo of his words. Arriving home, he discovers his sweetheart has died calling out his name.

744. *What were the dying words of Chief Crowfoot?*

Crowfoot, Blackfoot leader and the last of the great Indian chiefs, died overlooking the Bow River, Alberta, April 25, 1890. His dying words are very moving. "A little while and I will be gone from among you, whither I cannot tell. From nowhere we came, into nowhere we go. What is life? It is a flash of a firefly in the

night. It is a breath of a buffalo in the wintertime. It is as the little
shadow that runs across the grass and loses itself in the sunset.''

745. *Is there any evidence for the existence of the Sasquatch?*
The Sasquatch is a mysterious apelike creature said to inhabit the
remoter regions of the Pacific northwest. The word *sasquatch* is
Salish for "wild men" or "hairy men." In northern California,
the Sasquatch is known as Big Foot.

Evidence for the existence of the Sasquatch in British Columbia
and Alberta consists of references in Indian legend, passages in
the journals of David Thompson and Paul Kane, casts of alleged
footprints, and reports of sightings from early times to the present
day. The Sasquatch seems as elusive as his country cousin, Big
Foot, and his distant relation, the Yeti or Abominable Snowman
of the Himalayas.

746. *Where is the fabled Kingdom of Saguenay?*
The Kingdom of Saguenay, the fabled region between the Saguenay
River and the Ottawa River, was described to Jacques Cartier on
his voyages of 1534 and 1535. The Indians reported that the
"kingdom" contained precious metals and stones. The myth of
the riches of the Saguenay was still alive in 1609 when Marc
Lescarbot wrote of the region "where is infinite gold, rubies and
other riches, and where the men are as white as in France, and
clad in wool."

747. *Where is the legendary Headless Valley said to be?*
The legendary Headless Valley, or Valley of Mystery, is said to be
in a deep canyon along the South Nahanni River in the Yukon
Territory. Certainly the river valley, which runs through the rugged terrain of Nahanni National Park, is all but inaccessible except
by boat or plane. Its remoteness has given rise to legend, sparked
by the discovery in 1917 along the Nahanni of the decapitated

body of a prospector. Headless Valley remains "a land that time forgot" — a legendary region rich in tropical vegetation, fed by volcanic springs, with prehistoric beasts, and a lost race ruled over by a white queen.

748. *Does Santa Claus live in Canada?*

Santa Claus is said to reside the year round at the North Pole. Here, in an ice castle, he lives and works with his elves in his toyshop, making toys for good little boys and girls. Any child who writes to him — Santa Claus, North Pole, Canada, H0H 0H0 — will receive a reply (courtesy of Canada Post).

749. *Is there a Mount Rudolph the Red-nosed Reindeer?*

No. The Canadian Permanent Committee on Geographical Names rejected the suggestion that a mountain between Newcastle and Grand Falls, N.B., be named after the subject of the popular Christmas song "Rudolph the Red-nosed Reindeer." Instead, the Committee, in 1964, called the mountain Mount St. Nicholas. The name is in keeping with the official names of other peaks in the vicinity — Dasher, Dancer, Prancer, Vixen, Comet, Cupid, Donner, and Blitzen — from Clement C. Moore's narrative poem "A Visit from St. Nicholas."

750. *What is the oldest folk song about a Canadian incident?*

The first folk song about an incident that took place in early Canada is considered to be "*Petit Rocher*" ("Little Rock"). It is the lament of the trapper Jean Cadieux, who, though mortally wounded during an Iroquois attack in 1709, lived long enough to dig his own grave on the bank of the Ottawa River, and write his lament on birch bark in his own blood.

751. *Who was called "La Corriveau" and why was she feared?*
"La Corriveau" was the nickname of Marie-Josephte Corriveau (1733–1763), who was tried in Quebec and condemned to death for murdering her husband after she confessed to hitting him on the head twice with an axe while he was asleep. She was hanged near the Plains of Abraham on April 18, 1763, and her body was publicly exposed in an iron cage. The discovery of the iron cage in 1850 rekindled interest in "La Corriveau," and she entered into Quebec legend and literature as something of a witch.

752. *What is the name of "the girl who danced with the devil"?*
The French-Canadian legend of "the girl who danced with the devil" was common throughout the Gaspé in the eighteenth and nineteenth centuries. Although she dared to dance with the devil on Saturday night, she was saved by the power of love on Sunday morning. The traditional name of the spirited girl is Rose Latulippe.

753. *What is the French-Canadian legend of* La Chasse-Galerie*?*
The legend of *La Chasse-Galerie*, or the Flying Canoe was popular in Quebec in the nineteenth century. A French-Canadian *voyageur* bargains with the devil to take him in his Flying Canoe for a quick visit with his sweetheart. In exchange, the devil demands the young man's soul, but is foiled in his attempt to claim it. The legend may be based on an old French story of a "Monsieur Galéry" who, as punishment for hunting rather than attending Mass on Sunday, was condemned to hunt through the skies at midnight until the world ended.

754. *Who is Paul Bunyan and where did he come from?*
Paul Bunyan is the giant lumberjack of folklore, the subject of tall tales told in lumber camps in New Brunswick and Maine in the late nineteenth century. With his "fabulous blue ox, Babe," Bunyan is said to have created the tides in the Bay of Fundy, hollowed

out the Great Lakes, raised the Rocky Mountains, etc. The comic figure and his preposterous adventures may be an adaptation of the Glooscap cycle of the Micmacs; a corruption of the French-Canadian Ti-Jean, "Beau Jean," or Bonhomme figure; a tribute to a "giant warrior" recalled from the Rebellion of 1837 in Lower Canada; or an oral-literary creation employed by various writers from 1910 on.

755. *There is a cairn at Spencer's Island, N.S., that refers to "the world's most famous mystery ship." Why?*
One of the great mysteries of the sea — one of the most intriguing mysteries of all time — was the sudden abandonment, on open waters, of the *Mary Celeste*. On December 5, 1872, the twin-masted brigantine was encountered drifting ghost-like, sans crew but cargo intact, on the Atlantic Ocean between the Azores and the Portuguese coast. Speculation as to the vessel's fate and the whereabouts of its crew has continued to this day. Stories, essays, books, and even a Hollywood movie have sought to "explain" the mystery.

The reason there is a cairn at Spencer's Island, near Parrsborough, N.S., is that the *Mary Celeste* was built and launched there in 1861, when the vessel was christened the *Amazon*.

756. *Who was the "witch doctor" of Long Point?*
The semi-legendary "witch doctor" of Long Point, which extends into Lake Erie south of Simcoe, Ont., is Dr. John Frederick Troyer (1753–1842), the first permanent resident of what is now Norfolk County. Legends linger about this self-styled doctor, "witch doctor," and herbalist. It is said he possessed a magical "moonstone" and a "witch trap." It is claimed he travelled to Baldoon, on Lake St. Clair, to put an end to the poltergeist-like haunting of the farmhouse of John McDonald in 1829–31. Some of Troyer's effects may be seen at the Eva Brook Donly Museum, Long Point, Ont.

757. *Who was Nelvana of the Northern Lights?*
Nelvana of the Northern Lights was a comic book heroine created by the Toronto artist Adrian Dingle in 1940–45. The statuesque Nelvana was the "daughter of the Northern Lights." She had long, raven-black hair, she sported a cape, and she wore a fur-trimmed miniskirt much ahead of its time. Nelvana was the protectress of the Eskimo people, and she could cause the caribou to roam again. Nelvana appeared in the so-called Canadian whites, comic books produced in Canada in black and white to replace the full-colour American comic books embargoed during World War II. She was the most imaginative and well drawn of the heroes, heroines, superheroes, and superheroines of the Canadian whites.

758. *What popular board game was devised by a sportswriter and a photo editor?*
One December evening in 1979, Scott Abbott, sportswriter for Canadian Press, and Chris Haney, photo editor of the Montreal *Gazette*, spent forty-five profitable minutes devising the basic rules and board design of Trivial Pursuit. They test-marketed 1,200 sets in the fall of 1981. After risks and setbacks, the game went into full-scale production. By 1984, worldwide retail sales had reached $1 billion.

759. *Where was Jumbo the Circus Elephant killed?*
Jumbo the Circus Elephant was struck down and killed by a Grand Trunk train at St. Thomas, south of London, Ont. The mammoth, African-born pachyderm, the featured performer with the Barnum and Bailey Circus, was killed on September 15, 1885. A gigantic statue of Jumbo in St. Thomas recalls the incident.

760. *What are the six safety rules of Elmer the Safety Elephant?*
Elmer the Safety Elephant is the symbol of the national safety program for school children. The grey elephant with the green

suit and orange hat and tie "never forgets" the safety rules. The Canada Safety Council has used the mascot since 1949 on flags, pamphlets, posters, crests, booklets, etc. Elmer's six safety rules are as follow: "Always look before you cross the road. Keep away from all parked cars. Ride your bike safely and obey all signs and signals. Play your games in a safe place away from traffic. Walk, don't run, when you cross the road. Where there are no sidewalks, walk off the road to the left and face oncoming traffic."

761. *Who were the most despised Canadians of all time?*
No list of this nature could ever be complete or even representative. Yet all the men whose names appear below — there are no names of women — have aroused the enmity of their fellow Canadians. It should be noted that some of the despised Canadians acted out of conviction, others out of convenience. There are no common criminals among them; criminals are dealt with in the next list.

1. François Bigot, corrupt intendant of New France
2. Charles Lawrence, governor responsible for the Acadian expulsion
3. Lord Durham, author of the famous (or infamous) *Report*
4. Sir Francis Bond Head, reactionary lieutenant governor
5. Louis Riel, Métis leader and insurrectionist
6. C.P.T. Chiniquy, professional anti-Papist
7. Sir Joseph Flavelle, war profiteer
8. Adrien Arcand, Quebec fascist and anti-Semite
9. Charles E. Coughlin, the "Radio Priest," fascist
10. R. B. Bennett, Prime Minister during the Depression
11. F. C. Blair, bureaucrat in the Department of Immigration
12. Fred Rose, Communist member of the House of Commons convicted of espionage
13. Paul Rose, plus other FLQ members and murderers of Pierre Laporte

762. *Who are some of the country's most notorious criminals?*
Here is a list of thirteen common and uncommon criminals. Unlucky baker's dozen! The crimes committed by these men and women received widespread publicity, yet doubts persist about the guilt of two of them (Wilbert Coffin and Stephen Truscott), and two others (Almighty Voice and the Megantic Outlaw) are regarded more as symbols of resistance to arbitrary authority than of criminality.

1. Marie-Josephte Corriveau, Quebec axe murderess, witch
2. J. Reginald Birchall, confidence man and murderer
3. Donald Morrison, called the Megantic Outlaw
4. Almighty Voice, Cree Indian escapee
5. Edwin Alonzo Boyd, bankrobber and leader of the Boyd Gang
6. Albert Johnson, known as the Mad Trapper of Rat River
7. Norman (Red) Ryan, supposedly reformed bankrobber
8. Evelyn Dick, murderess
9. Albert Guay, jeweller who blew up a CP DC-3 to kill his wife
10. Wilbert Coffin, prospector and supposed murderer
11. Stephen Truscott, convicted of rape and murder at 14
12. Peter Demeter, developer and murderer
13. Clifford Olson, serial murderer

763. *Who were "the Black Donnellys"?*
The so-called Black Donnellys were members of an Irish-Catholic family, slain the night of February 4, 1880. James, his wife Johannah, their sons Thomas and John, and their niece Bridget, were all murdered in the Donnelly farmhouse at Lucan, northwest of London, Ont. The assailants were vigilante nightriders intent on continuing a blood feud introduced from Tipperary, Ireland. No one was ever found guilty of the massacre. The feud continued and claimed an estimated twenty more lives.

764. *Who was "The Great Detective"?*
The description fits John Wilson Murray (1840–1906), Chief

Inspector of the Ontario Criminal Justice Department, who recounted his old cases in the somewhat immodestly titled book *Memoirs of a Great Detective* (1904). Murray solved the sensational Birchall Case of 1890. He is played with gusto by Douglas Campbell on the CBC-TV series "The Great Detective."

765. Who murdered whom in Blenheim Swamp?

The body of F. C. Benwell, an English remittance man, was found on February 21, 1890, in Blenheim Swamp, midway between Woodstock and Paris, Ont. John Wilson Murray, the so-called Great Detective, investigated the slaying. The case attracted considerable international attention as Benwell had been lured to Canada by J. Reginald Birchall, an English embezzler and murderer who posed as "Lord Somerset." Birchall was found guilty and was hanged at Woodstock later that year.

766. Who was the Megantic Outlaw?

The so-called Megantic Outlaw was Donald Morrison (1858–1894), a Scottish settler in Megantic County in the Eastern Townships of Quebec. Cheated of the family farm, he accidentally killed an inspector who had been attempting to arrest him in 1888 on suspicion of having set it on fire. What followed was a three-year manhunt, with the Scottish settlers conspiring to protect Morrison from the law. He was caught, found guilty of manslaughter, and died three years later in St. Vincent de Paul Penitentiary. Ballads, stories, and novels have been written about Morrison, whose experience somewhat parallels that of Almighty Voice in the West.

767. What was the crime of Almighty Voice?

Almighty Voice, who became a Cree hero and martyr, was initially arrested for stealing and slaughtering a cow on the Cree reserve near Duck Lake, Sask. In escaping from prison he shot and killed his captor, a North West Mounted Police officer. He eluded arrest for two years but was finally cornered and perished in a shoot-out on May 30, 1897. He stood in defiance of arbitrary white authority.

768. Who was "the Mad Trapper"?

The Mad Trapper was the sobriquet of a man sometimes identified as Albert Johnson, of whom little is known. Legend would have that he was a somewhat demented sharpshooter who murdered prospectors for the gold in their teeth; although this is disputed. He did murder an RCMP officer in the Fort McPherson area, and this led to a massive manhunt in the Yukon. Johnson was killed in a shoot-out in the Eagle River district on February 17, 1932.

769. Who was "the Grey Fox"?

Bill Miner (1847–1914) was an American-born stagecoach robber who emigrated to Canada. Since there were no stagecoaches to rob, he held up railway trains in the Kamloops area of British Columbia. He was known as "the Grey Fox" for his silver locks and his cunning. He was portrayed by the stuntman and actor Richard Farnsworth in the 1983 movie *The Grey Fox*.

770. Who was the country's most famous missing person?

Ambrose Small, the millionaire theatre owner who disappeared from downtown Toronto on December 2, 1919, was the country's most famous missing person. Rumours of his whereabouts or fate circulated for decades following his disappearance.

771. Who was the dreaded Arthur Ellis?

There never was an Arthur Ellis. This was the traditional name of the official executioner, or hangman, who travelled the country performing his service until the effective abolition of capital punishment in 1962. The Arthur Ellis alias was used in the 1930s and 1940s by Arthur Bartholomew English, who enjoyed meeting the press. He even granted the poet A. M. Klein the right to write his biography. In 1984, the Crime Writers of Canada instituted the Arthur Ellis Award for the author of the year's best crime novel. It is in the shape of a tiny gibbet.

772. *Who murdered Sir Harry Oakes?*

No one knows who murdered Sir Harry Oakes (1874–1943), the millionaire mining magnate who was brutally slain in the bedroom of his villa near Nassau, Bahamas, on July 8, 1943. Theories are legion as to why Oakes, who made a major gold strike in 1912 near Kirkland Lake, Ont., was murdered. They range from family quarrels (Sir Harry was a tempestuous person) to Mafia business (Sir Harry was against gambling). Numerous books have been written about the man, largely about his tragic demise.

773. *Who was the tallest man in the world?*

The tallest man in the world was Angus McAskill (1825-1863), the so-called Cape Breton Giant, who stood 236 cm, or 7 feet 9 inches, and weighed 193 kg, or 425 pounds. Born in the Outer Hebrides of Scotland, he was raised in St. Anns, Cape Breton Island, N.S., where he died, aged thirty-eight. Some of his effects may be seen at the Giant McAskill-Highland Pioneers Museum at St. Anns. He is described as "the tallest recorded 'true' (non-pathological) giant" in the *Guinness Book of Records* (1971).

One of the tallest women of her day was Anna Swan (1846–1888), a native of Nova Scotia, who was exhibited by P. T. Barnum. She was 228 cm, or 7 feet 6 inches tall, and weighed 160 kg, or 352 pounds. She married Martin van Buren Bates, the Kentucky giant.

774. *Who was nicknamed "Fox Populi"?*

The nickname was accorded Sir John A. Macdonald (1815–1891) on account of his cunning and popularity. It is a clever variation on the common phrase *vox populi*, Latin for "voice of the people." It attests to the affection of the Canadian people for their first Prime Minister and their willingness to overlook such excesses as his heavy drinking.

775. *In what words did Sir John A. Macdonald affirm his loyalty to Britain?*

Prime Minister Sir John A. Macdonald said in his last electoral address in Ottawa on February 7, 1891, "As for myself, my course is clear. A British subject I was born — a British subject I will die."

776. *In what words did Sir Wilfrid Laurier express his confidence in the future of Canada?*

In the course of an address to the Canadian Club of Ottawa, January 18, 1904, Prime Minister Sir Wilfrid Laurier stated, "The twentieth century belongs to Canada." The expression is a touchstone of national aspiration. Brian Moore, the novelist, noted: "The twentieth century *did* belong to Canada." Earle Birney, the poet, suggested, "The 20th Century belongs to the Moon." Don Harron, the comedian, quipped, "Twentieth-Century still belongs to Fox (whoever he is)." And Pierre Elliott Trudeau observed, "The future really belongs to those who will build it. The future can be promised to no one."

777. *Who is the religious thinker who first used the term "cosmic consciousness"?*

The term "cosmic consciousness" was first used to describe "a higher form of consciousness than that possessed by the ordinary man" by Dr. Richard Maurice Bucke (1837–1902), a religious thinker and authority in the field of mental illness. He focussed attention on the religious, mystical, ecstatic, or transpersonal experience in his major work *Cosmic Consciousness: A Study in the Evolution of the Human Mind* (1901). He first used the phrase in 1894. Bucke was superintendent of the asylum at London, Ont., and a personal friend of Walt Whitman. Bucke arranged Whitman's visit to Ontario and Quebec in 1880.

778. Who were the Dionne Quintuplets and why were they so popular in the 1930s?

The Dionne Quintuplets were five daughters born on May 28, 1934, to a farming couple, Oliva and Elzire Dionne, at Callander, southeast of North Bay, Ont. The names of the Quints are Yvonne, Annette, Cecile, Emilie, and Marie. Their pediatrician was Dr. Alan Roy Dafoe. The birth created a sensation in the 1930s. Multiple births of this magnitude were relatively rare prior to the use of fertility drugs in the 1960s, and the Dionnes were the first family in which all five infants survived. The children were exploited by the media (anxious for happy stories during the Depression), by baby-products manufacturers, and by Hollywood, which based three films on their birth. Pierre Berton called the Dionne Quints "a Thirties Melodrama."

779. Who was known as "King of the Klondike" and "Uncrowned King of Romania"?

Joseph W. Boyle (1867–1923) was an adventurer whose exploits took him from the Yukon to the Balkans. He founded a profitable gold-dredging operation in the Yukon in 1897. As an Allied agent in Russia in 1917, he made an unsuccessful attempt to rescue the Czar and his family. Thereafter he became a confidant of Queen Marie of Romania and was rumoured to be the power behind the throne. He died in England and was buried in London, but in April, 1983, his remains were reburied in the family plot at Woodstock, Ont.

780. *Who was known around the world as the Bird Man of Kingsville?*

The sobriquet fits Jack Miner (1865–1944), the country's best-known ornithologist. He grew up in Kingsville (the most southern town in Canada; it is 48 km, or 30 miles, south of Windsor, Ont., and located on Lake Erie). In 1904, he opened a wildlife sanctuary and began banding birds to trace migratory paths. Thousands of tourists flocked to the Jack Miner Bird Foundation, an 800-ha, or 2,000-acre, wilderness tract, for unparalleled viewing of millions of wild birds and to catch a glimpse of a greatly revered naturalist and conservationist.

781. *Who was Canada's foremost folklorist?*

The leading Canadian folklorist was unquestionably Marius Barbeau (1883–1969), the Quebec-born ethnologist at the National Museum of Canada from 1911 to 1958. He wrote in detail and at length about Indian culture and Quebec folklore, inspiring all subsequent collectors of Canadian folklore. He collected 195 Eskimo songs, 300 Indian songs, 1,500 old English songs, and 7,000 French-Canadian songs.

782. *Who compressed his philosophy into the aphorism, "Literature is conscious mythology"?*

The aphorism is that of Northrop Frye (b. 1912), literary critic at the University of Toronto. He evolved the theory that literature reveals archetypes that belong to a mythology in which man has a place in both the natural world and the world of ideas.

783. *Who first said, "The medium is the message," and what does the statement mean?*

The statement was first made in Vancouver on July 30, 1959, by Marshall McLuhan, a professor of English at the University of

Toronto and a specialist in the effects of the media. It became one of the catch phrases of the 1960s and remains one of the few aphorisms of Canadian origin known around the world. What McLuhan is saying is that the way information is conveyed determines the kind of information that can be conveyed. One *reads* a book, but *watches* television, so the content of a book cannot be directly conveyed in a television program, and vice versa. In later years McLuhan delighted in punning on his famous formulation: "The medium is the massage," "The medium is the mess-age," etc.

784. *Who is "Honest Ed"?*

"Honest Ed" is the sobriquet of Edwin Mirvish, a Toronto businessman and theatre owner. He founded Honest Ed's, the world's first discount department store, in Toronto in 1948. He acquired and refurnished the Royal Alexandra Theatre, which was slated for demolition, in 1963. He acquired the celebrated Old Vic, first opened in London, England, in 1818, refurnished it, and reopened it on November 8, 1983. Since then he has successfully operated both theatres.

785. *Who are the regular panelists on "Front Page Challenge"?*

"Front Page Challenge" is the longest-running entertainment show on Canadian television. It made its debut on the CBC-TV network as a summer replacement on June 24, 1957, and has appeared weekly since then. Fred Davis, as host-moderator, challenges the panelists to identify the week's "mystery guest," whose identity is gradually revealed through clues about his or her association with a headline-making news event of the past or present. Veteran panelists include Pierre Berton, Betty Kennedy, and Gordon Sinclair, all journalists. Allan Fotheringham, another journalist, replaced Gordon Sinclair, who died in 1984.

786. Who said, "When I die, I'm going to take New Year's with me"?
The remark was jokingly made by Guy Lombardo (1902–1977), the popular bandleader. Born in London, Ont., he formed the Royal Canadians dance band in the early 1920s. The band played "the sweetest music this side of heaven," and was the featured attraction for decades at New York's Waldorf Astoria Hotel, where Lombardo greeted the New Year with "Auld Lang Syne" and other sentimental melodies on behalf of the hotel guests and television watchers across the continent.

787. Is it true that both Buffy Sainte-Marie and Joni Mitchell were born in western Canada?
Yes, the two singer/songwriters are natives of western Canada. Buffy Sainte-Marie was born in 1941 at the Piapot Reserve, west of Fort Qu'Appelle, Sask. She was raised by adoptive parents in Massachusetts, and went on to compose some fine songs, including "Universal Soldier" in 1963. Joni Mitchell was born in 1944 in Fort Macleod, Alta., and wrote "Both Sides Now" in 1968. Both are international recording artists who live in the United States.

788. Who was the most admired and respected Canadian of the 1980s?
Most people would agree that the most admired and respected Canadian of the 1980s was Terry Fox (1958–1981). This determined young man from New Westminster, B.C., who lost a leg to cancer, resolved to raise money for research into the disease by jogging across Canada. With the blessing of the Canadian Cancer Society, he ran from Cape Spear, Nfld., to just east of Thunder Bay, Ont., on his "Marathon of Hope." He had crossed more than half the country when a recurrence of the disease forced him to stop. (The point at which he halted is now called the Terry Fox Scenic Lookout. It is marked by a 3-m, or 9-foot, statue of the

runner.) He died later that year in New Westminster, but his determination and idealism raised $24 million for cancer research (he attained his goal of one dollar for every Canadian) and inspired the annual Terry Fox Run. Terry Fox also inspired Steve Fonyo, who likewise lost his left leg to the disease, to run from the Atlantic to the Pacific. It took Fonyo fourteen months to complete his "Journey for Lives" in 1985. As Fonyo explained, "I'm not a hero. I'm just a nineteen-year-old guy who got cancer."

789. Who is Canada's best known chef?
Although many men and women could claim the distinction, the chef's hat is most delightfully worn by Madame Benoît. A native of Quebec, Jehane Benoît received a degree in food chemistry from the Sorbonne in Paris and experience at the Cordon Bleu school there. She established her own cooking school in Montreal in 1931 and is nationally known for her appearances on radio and television and for her many books, including *The Encyclopedia of Canadian Cuisine* (1963), which extol the merits of Quebec and Canadian cookery.

790. Who planted the Canadian flag on the summit of Mount Everest?
Laurie Skreslet, a skier from Calgary, was the first Canadian to climb to the top of Mount Everest. He led a Canadian team to scale the world's highest mountain, attaining the summit at 11:50 P.M., October 4, 1982, where he planted the maple leaf flag.

791. How did Pierre Elliott Trudeau express the disparity of the relationship between Canada and the United States?
In a widely reported address to the National Press Club in Washington, D.C., on March 26, 1969, Prime Minister Trudeau said, imaginatively: "Living next to you is in some ways like sleeping with an elephant. No matter how friendly and even-tempered is

the beast, if I can call it that, one is affected by every twitch and grunt."

792. *Who was Charlie Grant, the hero of* Charlie Grant's War?
Charlie Grant's War was a made-for-television movie produced by CBC-TV and first shown in January 1985. It added a new hero to the Canadian pantheon. Written by Anna Sandor, produced by William Gough, and directed by Martin Lavut, the drama starred R. H. Thomson as Charles Aubrey Grant (1900–1980), a Gentile who, like the Swedish diplomat Raoul Wallenberg, is credited with saving the lives of Jewish people in Nazi-occupied Europe. In the movie Grant is a Toronto-born diamond merchant in Vienna in 1938. Acquiring illegally 647 blank passport and visa forms, he supplies them to members of the Jewish community who would otherwise have died at the hands of the Nazis. Caught by the Gestapo, Grant is imprisoned from 1938 to 1945. After the war he returns to Canada where he is active as a spokesman on behalf of brotherhood. It was not until the television movie, released five years after his death, that his deeds became public knowledge.

793. *What are the Women's Institutes?*
The Women's Institutes are a federation of educational organizations founded in Canada and established in sixty-six countries around the world. The first Women's Institute was founded by Adelaide Hunter Hoodless and Erland Lee at Stoney Creek, Ont., on February 18, 1897, to assist farm women in household science. Mrs. Hoodless had lost a child because of contaminated milk and resolved to help other mothers. The Federated Women's Institutes of Canada was formed in Winnipeg in 1919. It advises on home economics, citizenship, agriculture, and industry. The home of Erland Lee, near Stoney Creek, where the original constitution was penned, has been preserved as a WI museum.

794. *What do the initials WCTU stand for?*
The initials stand for the Women's Christian Temperance Union, a prohibition-minded association formed in 1874, which became a social service agency. It was said WCTU meant "Women Continually Torment Us."

795. *What was the so-called Women's Parliament?*
The Women's Parliament was a mock parliament staged by a group of militant suffragettes, led by Nellie L. McClung. It was held the evening of January 28, 1914, at the old Walker Theatre in Winnipeg. The women mocked the all-male provincial legislature, especially its arch-conservative leader, and pointed out the lack of female franchise. The event, staged twice more, led to the unseating of the premier and ultimately to Manitoba women securing the franchise.

796. *When did women "get the vote" in Canada?*
Feminists had to form a women's suffrage movement in the West in 1910 before they were granted the franchise, the right to vote in elections. Even then it was slow in coming. The federal franchise was not extended to women until 1918. Provincially, Manitoba was the first province to grant women the right to vote in 1916, Quebec the last in 1940.

797. *What are some women's "firsts"?*
Here are some "firsts" for Canadian women in public life. In 1917, Louise G. McKinney became the first woman elected to a provincial legislature in the British Empire. It was the Alberta legislature. In 1921, Agnes Macphail became the first woman elected to the House of Commons. In 1930, Cairine Wilson became the first woman summoned to the Senate. In 1957, Ellen Fairclough became the first woman elected to the House of Commons to

serve in the Cabinet. In 1973, Pauline McGibbon became the first woman to serve as a lieutenant-governor. She was appointed lieutenant-governor of Ontario. In 1982, Bertha Wilson was the first woman appointed to the Supreme Court of Canada. In 1980, Jeanne Sauvé became the first woman to serve as Speaker of the House of Commons. In 1984, she became the first woman to serve as Governor General of Canada.

798. *Who was the first Canadian to win three medals at one Olympics?*

The first Canadian to win three medals at one Olympics is the speedskater Gaetan Boucher. At the 1984 Olympic Winter Games at Sarajevo, the athlete won a Gold in the 500-m,or 550-yard, race, a Gold in the 1,000-m, or 1,100-yard, race, and a Bronze in the 1,500-m, or 1,650-yard, race.

799. *How has Canada fared at the Olympic Games?*

While individual Canadians have excelled at Olympic competitions, Canada as a country has performed rather poorly at the Olympic Games. There are many explanations for this failure, but the likeliest reason is the lack of a truly committed national sports organization to encourage young athletes.

How well has Canada done? In a list of nations that won Olympic medals in summer and winter Games held between 1896 and 1980 inclusive, Canada placed eighteenth. It ranked between Austria and Czechoslovakia in total medals awarded. Canadians won 155 Gold, Silver, and Bronze medals. In the same competitions, the United States, the winning nation, gathered 1,621 medals; and the second-place nation, the USSR collected 1,026.

800. *Has a Canadian city ever hosted the Olympic Games?*

The Games of the XXI Summer Olympics were hosted by Montreal from July 17 to August 1, 1976. The Games were a success despite cost overruns and an eleventh-hour boycott by twenty

Third World nations. Twenty-one sports attracted over 250,000 spectators. Women's basketball was introduced at the Montreal Olympics. Until Montreal, the Olympic flame was borne by a single bearer. There were two bearers at Montreal — fifteen-year-old youths Stéphane Préfontaine and Sandra Henderson, who, some years later, were wed.

801. *Will a Canadian city host the Winter Olympics?*
The bid of the city of Calgary to host the Games of the XV Winter Olympics was accepted. The dates set for the event are February 23 to March 1, 1988.

802. *Was lacrosse ever a recognized Olympic sport?*
Lacrosse was recognized as an Olympic sport at the 1904 Games in St. Louis and at the 1908 Games in London. Both tournaments were won by Canada. The sport was discontinued, but noncompetitive demonstrations were held in 1928, 1932, and 1948.

803. *Lacrosse is sometimes called "the national game of Canada." Is it?*
The Indians of eastern Canada played a field game with sticks called *baggataway*, and during the nineteenth century it evolved into lacrosse. William George Beers, a Montreal dental surgeon, codified the rules of the game in 1867, and two years later he published a book called *Lacrosse: The National Game of Canada*. Beers so loved the game, he wanted to think that all Canadians had taken it to their hearts, but neither lacrosse nor any other game has ever been officially designated as "national." In 1876, Beers organized the first lacrosse team to visit the British Isles. In 1925, the Canadian Lacrosse Association was formed. The Mann Cup is awarded each year to the senior winning team, the Minto Cup to the junior winning team. There is a Lacrosse Hall of Fame, with a suitable acknowledgement of Beer's contribution, at New Westminster, B.C.

804. *Was ice hockey ever a recognized Olympic sport?*
Ice hockey was never recognized as an Olympic sport. However, the Olympic committee accepted it as a demonstration sport. The first demonstration game was played at the 1920 Games in Antwerp. The Canadian team won Gold medals in 1920, 1924, 1928, 1932, 1948 and 1952. It won Silver medals in 1936 and 1960 and Bronze medals in 1956 and 1968. It finished out of the medals in 1964. Canada withdrew from the sport after 1968, objecting to the "professional" status of the players from Eastern Europe.

805. *Where and when was the first game of ice hockey played?*
The first recorded game of ice hockey was played by members of the regiment of the Royal Canadian Rifles at Tête du Pont Barracks, Kingston, U.C. (Ont.), December 25, 1855. They cleared an expanse of snow from the harbour, tied blades to their boots, borrowed field hockey sticks, and proceeded to play field hockey on ice with sticks and a lacrosse ball.

Kingston is thus the birthplace of ice hockey. It is appropriately the home of the International Hockey Hall of Fame. On display in the Hall is a hockey stick used in one of the first organized hockey games played on Kingston Harbour in the winter of 1885–86 by Royal Military College cadets and Queen's College students. Also on display is the puck — a square-cut lacrosse ball.

Ken Dryden, writing in *The Game* (1983), noted that the first public exhibition of the game was held at Montreal's Victoria Skating Rink on March 3, 1875, when the game was played with shinny sticks and followed rules derived from English rugby. "This was the sport's true departure point," he explained.

806. *Is it true that Canadians invented or developed the games of hockey, lacrosse, basketball, football, and baseball?*
Yes. While there is no need to mimic patriotic Russians who throughout the 1950s made extravagant boasts to have invented everything worth inventing, the claims may be substantiated that

Canadians invented or developed the games of hockey, lacrosse, basketball, football, and baseball.

There is no question that hockey, the quintessential Canadian game, developed from the form of lacrosse played on ice at Kingston on Christmas Day, 1855.

Lacrosse, once called Canada's national game, was the first organized sport in North America. It developed in this country from the Indian game of *baggataway*. The French who played it called it *la crosse*, after the wooden lacrosse stick shaped like a bishop's crozier. Rules were formulated by Montrealer George Beers in 1867. The preferred lacrosse sticks are still those manufactured at the Akwasasne (St. Regis) Indian Reserve, Que.

Basketball was invented by James A. Naismith, a Canadian, in January, 1892. He devised thirteen rules and called it "a new game of ball." Its growth was fast and furious.

Football, an American game popular in Canada, was irrevocably influenced in form of play by Canadians. Canadians play twelve players, Americans play eleven. Americans played twelve players until 1874, when students at Harvard, to accommodate the visiting McGill team, which was one man short, fielded eleven players. Although the visiting team lost the two games it played, the Harvard precedent influenced all subsequent American play.

The world accepts baseball as an American game — *the* American game. The invention of the game is credited to one Abner Doubleday in Cooperstown, N.Y., in 1839. But in Ingersoll, U.C. (Ont.), on June 4, 1838, there was a baseball match played between the Beachville Club and the Zorras. The fact is recorded by sports historian William Humber, who calls baseball "the people's game."

807. Which is larger, the Montreal Forum or Maple Leaf Gardens?

The Montreal Forum and Maple Leaf Gardens are Canada's best known sports arenas. The former is the home of the Montreal Canadiens, the latter of the Toronto Maple Leafs. The Forum, opened at its present site in Montreal in 1924, has 16,076 seats.

The Gardens, opened in Toronto in 1931, has 16,000 seats, so the Forum is larger than the Gardens.

808. *In the Montreal Forum, what do the letters* CH *at centre ice stand for?*
It was jokingly suggested that *CH* stands for "centre hice," but the letters are the abbreviation of Club de Hockey Canadien, Inc., the organization that owns the Montreal Canadiens (who are also known as the Habs, for *habitants*).

809. *Who said, "He shoots! He scores!"?*
Hockey broadcaster Foster Hewitt was a twenty-nine-year-old announcer and as exhausted as the players when he covered the Toronto Maple Leaf–Boston Bruins game at Toronto's Maple Leaf Gardens. The game went into overtime, April 4, 1933, when Ken Doraty, the smallest player on either team, whipped the puck into the Boston net. "He shoots! He scores!" Hewitt murmured, exhausted, little knowing that the phrase would be associated with him for decades to come.

810. *What is the fastest contact sport?*
Hockey is often called the fastest contact sport — and with justice. Bobby Hull was once clocked skating at 47.7 km/h, or 29.7 mph. One of his left-handed slapshots sped by at 190.3 km/h, or 118.3 mph.

811. *What happened in Moscow on September 28, 1972, that made headlines across Canada?*
Paul Henderson, left wing on Team Canada, scored the winning goal against goalkeeper Vladislaw Tretiak in the last thirty-four seconds of the eighth and final game in the first Team Canada–

USSR hockey series. With that win, Canadians could claim world hockey supremacy — at least until the second series of games.

812. *Who, according to Brian McFarlane, is the most exciting hockey player of the 1980s?*

According to hockey personality Brian McFarlane, the game's most exciting player in the 1980s is Wayne Gretzky. McFarlane has argued that every ten years or so a player emerges who is a notch or two above every other player. The 1940s belonged to Maurice (Rocket) Richard; the 1950s to Gordie Howe; the 1960s to Bobby Hull; the 1970s to Bobby Orr; and the 1980s to Wayne Gretzky. Born in Brantford, Ont., on January 26, 1961, Gretzky was an enthusiastic amateur player who turned professional at seventeen. He joined the Edmonton Oilers in 1978, plays centre, wears sweater No. 99, and is a record-breaking scorer.

813. *How many sweater numbers have been retired?*

Some outstanding hockey players have been honoured by having their sweater numbers retired from active play. NHL teams have declared out of use thirty-two sweater numbers, including Montreal's retirement of Guy Lafleur's No. 10 in February, 1985.

Here are a few other retirements: Boston's Bobby Orr (4) and Dit Clapper (5), Detroit and Hartford's Gordie Howe (9), Philadelphia's Bernie Parent (1), Quebec's J. C. Tremblay (3), Montreal's Jean Beliveau (4), Howie Morenz (7), Maurice Richard (9), and Henri Richard (16). Toronto retired two numbers: Bill Barilko (5) and Ace Bailey (6). Bailey, however, took his sweater number out of retirement and gave it to Ron Ellis, so it is ex-retired.

814. *Who is Peter Puck?*

Peter Puck is an appealing, impish cartoon character created by Toronto sportswriter and broadcaster Brian McFarlane. Since 1974,

Peter Puck has taught hockey basics and safety tips to young hockey fans on CBC-TV's *Hockey Night in Canada*.

815. *How many teams constitute the National Hockey League?*
There were twenty-one professional hockey teams franchised by the National Hockey League in 1985. The NHL, founded in Montreal on November 22, 1917, grew to six teams in the 1940s and then to twelve in the 1960s. Further expansion was underway when the World Hockey Association was created in 1971. The WHL franchised fifteen teams, five of them Canadian, before it folded in 1978. With its demise, the NHL absorbed some of the newly created teams until it reached its present membership of twenty-one. The NHL is composed of two conferences and four divisions. They are the Prince of Wales Conference (Patrick Division, Adams Division) and the Clarence Campbell Conference (Norris Division, Smythe Division).

816. *What is the highest award in professional hockey?*
The highest award in professional hockey is the Stanley Cup, which is presented annually by the National Hockey League to its championship team. The Stanley Cup, a sterling bowl presented by Governor General Lord Stanley in 1893, is the oldest trophy for which professional athletes compete in North America. It is said to be "symbolic of the World's Hockey Championship."

817. *What is the amateur counterpart of the Stanley Cup?*
The Stanley Cup is the highest award in professional hockey. The Allan Cup, which is awarded by the Canadian Amateur Hockey Association, is the highest award in amateur hockey. The silver bowl was donated in 1908 by Sir Hugh Montague Allan, a Montreal financier.

818. *Which is larger, the Canadian or the American football field?*

The regulation Canadian football field is larger than the regulation American football field. The dimensions of the Canadian field are 99 m by 58.5 m, or 110 yards by 65 yards. The American field measures 90 m by 47.7 m, or 100 yards by 53 yards.

819. *Is it true that there are two Grey Cups?*

There are, indeed, two Grey Cups. The original silver cup, donated by and named after Governor General Lord Grey in 1909, is on permanent display at the Canadian Football Hall of Fame in Hamilton, Ont. It is the replica of the original cup that resides with the winning football team for a year. Custodian of both cups is the Canadian Football League, which annually awards the cup to the best professional football team in eastern or western Canada. The championship game and the awarding of the highly coveted cup take place in late November or early December each year.

820. *Who was Percy Page of the Edmonton Grads?*

Percy Page (1877–1973) was the celebrated coach of the famed Edmonton Grads, the leading women's basketball team of the day. He founded the team with undergraduates and graduates from McDougall Commercial High School in Edmonton, where he taught, in 1915. The Grads won every possible North American and European basketball title until the team was officially disbanded in 1940. In all, the Grads won all but 20 of the 522 games they played. Page went on to sit in the Alberta legislature and to serve as lieutenant-governor of the province.

821. *Who is the inventor of basketball?*

The game of basketball was invented by James A. Naismith, an Ontario-born medical doctor. He was an instructor at the International YMCA Training School, now Springfield College, Massachusetts, where the need for a competitive indoor team sport led him to devise, in January, 1892, a game played under thirteen basic rules with a ball and round hoops. The original basketball was a soccer ball, and the original hoops were a pair of peach baskets. The game is now popular around the world.

822. *What is the oldest continuously run turf event in North America?*

The Queen's Plate, North America's oldest continuously run turf event, dates from 1859, when Queen Victoria arranged for an annual grant to be presented to the winner of a horserace to be run at Toronto or some other location in today's Ontario. The Queen's Plate is run each June at New Woodbine Racetrack. The annual event remains one of the most popular horseraces on the continent. One of the most famous racers was Northern Dancer, winner of the Queen's Plate in 1964. Perhaps the most famous breeder is E. P. Taylor, owner of Northern Dancer and of Windfields Farm.

823. *In which sports did Ken Watson and Whipper Billy Watson excel?*

Ken Watson is a Manitoba-born curler. He skipped his rink to victory in six consecutive Manitoba Bonspiel championships, and in 1936, 1942, and 1949 took the Macdonald Brier (emblematic of Canadian supremacy in curling).

Whipper Billy Watson is the professional name of Toronto-born William Potts. An outstanding wrestler, he twice (in 1946 and 1956) held the world heavyweight wrestling championship. He devised two holds, the Canadian Avalanche (he performs cartwheels before his opponent) and the Canuck Commando Unconscious (he grasps the opponent's carotid artery).

824. *Which Canadian boxer was never knocked off his feet?*

George Chuvalo, the Toronto-born boxer, has boxed with the best in the world, including Muhammed Ali, Floyd Patterson, Ernie

Terrell, Joe Frazier, and George Foreman, but he was never knocked off his feet. He went the full fifteen rounds with Muhammed Ali but never took the world heavyweight championship.

825. *Who won within thirty days the European, Olympic, and World ladies' figure skating championships?*

Barbara Ann Scott won three top figure skating championships between January 15 and February 15, 1948. The European title she took at Prague, the Olympic Gold Medal at St. Moritz, and the World championship at Davos. Seventy thousand people welcomed her when she returned to Ottawa.

826. *Who is the figure skater who said, "I skate the way I think Isadora Duncan danced"?*

The remark was made by Toller Cranston, a native of Kirkland Lake, Ont., who took the Canadian men's figure skating championship in 1971 and a Bronze medal at the 1976 Winter Olympics. His skating style is exceptionally free and expressive, like the dancing of Isadora Duncan.

827. *In which sports do Neil Lumsden and Cliff Lumsdon excel?*

Neil Lumsden, who was born in 1952 in London, Ont., is an outstanding football player. He joined the Toronto Argonauts in 1976. Cliff Lumsdon, who was born in Toronto in 1931, is an outstanding swimmer. He conquered the Straits of Juan de Fuca in 1956 and coached his daughter Kim Lumsdon, born in 1957, also an outstanding swimmer.

828. *Who introduced North Americans to cross-country skiing?*

No single person can claim all the credit for introducing the popular sport of cross-country skiing to North Americans. But credit is often given to the Norwegian-born Canadian skier Herman Smith-Johannsen, who began cross-country skiing when he settled in North Bay in 1902. When he moved to Montreal in 1906, he introduced the sport there. In the 1930s, he laid out the 144-km, or 90-mile, Maple Leaf Trail between Labelle and Shawbridge, Que. Admirers published a book about him, *Jack-rabbit*, in 1975, to celebrate his hundredth birthday on June 15.

829. *Is five-pin bowling a Canadian invention?*

The game of five-pin bowling, a popular version of ten-pin bowling, was invented by Thomas E. Ryan (1872–1961), a native of Guelph, Ont. Tommy Ryan was operating a Toronto bowling alley in 1908–9 when, to make the game of indoor bowling more attractive to a larger group of players, he diminished the size and weight of the bowling ball, eliminated the need for finger holes, reduced the size and number of pins from ten to five, and simplified the scoring. Five-pin bowling was an immediate success. Wherever the popular recreational and tournament game is played, Ryan is recognized as its "father."

830. *What are the Arctic Winter Games and the Northern Games?*

The Arctic Winter Games are a series of competitive events held every two years for residents North of Sixty. The Games were first held in Yellowknife, N.W.T., in 1970. The games themselves are a mix of winter sports (hockey, curling), summer sports (badminton, volleyball), and native activities (dog-sledding, drum-dancing), etc. They are open to all residents of the Canadian North and Alaska and Greenland.

The Northern Games are a series of competitive events held every two years for Indians and Eskimos of Canada and Alaska. The Games are a summer event and were first held at Inuvik, N.W.T., in 1970. Participants engage in traditional skills and activities like harpoon-throwing, blanket-tossing, dog-racing, and drum-dancing.

831. *Who was the first person to swim across Lake Ontario?*
The feat was first accomplished by Marilyn Bell, a sixteen-year-old marathon swimmer. She crossed the turbulent waters of Lake Ontario from Youngstown, N.Y., to Toronto's CNE Grounds on September 9, 1954. The following year, on her second try, she became the youngest swimmer to conquer the English Channel. When asked why she decided to brave Lake Ontario, she exclaimed: "I did it for Canada!"

832. *Have the Commonwealth Games and the Pan-Am Games ever been held in Canada?*
They have. Both series are scheduled at four-year intervals. The Commonwealth Games, then called the British Empire Games, go back to 1911, but the modern series dates from 1930. The first series was held that year in Hamilton, Ont. The fifth series was held in Vancouver in 1954, and the eleventh series in Edmonton in 1978. Vancouver has bid to hold the fifteenth series in 1994.

The Pan-American Games, for nations of the Western Hemisphere, were first held in Buenos Aires in 1951. The fifth Pan-Am Games were held in Winnipeg in 1967. The eleventh Pan-Am Games are scheduled to be held in 1991 in London, Ont.

833. *What is the name of the award given to the most outstanding athlete of the year?*
The Lou Marsh Trophy is awarded to Canada's most outstanding male or female athlete, amateur or professional, of the year. The trophy is a silver memorial cup named after Lou Marsh, longtime sports editor of *The Toronto Star*. The winner, selected by a committee of sports editors, is announced each December. The trophy was first presented in 1936. Here is a list of award winners (with area of accomplishment).

1936 Dr. Phil Edwards (track)
1937 W. Marshall Cleland (equestrian)
1938 Bobby Pearce (rowing)
1939 Bob Pirie (swimming)
1940 Gerard Côté (track)
1941 Theo Dubois (rowing)
1942–44 Dedicated to Athletes who made the supreme sacrifice during World War II
1945 Barbara Ann Scott (skating)
1946 Joe Krol (football)
1947 Barbara Ann Scott (skating)
1948 Barbara Ann Scott (skating)
1949 Cliff Lumsdon (swimming)
1950 Bob McFarlane (track)
1951 Marlene Stewart Streit (golf)
1952 George Genereux (trapshooting)
1953 Doug Hepburn (weightlifting)
1954 Marilyn Bell (swimming)
1955 Beth Whittall (swimming)
1956 Marlene Stewart Streit (golf)
1957 Maurice Richard (hockey)
1958 Lucille Wheeler (skiing)
1959 Barbara Wagner & Bob Paul (skating)

1960 Anne Heggtveit (skiing)
1961 Bruce Kidd (track)
1962 Donald Jackson (skating)
1963 Bill Crothers (track)
1964 George Hungerford & Roger Jackson (rowing)
1965 Petra Burka (skating)
1966 Elaine Tanner (swimming)
1967 Nancy Greene (skiing)
1968 Nancy Greene (skiing)
1969 Russell Jackson (football)
1970 Bobby Orr (hockey)
1971 Hervé Filion (harness racing)
1972 Phil Esposito (hockey)
1973 Sandy Hawley (horse racing)
1974 Ferguson Jenkins (baseball)
1975 Bobby Clarke (hockey)
1976 Sandy Hawley (horse racing)
1977 Guy Lafleur (hockey)
1978 Graham Smith (swimming) & Ken Reid (skiing)
1979 Sandy Post (golf)
1980 Terry Fox (track)
1981 Susan Nattrass (trapshooting)
1982 Wayne Gretzky (hockey)
1983 Wayne Gretzky (hockey)
1984 Gaetan Boucher (skating)
1985 Wayne Gretzky (hockey)

834. *What is a "carded" athlete?*

A "carded" athlete is an amateur athlete who is assisted through Sport Canada's athlete assistance program. The program of assistance was established in 1977 by the Fitness and Amateur Sport Canada branch of the Department of National Health and Welfare. Its predecessor was Game Canada's program of preparation for the 1976 Olympics.

Through the program of "carding," an athlete's living and training expenses are partly defrayed to assist him or her to meet competitive requirements to better represent Canada in international competitions. The "carding" (or grading) occurs on three levels based on world ranking. A-level athletes received $650 a month, B-level $550, and C-level $450 in 1985. Grants are reviewed annually. Some seven hundred and fifty athletes of promise and dedication are part of the program.

835. *Who is the least admired sports figure in the country?*

Harold Ballard fits the bill. He may be "Pal Hal" to employees and players of the Maple Leaf hockey club, Maple Leaf Gardens, and the Hamilton Tiger-Cats, all of which he owns, but to the rest of the Canadian public the behaviour of this sports figure, who was born in Toronto in 1903, is boorish.

836. *Which city erected the country's first domed stadium?*

Vancouver erected the country's first domed stadium in 1983. B.C. Place is large enough to seat 60,000 spectators under a permanent, air-supported fabric roof or dome. Montreal's Olympic Stadium, built in 1976, was designed for a retractable roof or dome but has yet to receive one. Seating capacity is about the same as Vancouver's. Plans were approved in 1986 to build a domed stadium, with or without a retractable roof, in Toronto. Nine domed stadiums have been built in North America since the erection of the Astrodome in Houston, Texas, in 1965.

837. *How many members has Canada's Sports Hall of Fame?*
Canada's Sports Hall of Fame was established at Toronto's Exhibition Place in 1955. Each August, a selection committee of sportswriters inducts six or so athletes and builders (non-athletes who promote the game) who have demonstrated competitive excellence. Included are all Canadian Olympic gold medallists and World championship holders. In 1984, there were 320 members representing competitive excellence in forty types of sport. Included as nonhuman members are a sailing ship (*The Bluenose*), a powerboat (*Miss Supertest*), and a thoroughbred (Northern Dancer).

Canada's Sports Hall of Fame is not the country's only recognized hall of fame. It shares premises at Exhibition Place with the Hockey Hall of Fame and Museum, opened in 1961. The International Hockey Hall of Fame, founded in 1943, is in Kingston, Ont. The Canadian Lacrosse Hall of Fame was opened in 1965 in New Westminster, B.C., and the Canadian Football Hall of Fame and Museum was established in 1972 in Hamilton, Ont.

838. *Is it true that a thirty-year-old Canadian is as fit as a sixty-year-old Swede?*
This question was raised by many who watched the brilliant commercial sponsored by the federal fitness program called PARTICIPaction and shown on national television a total of six times in the fall of 1973.

It showed a Canadian and a Swede, and the narration ran: "These men are about evenly matched. That's because the average thirty-year-old Canadian is in about the same shape as the average sixty-year-old Swede. . . . Run. Walk. Cycle. Let's get Canada moving again. This message is from the Canadian movement for personal fitness, PARTICIPaction."

The answer to the question is that the commercial was based on no research. Yet it struck a responsive chord in the psyches of Canadians.

9. CULTURE

839. *Which literary figure has more statues erected in his honour than any other?*

The Scots poet Robert Burns (1759–1796) has more statues erected in his honour across the country than any other author, living or dead, Canadian or foreign. He is the country's most honoured literary figure. There are statues, monuments, memorials, or reminders of Burns's popularity as a poet and a man in the following centres: Halifax, N.S.; Fredericton, N.B.; Burlington, P.E.I.; Montreal, Que.; Toronto, Ont.; Winnipeg, Man.; Vancouver, B.C.; Victoria, B.C.

840. *Does William Shakespeare refer to Canada in any of his plays?*

There are no specific references to early Canada in any of the plays or poems of William Shakespeare. However, in *The Comedy of Errors* (about 1591), one of the characters asks another, "Where America, the Indies?" In *Hamlet, Prince of Denmark* (about 1601), the melancholy Dane says, "I am mad north-north-west; when the wind is southerly, I know a hawk from a handsaw." This may be an oblique reference to the Northwest Passage, which was certainly familiar to the Bard's contemporaries.

841. *Who wrote the first book of verse in North America?*

Robert Hayman (1575–1629) was governor of the first permanent colony in Newfoundland, at Harbour Grace on Conception

Bay, between 1618 and 1628. He had little to do other than to write epigrams and verses, some about local conditions, others translations from the French. When he returned to London in 1628, he published a collection of his verses called *Quodlibets*. The slim book is the first book of verse written in North America.

842. *What is the special importance of* The History of Emily Montague*?*
The History of Emily Montague is considered the first Canadian novel. The epistolary novel is set in eighteenth-century Quebec and describes the society and countryside in some detail. It was written and published in four volumes in 1769 by Frances Brooke (1723–1789), an English essayist, novelist, and dramatist who sojourned in Quebec in 1763–68 and, as the wife of the chaplain of the garrison, observed high society. The work has remained in print to this day, although the contemporary reader may find it of more social than dramatic interest.

843. *What was the first novel by a native-born author to be published in British North America?*
That distinction belongs to *St. Ursula's Convent*, which was published in Kingston in 1824. The author was Julia Catherine Hart (1796–1867), a native of Fredericton, N.B., but a resident of Kingston at the time of publication. Her novel, subtitled *The Nun of Canada*, was described by one critic as "introducing shipwrecks, kidnappers, exchanged babies, and a false priest into a sentimental story of Quebec seigneurial and convent life."

844. *There are two so-called Canadian boat songs. What are they?*
A number of Canadian boat songs were popular in Canada and Britain in the nineteenth century, but two are of particular importance.

One was composed by an Irish poet, the other by a Scots versifier. The Irish poet was Thomas Moore, who at Sainte-Anne-de-Bellevue, south of Montreal, in 1804, composed "A Canadian Boat Song: Written on the River St. Lawrence." The last two lines are particularly lilting: "Blow, breezes, blow, the stream runs fast, / The Rapids are near and the daylight's past."

The Scottish versifier, who never visited North America, is David Macbeth Moir. In 1829, he published, anonymously, "Canadian Boat-Song (from the Gaelic)" which is sometimes called "The Lone Shieling." It is the lament of a Hebridian exiled in Upper Canada, and the last lines run: "Fair these broad meads — these hoary woods are grand; / But we are exiles from our fathers' land."

845. *Who were the literary-minded Strickland sisters?*
The Strickland sisters were two literary-minded women who emigrated from Britain with their husbands and became pioneer farmers in Upper Canada in the 1830s. Their names are Catharine Parr Traill (1802–1899) and Susanna Moodie (1803–1885). They established backwoods farms in Douro Township, near Lakefield, Ont., close to the farm of their brother, Colonel Samuel Strickland (1804–1867), who had emigrated earlier and became a writer in his own right.

The Stricklands, all three of them, wrote the earliest books about living and working conditions in the backwoods. These studies of pioneer conditions were published in the old country as guides to prospective immigrants. Strickland's memoir was called *Twenty-Seven Years in Canada West* (1853). Among the many books by the two sisters, the best known are Traill's *The Backwoods of Canada* (1836) and Moodie's *Roughing It in the Bush* (1852) and *Life in the Clearings* (1853). All these books are available today in reprint editions.

846. *Who was Sam Slick?*
Sam Slick was a memorable comic character created by the Nova

Scotia judge and humorist Thomas Chandler Haliburton (1796–1865). Sam, a Yankee pedlar of clocks, travels around Nova Scotia, giving his views in salty language on all manner of social concerns. He appears in *The Clockmaker* (1836), the first of four collections of sketches. The Sam Slick books give a good view of Nova Scotian society in the mid-nineteenth century.

847. *People laugh at any mention of "the Four Jameses." Who were they?*

The so-called four Jameses were four versifiers who lived in nineteenth-century Canada whose verses were so excruciatingly bad that they are fun to read today. The poetasters (with their titles) are: James Gay, "Poet Laureate of Canada, and Master of all Poets"; James McIntyre, "The Cheese Poet"; James P. Gillis, "A Man of Parts"; and James MacRae, "The Man from Glengarry." They were first grouped together by William Arthur Deacon in *The Four Jameses* (1927).

848. *One frequently hears the remark, "O God! O Montreal!" What is its origin?*

The remark is the refrain of a satiric poem written by the English author Samuel Butler on a business trip to Montreal in 1875. The poem, called "A Psalm of Montreal," concerns Butler's experience at the Montreal Museum of Natural History. He came upon a plaster copy of the Greek statue known as the *Discobolus*. It depicts a nude athlete holding a discus, and is used in art schools wherever drawing is taught. But in Montreal it was "banished from public view" because it was deemed "rather vulgar." Butler, noting that Montrealers "are as yet too busy with commerce to care greatly about the masterpieces of old Greek art," concluded: "O God! O Montreal!" The poem ridicules prudery and pretension.

849. *In which city will you find the famous "Golden Dog" inscription?*

Visitors to Quebec City frequently pause in front of the Upper Town Post Office where the "Golden Dog" inscription is part of the pediment. The bas-relief sculpture depicts a dog gnawing on a bone, beneath which appear the lines (translated into English): "I am a dog that gnaws his bone / I crouch and gnaw it all alone / The time will come which is not yet / When I'll bite him by whom I'm bit." The inscription refers to an eighteenth-century Quebec tale of love and murder employed by the novelist William Kirby in his historical romance *The Golden Dog* (1877).

850. *Who is the versifier who wrote the poem that begins: "In the seaport of Saint Malo, 'twas a smiling morn in May"?*

Generations of school children were familiar with this poem. They were forced to memorize all seven stirring stanzas of it for patriotic as well as poetic reasons. The poem is called "Jacques Cartier" and it tells how "the Commodore Jacques Cartier to the westward sail'd away." It was written a few years before his death by Thomas D'Arcy McGee (1825–1868), ardent nationalist and Father of Confederation, and it celebrates the early exploration of the east coast of Canada.

851. *Who was "the Poet of the Yukon"?*

The title belongs to Robert W. Service (1874–1958), who was so modest he preferred to be called a verse-maker or a rhymester rather than a poet. Born in England, raised in Scotland, he worked as a bank clerk in Whitehorse and Dawson City, Y.T., half a decade after the Klondike Gold Rush of 1896. Service caught the romance of the period in two ballads, "The Shooting of Dan McGrew" and "The Cremation of Sam McGee," published in *Songs of a Sourdough* (1907). The collection, immensely popular, was followed by many other collections of ballads about prospectors and bohemians, vagabonds and lovers. Service left the snows of the

Yukon for good in 1909. He worked as a correspondent, settled at Monte Carlo on the Riviera, and lies buried at Lancieux, Brittany, France. His former cabin in Dawson has been restored to represent his period of occupancy, and during the tourist season, actors recite his lively ballads.

852. What popular children's book grew out of the following notebook entry: "Elderly couple apply to orphan asylum for a boy; a girl is sent them"?
The novel is the ever-popular *Anne of Green Gables* (1908), written by L. M. Montgomery, which chronicles the experiences of the young orphan girl, Anne Shirley, who grows up at Avonlea. The novel was followed by seven sequels, and two Hollywood films and a musical comedy have been based on the beguiling story. The author based at least some of Anne's experiences on her own childhood, part of which was spent living at "Green Gables" at Cavendish, P.E.I. Each year thousands of copies of the Anne books are sold, and thousands of tourists visit the charming green and white house in which the author lived with her grandparents, in Cavendish National Park.

853. Who was Maria Chapdelaine and what was her dilemma?
Maria Chapdelaine was the fictional creation of the French novelist Louis Hémon. In the novel *Maria Chapdelaine*, which Hémon based on his farming experiences at Péribonca in the Lac Saint-Jean area of Quebec, Maria is the daughter of a *habitant* who must choose between two suitors: Lorenzo Surprenant, who will take her to a life of ease in Boston, and Eutrope Gagnon, a young farmer who can offer her only the life of her ancestors. She accepts the latter destiny for "in this land of Quebec naught shall die and naught change." Although much has changed in Quebec since the novel was completed in 1913, Maria's dilemma continues to bedevil *les Québécois*. The novel was translated into English in 1921 and has been filmed on three occasions.

854. *Who wrote the familiar poem "The Song My Paddle Sings"?*
"The Song My Paddle Sings," about the excitement of paddling a
canoe in rough water, was one of many poems on native and
wilderness themes written by Pauline Johnson (1861–1913), poet
and writer, whose Mohawk name, Tekahionwake, means "Smoke
from Many Campfires." Johnson's mother was an Englishwoman,
her father the hereditary Mohawk chief of the Six Nations Reserve,
near Brantford, Ont. Chiefswood, her family home, is now a
national historic site and museum. She toured the country, performing her poems in authentic Indian garb, insisting that Canadians generally must show greater knowledge and understanding of
Indian ways. She died in Vancouver and her ashes were scattered
around Siwash Rock, Stanley Park. The title of her collected
poems is *Flint and Feather* (1912).

855. *Who were the country's two leading "animal story" writers?*
Two writers who knew the Canadian woods intimately and wrote
vividly about its wildlife are Ernest Thompson Seton (1860–1946)
and Sir Charles G. D. Roberts (1860–1943). Seton wrote and
illustrated the stories in *Wild Animals I Have Known* (1898). He
described each animal in such a way that it acquired a personality
of its own. Roberts went even further in such books as *Earth's
Enigmas* (1896), endowing each animal with quasi-human thoughts
and feelings.

856. *Was Grey Owl an Indian?*
The naturalist and author who signed his books Grey Owl was
born an Englishman named Archibald Stansfeld Belaney (1888–
1938). He immigrated to Canada in 1903 and became a guide and
trapper in northern Ontario. He passed as a half-breed and was
adopted by the Ojibwa as one of their own. Entering government
service, he worked as a warden at Riding Mountain National Park
in Manitoba and Prince Albert National Park in Saskatchewan.
When he died, Greg Clark, the journalist, broke the story that

Grey Owl was an Englishman and not an Indian. The revelation did nothing to diminish his message that man must co-exist with nature, presented in such books as *Pilgrims of the Wild* (1934) and *Tales of an Empty Cabin* (1936).

857. *Was Frederick Philip Grove a Swedish writer born in Russia or a German writer born in Prussia?*

There is considerable confusion on the matter of the early life of the prairie novelist Frederick Philip Grove. Grove himself maintained he was born in Russia in 1871, but the literary scholar Douglas O. Spettigue established in his revisionist biographical inquiry *FPG: The European Years* (1973) that Grove was born in Prussia in 1879, that his real name was Felix Paul Greve, and that he was a German writer and translator years before he began teaching school in rural Manitoba in 1912.

Whatever his background and his reasons for hiding it, Grove began his Canadian literary career writing in English. His first book, *Over Prairie Trails* (1922), is a collection of nature essays. Such novels as *Settlers of the Marsh* (1925) and *The Master of the Mill* (1944) show him to be a compelling writer attracted to universal themes and open spaces.

858. *What celebrated country home is in Clarkson, Ont.?*

The most famous country home in Canadian literature is in the town of Clarkson, west of Toronto. The country home, built in 1857 by a British army officer, was named Benares after the city in India where he had served. The pleasing appearance of Benares, and its suggestion of gracious living, inspired the novelist Mazo de la Roche (1879–1961) to write her first famous novel, *Jalna* (1927), and its fourteen sequels. De la Roche chose her name, Jalna, from a gazetteer that listed British posts in India. The exterior scenes of the CBC-TV series *Whiteoaks of Jalna* were taken at Benares.

859. *Is there a real town called Mariposa?*

There is no town called Mariposa in Canada. But there is an imaginary town called Mariposa in *Sunshine Sketches of a Little Town*, a series of sketches of small-town life by the celebrated humorist Stephen Leacock (1869–1944), published in 1912. The author modelled his Mariposa on Orillia, Ont., where he summered. "Mariposa is not a real town," he warned his readers. "On the contrary, it is about seventy or eighty of them. You may find them all the way from Lake Superior to the sea, with the same square streets and the same maple trees and the same churches and hotels, and everywhere the sunshine of the land of hope." The author's handwritten manuscript of *Sunshine Sketches*, one of the few classics of Canadian humour, is on display at the Stephen Leacock Memorial Home, on Old Brewery Bay, in the east end of Orillia.

860. *Is Manawaka a real or a fictional place?*

Manawaka is a fictional town created by Margaret Laurence and described in such novels as *The Stone Angel* (1964) and *A Jest of God* (1966). The imaginary community bears a resemblance to the author's hometown of Neepawa, Man.

861. *Who was "the Sweet Songstress of Saskatchewan"?*

The so-called Sweet Songstress was Sarah Binks, poetess, born in "Willows," Sask., winner of the "Wheat Pool Medal" for such dreadful verses as "The Farmer is King" and "The Farmer and the Farmer's Wife." Sarah is no real person, of course, but the fictional creation of writer and teacher Paul Hiebert, author of *Sarah Binks* (1947) and *Willows Revisited* (1967). These two books are tongue-in-cheek satires of prairie life-styles, social pretension, and western Canadian literature. The actor Eric Donkin has toured in *The Wonderful World of Sarah Binks*, a one-man show in which he delights audiences across the country with his impersonation of the Sweet Songstress and her awful rhymes.

862. *Where is the Poets' Corner of Canada?*

The Historic Sites and Monuments Board of Canada has erected a plaque on the campus of the University of New Brunswick, Fredericton, N.B., to honour three poets. The three poets are Francis Sherman, Bliss Carman, and Sir Charles G. D. Roberts. The designation ''Poets' Corner'' is meant to apply to the city of Fredericton. The plaque was erected in 1947.

863. *Who was Canada's epic poet?*

If an epic poet is someone who writes about grand subjects in a heroic manner, then E. J. Pratt (1882–1964) could claim to be English Canada's epic poet. But Pratt, a Newfoundland-born Methodist minister and professor of English at Victoria College in Toronto, was a mild-mannered man and made no claims of his own. Readers of such narrative poems as *Brébeuf and His Brethren* (1940) and *Towards the Last Spike* (1952) attest to his epic importance, noting his larger-than-life interests (the Jesuit Martyrs of Huronia, the construction of the CPR), his narrative techniques, and his sense of destiny.

864. *Who wrote "David" and what is it about?*

''David'' is a well-known narrative poem, under two hundred lines in length, written by the poet Earle Birney and published in *David and Other Poems* (1942). It tells of a tragic incident of two climbers, David and Bob, while scaling ''the Finger of the Sawback'' in the Rocky Mountain range in Banff National Park. David saves Bob's life but in the process falls and is paralyzed. He begs Bob to roll him over the ledge to certain death, and Bob complies. The poem dramatizes an instance of mercy killing but does not endorse the practice. For many years certain schoolboards banned it from classroom use, and Birney himself gained the ill-deserved reputation of ''the man who would push his best friend over a cliff.''

865. *What is the origin of the phrase "two solitudes"?*
The phrase "two solitudes" was first used to refer to the French
and the English in Quebec by Hugh MacLennan in his novel *Two
Solitudes*, published in 1945. The title has entered the language
as an image of the mutual alienation of the founding peoples of
Canada. MacLennan took it from a letter written in 1904 by the
German poet Rainer Maria Rilke.

866. *Who created "the Plouffe Family"?*
"The Plouffe Family" was created by the Quebec novelist Roger
Lemelin. The adventures of this working-class family from Quebec
City's Lower Town are described in three novels. The titles in
English translation are *The Town Below* (1948), *The Plouffe Family*
(1950), and *The Crime of Ovide Plouffe* (1983). Members of the
family — Mama Josephine, Papa Théophile, Napoléon, Ovide,
Guillaume, and Cécile — are familiar to two generations of
Québécois through the novels, radio and television series based
on them, and the feature film *Les Plouffe* released in 1981.

867. *Did Malcolm Lowry write* **Under the Volcano** *in Canada?*
The English novelist Malcolm Lowry (1909–1957) lived in Canada
from 1939 to 1954, largely in a squatter's shack at Dollarton, now
part of Vancouver, B.C., where he worked on his classic novel
Under the Volcano (1947), not to mention other imaginative works
subsequently published. When the shack was levelled by developers
in June, 1944, he headed east, living briefly in Oakville and then
in the Old Kirby House, still standing in Niagara-on-the-Lake,
Ont. He stayed with his wife at the Riverside Inn, where, on
Christmas Eve, 1944, he completed his novel. The inn is now
called the Dew Drop Harbour Inn.

868. Which novelist has been called the Balzac of St. Urbain Street?

Montreal novelist Mordecai Richler has been called the Balzac of St. Urbain Street for his realistic descriptions of the ethnic area near the Main. In his novel *The Apprenticeship of Duddy Kravitz*, published in 1959, he described St. Urbain Street and Baron Byng High School, which he named Fletcher's Field. Once predominantly settled by Jews from Eastern Europe, the area is now inhabited by Greeks and Portuguese.

869. Who gave currency to the theme of "survival" in Canadian literature?

The poet and novelist Margaret Atwood published a study called *Survival: A Thematic Guide to Canadian Literature* (1972). In it she argued that in their imaginative literature Canadians appear to be "victims" fearful of success. *Survival* was one of the most influential social and literary texts of the seventies. The "survival" theme dovetailed English Canada's concern over cultural sovereignty vis-à-vis the United States and Quebec's continued reliance on *la survivance*, cultural survival.

870. Who is the author of the Deptford Trilogy?

The so-called Deptford Trilogy is a series of three novels by Robertson Davies, the prominent novelist, playwright, and man of letters. The intricately plotted novels are called *Fifth Business* (1970), *The Manticore* (1972), and *World of Wonders* (1975). They shed light on the mysteries of human character and trace the consequences of a prank — a child throwing a snowball on December 27, 1908, in Deptford, an imaginary Ontario village modelled on the author's birthplace of Thamesville, northeast of Chatham, Ontario.

871. Who is La Sagouine?

La sagouine means "the slattern." It is the nickname of a garrulous, foul-mouthed Acadian widow who speaks of her people's hopes and fears in a rich sixteenth century argot, traces of which still survive among the Acadians of New Brunswick. La Sagouine is the creation of the Acadian writer and scholar Antonine Maillet. La Sagouine's monologues appear in numerous books, beginning with *La Sagouine* (1971), and on the stage, performed by the actress Violet Léger.

872. *Who wrote the catchy verse called "Alligator Pie"?*

Kids enjoy chanting, "Alligator pie, alligator pie,/If I don't get some I think I'm gonna die." The lively lines come from the title poem of *Alligator Pie* (1974), a collection of children's verse by the Toronto writer and poet, Dennis Lee. The same year, Lee published *Nicholas Knock*, the title poem of which begins: "Nicholas Knock was a venturesome boy./He lived at Number Eight./He went for walks in the universe/And generally got home late."

873. *Which titles appeared on E. K. Brown's list of the ten best Canadian books?*

The distinguished literary critic E. K. Brown (1905–1951) drew up his own list of the ten "best" Canadian books written in English. (He put the word "best" in quotation marks, as an acknowledgement of the fact that the word has many meanings.) His list is dated February 28, 1948.

1. C. N. Cochrane: *Christianity and Classical Culture* (1940)
2. Mazo de la Roche: *Jalna* (1927)
3. Frederick Philip Grove: *Over Prairie Trails* (1922)
4. Archibald Lampman: *Poems* (1900)
5. Stephen Leacock: *Sunshine Sketches of a Little Town* (1912)
6. John Macnaughton: *Lord Strathcona* (1926)
7. Sir William Osler: *Aequanimitas and Other Addresses* (1904)
8. E. J. Pratt: *Collected Poems* (1944)
9. Sir Charles G. D. Roberts: *Animal Stories*
10. Duncan Campbell Scott: *Poems* (1926)

874. *What are the ten most significant Canadian novels of all time?*

This question is easier to ask than to answer. Carl F. Klinck, scholar and teacher, asked the question at a convention of teachers of Canadian literature at the University of Calgary in 1978. The teachers were asked to select "the most significant Canadian novels" and they did so. The "top ten" are listed here, in order of priority, with their authors.

1. *The Stone Angel*, Margaret Laurence
2. *Fifth Business*, Robertson Davies
3. *As for Me and My House*, Sinclair Ross
4. *The Mountain and the Valley*, Ernest Buckler
5. *The Tin Flute*, Gabrielle Roy
6. *The Apprenticeship of Duddy Kravitz*, Mordecai Richler
7. *The Double Hook*, Sheila Watson
8. *The Watch that Ends the Night*, Hugh MacLennan
9. *Who Has Seen the Wind*, W. O. Mitchell
10. *The Diviners*, Margaret Laurence

875. *Who is the most prolific author in Canada?*

The Canadian author who has published more books than any other is W. E. Dan Ross (b. 1912), a resident of Saint John, N.B. He has written over three hundred mass market paperbacks in the last quarter century, and in the last two decades more than seven hundred short stories published in popular magazines. His specialty is romantic fiction, and his works appear under such pseudonyms as "Marilyn Ross," "Dan Roberts," and "Rose Williams."

Many journalists have written voluminously. The popular journalist and author Greg Clark (1892–1977) estimated in 1963 that he had turned out 10,653,000 words for newspaper publication. Possibly the country's most productive *literary* figure is George Woodcock (b. 1912) who, between 1940 and 1984, produced over sixty biographical and literary studies, travel books, histories, and collections of verse. As one critic noted, "Woodcock has written more books than most people have read."

876. *Are Harlequin Romances published in Canada?*

Harlequin Books are published in Canada, but it seems the majority of the authors who write the Harlequin Romances live elsewhere. The Harlequin imprint first appeared on mass market paperbacks issued from Winnipeg in 1949. The line of popular romantic fiction caught on and the company was reconstituted in Toronto in the 1960s. The company has found international success in the commissioning and marketing of romantic fiction. One dozen new titles are issued each month for those who like their romantic encounters to take place in hospitals, castles, and other unlikely locations. The novels appear under pseudonyms and are written, it is said, by novelists — mostly women — in Britain and the United States.

877. *What are the country's oldest newspapers?*

The first newspaper published in early Canada was the *Halifax Gazette*. It was founded in Halifax, and the first issue appeared on March 23, 1752.

The *Chronicle Telegraph* was established in Quebec City in 1764. It ceased publication in 1971. It boasted that its first publisher was Benjamin Franklin.

The longest continuing newspaper in Canada, as well as in the United States, is *The Gazette*. It was established in 1778 in Montreal. It is being published today as the *Montreal Gazette*.

The oldest weekly newspaper is the *Cobourg Star*. It was founded in 1831 in Cobourg, U.C. (Ont.), and it appears today as the *Cobourg Sentinel Star*.

878. *What was* The Eye Opener *and who published it?*

The Eye Opener was the weekly newspaper written and published by Bob Edwards (1864–1922), pioneer journalist and satirist. The paper appeared between 1902 and 1922, mainly from Calgary, and it specialized in poking fun at politicians, public figures, and prohibitionists. Samples of his aphoristic humour: "One trouble with being efficient is that it makes everybody hate you so." "Some men spoil a good story by sticking to the facts." "Never exaggerate your faults; your friends will attend to that." "Hope for the best, then hustle for it."

879. Who was "Ma" Murray?
Margaret "Ma" Murray (1888–1982) was a feisty pioneer newspaper editor and publisher. From the 1940s to the 1980s, she published and largely wrote first *The Alaska Highway News* from Fort St. John, B.C., and then *Bridge River–Lillooet News* from Lillooet, B.C. She never shrank from expressing salty opinions. "This week's circulation 1,769, and every bloody one of them paid for."

880. Did Ernest Hemingway write for The Toronto Star?
Ernest Hemingway (1899-1961), who received the Nobel Prize for literature in 1954, wrote for both the daily *Star* and the *Star Weekly* in Toronto. He lived in Toronto on two occasions, briefly in 1919 and for a short period in 1923–24. The second time he came with his pregnant wife Hadley; their son John Hadley Hemingway, called "Mr. Bumby," was born in Toronto on October 10, 1923. Between the visits Hemingway was the *Star*'s Paris correspondent. The pieces he wrote for the *Star* were collected by William White and published in 1967.

881. What is the present name of the popular magazine founded in 1905 as The Business Magazine, later retitled The Busy Man's Magazine?
Believe it or not, *Maclean's* magazine was founded in Toronto in October, 1905, as *The Business Magazine* and soon after renamed

The Busy Man's Magazine. It was a twenty-cent digest of extracts and reprints which billed itself as "The Cream of the World's Magazines Reproduced for Busy People." The print run was 5,000 copies.

Today *Maclean's* is a national newsmagazine. Each week it reaches 2,399,000 readers. The total paid circulation reported in 1985 was approximately 650,000 copies.

882. *Is it true that Goya painted two Canadian scenes?*

Although Francisco de Goya (1746–1828) never visited the New World, the great Spanish artist was moved by the fate of the Jesuit Martyrs and painted two panels in oil called *The Martyrdom of Saints Jean de Brébeuf and Gabriel Lalemant at the Hands of the Iroquois*. The first represents the Iroquois flaying and hanging their victims, the second shows the two bodies in a mutilated state. The grim scenes were completed about 1810 and recall Goya's series *The Disasters of War*.

883. *What is the most valuable Canadian painting?*

There is no way to determine the commercial value of a work of art short of offering it for sale. Yet art experts have expressed the opinion that there is one painting that is probably more valued by collectors than all the rest, and that if it were offered for sale in the mid-1980s, it would be guaranteed to fetch over a million dollars. That canvas is *Merrymaking*, which was painted in 1860 by the Dutch-born Canadian artist Cornelius Krieghoff. The canvas, acquired by the Beaverbrook Art Gallery in Fredericton, N.B., for $25,000 in 1958, depicts the Jolifou Inn of Quebec with an animated assemblage of *habitants*, horses, and sleighs.

884. *Who painted* Sunrise on the Saguenay *and why was it so popular?*

Sunrise on the Saguenay was painted in 1880 by Lucius R. O'Brien (1832–1899). Among the first important canvases depicting

Canadian landscapes, a serene celebration of the sublime in nature, it depicts great cliffs overlooking the Saguenay River, softened by a pink sunrise. It is in the National Gallery of Canada.

885. *Who painted* The West Wind*?*
Perhaps the best known image in Canadian art is *The West Wind*, a canvas painted by Tom Thomson (1877–1917). It was based on a sketch made at Lake Cauchon, Algonquin Park, Ont., in 1916. Thomson painted the branches of a lone pine tree bent by the wind against a background of white-capped water and storm-laden clouds. It is owned by the Art Gallery of Ontario.

886. *How did Tom Thomson die?*
Tom Thomson, the painter who found his true home in the woods, drowned in July, 1917, at Canoe Lake, Algonquin Park, Ont. His death remains something of a mystery to this day. Why would an experienced woodsman fall out of his own canoe and drown? There are suggestions — but little in the way of evidence — that he was murdered or that he committed suicide. His death remains mysterious, if not precisely a mystery.

887. *How many artists were there in the Group of Seven?*
If the question seems silly, it is because the answer seems even sillier. The Group of Seven was eventually comprised of eleven members. What began as a school of seven like-minded painters over the years expanded to embrace new and old members.

The Group of Seven was the most influential of all movements in Canadian art. Members, who first exhibited collectively in Toronto in 1920, were inspired by the landscape of northern Ontario. They evolved a distinctive style to match the rugged subject matter. They were inspired by the dedication of their fellow artist Tom Thomson, who painted the landscape in vivid colours and bold outlines. Thomson is often exhibited with and discussed in context with the group, but was not originally a member.

The original seven members (with birth and death dates) are the following: Franklin Carmichael (1890–1945), Lawren Harris (1885–1970), A. Y. Jackson (1882–1974), Frank H. Johnston (1888–1949), Arthur Lismer (1885–1969), J. E. H. MacDonald (1873–1932), and Frederick H. Varley (1881–1969). Tom Thomson (1877–1917), who died before the formation of the group, was its chief inspiration. The three later members (with dates) are A. J. Casson (b. 1898), Edwin H. Holgate (1892-1977), and LeMoine FitzGerald (1890–1956).

The McMichael Canadian Collection is a gallery inspired by their vision and devoted to their work. It was founded by Robert and Signe McMichael as a memorial to the Group of Seven in the village of Kleinburg, north of Toronto, in 1954.

888. *What painter was known as Klee Wyck?*

Emily Carr (1871–1945) was called Klee Wyck, or "laughing one," by the Nootka Indians. From 1898, her art was influenced by the monumental sculptures of the northwest coast Indians, as it had earlier been influenced by the French impressionists and would later be influenced by the Group of Seven. "Indian art broadened my seeing, loosened the formal tightness," she once wrote. No gallery in the country has a complete collection without at least one of her paintings or drawings.

889. *What is the significance of the manifesto called* Refus global?

The appearance of this manifesto marked the beginning of a modern Quebec, according to social historians, and to art historians it announced the appearance in Canada of a new aesthetic spirit. Four hundred copies of the mimeographed manifesto *Refus global* were issued in Montreal on August 9, 1948, by Paul-Emile Borduas and fifteen other artists. Their "global refusal" was an unwillingness to be constrained by the past. In its place they celebrated "the joyful fulfillment of our fierce desire for freedom."

890. *Who painted* Horse and Train?

This famous painting, which depicts a saddleless horse running along a railway track towards an onrushing train, was painted in tempera on board by Alex Colville in 1954. The realist painting, in the Art Gallery of Ontario, is a meticulously detailed image that might be seen in a dream.

891. *Who drew the pen and ink sketches of Canadian historical scenes that appear in many history textbooks?*

C. W. Jefferys (1869–1951) is the artist and illustrator who specialized in illustrating important incidents in Canadian history. With his lean style, verging on caricature, he prepared the 2,000 well-researched sketches that appear in *The Picture Gallery of Canadian History*, published in three volumes in 1942–50. The image one has of many historical events is attributable to Jefferys's skill and imagination.

892. *Who are Canada's best known political cartoonists?*

Space does not permit the listing of all of them. There are brief biographies of 170 Canadian political cartoonists of the past and present in Peter Desbarats and Terry Mosher's study *The Hecklers: A History of Canadian Political Cartooning and a Cartoonists' History of Canada* (1979). No reference to past cartoonists would be complete without taking into account the work of Henri Julien, J. W. Bengough, and Charles W. Jefferys. Similarly, current cartoonists of note include Aislin (pen name of Terry Mosher), Berthio (Roland Berthiaume), Robert LaPalme, Duncan Macpherson, Len Norris, Roy Peterson, and Ben Wicks. That list of ten leaves 160 whose work is of note!

893. *Who painted the controversial "Queen on Moose" series?*
The Toronto artist Charles Pachter painted "Queen on Moose," a series of acrylic sketches of Queen Elizabeth II riding a moose side-saddle. The sketches were exhibited during the royal visit of 1973 to much controversy, as many felt them to be insulting to the Queen. The images were based on a child's recollections of earlier royal visits.

894. *When was the Golden Age of Canadian Radio?*
The so-called Golden Age of Canadian Radio was the period between 1940 and 1955. For fifteen years Canadian radio listeners were offered variety and vitality in programming. Private radio did its part on a regional basis, but it was the national programming of the CBC that offered the most. National news broadcasts commenced in 1940. The terminal date is fixed at 1955, as this was the year television began to eat into the budgets of "the senior service" (as radio was called).

The program series that best epitomizes the Golden Age was CBC Radio's "CBC Stage." This series of weekly programs, at first thirty minutes in length, then sixty minutes, was produced by Andrew Allan until 1955 when Essa W. Ljungh took over. The Allan years set a high-water mark in production values and in the commissioning of original radio plays and adaptations and dramatizations of other literary works. Such writers and actors as Harry J. Boyle, Tommy Tweed, Lister Sinclair, and John Drainie were regulars.

895. *Who was "the king of happiness" on "The Happy Gang"?*
The so-called king of happiness on "The Happy Gang," CBC Radio's long-running musical comedy program, was Bert Pearl, who acted as master of ceremonies. He was billed as "that five-foot-two-and-a-half of sunshine."

"The Happy Gang" began as a summer replacement in 1937 and lasted until 1959. The thirty-minute program was heard five days a week in the early afternoon and, at its peak in the late 1940s, was regularly enjoyed by 2.5 million listeners. It featured trumpeter Bob Farnon, violinist Blain Mathé, organist Kay Stokes, plus other regulars, in addition to Pearl. It was sponsored by Colgate-Palmolive-Peet, and the program remains green in the memories of countless Canadian radio listeners.

896. Who are Canada's favourite comedians?
More Canadians have laughed longer and louder at the comedy routines of Johnny Wayne and Frank Shuster than at any other performers. (Their only rivals today are the band of men and women who produce CBC Radio's "Royal Canadian Air Farce.") Wayne and Shuster occupy a special place in the affections of Canadians. Born in Toronto, they got their start in war shows, went on CBC Radio in 1948 and CBC-TV in 1954, and performed as featured guests on CBS's "The Ed Sullivan Show" more often than any other act. Now they limit themselves to four television specials a year featuring skits that parody current concerns.

897. What have these following newscasters in common: Larry Henderson, Earl Cameron, Stanley Burke, Warren Davis, Lloyd Robertson, Peter Kent, and Knowlton Nash?
At one time or another all these newscasters have delivered the late-evening CBC-TV news program now called "The National."

898. What was the first theatrical presentation in North America?
"The Theatre of Neptune" was the first non-native theatrical presentation in North America north of Mexico. It was a masque, or play with music and dialogue, written in French verse forms by Marc Lescarbot (1570–1642), a lawyer and poetaster. Lescarbot staged it on November 14, 1607, at Port Royal, in present-day Nova Scotia, to mark the return by ship of the colonist Poutrincourt to Acadia. It was quite theatrical, and the cast included dozens of

French colonists and even some Micmac Indians. Over three centuries later, a regional repertory theatre was opened in Halifax in 1962. It was called the Neptune Theatre in honour of Lescarbot's pioneering entertainment.

899. *What was the Dominion Drama Festival?*

The Dominion Drama Festival, an association of amateur and semi-professional theatrical groups from across Canada, flourished between 1932 and 1969. Little theatre groups and community companies vied for regional and national awards. The DDF became Theatre Canada in 1970, but by then the audience for the little theatre movement was attracted to the professional productions offered by the so-called regional theatres, the earliest of which was the Manitoba Theatre Centre, founded in Winnipeg in 1958.

900. *Who is Johnny Belinda?*

Johnny Belinda is the baby boy born to a deaf mute following a rape, in the three-act play *Johnny Belinda*, premiered on Broadway in 1940. The play, written by the American playwright Elmer Harris, deals with the separation of the mother and child. Harris was a summer resident at Bay Fortune, P.E.I., and based the play on an incident that took place not far from there. The play is set in the year 1900 in Souris, P.E.I. It was filmed and made the basis of a musical.

901. *Who are Fridolin and Tit-Coq?*

Fridolin and Tit-Coq are characters created by the Quebec dramatist and actor Gratien Gélinas. Through them he expressed his passion for Quebec and the pathos of the human condition.

Gélinas appeared as Fridolin in a series of annual satiric reviews staged in Montreal from 1938 to 1946. Through Fridolin, Gélinas lovingly ridiculed Quebec society and its shibboleths.

Tit-Coq means "little rooster." It is the nickname of the familyless soldier who returns from the war to find his girlfriend married to another man. *Tit-Coq* is a full-length play by Gélinas. He created the role in French in 1948, then in English in 1950. The production went to Broadway and the play was filmed in 1953.

902. *The evening of July 13, 1953, has been described as "the most exciting night in the history of Canadian theatre." What happened that evening?*

That evening, at 8:00 P.M., under a gigantic, circus-style tent, the lights went up and the British actor Alec Guinness stepped out on the thrust stage and began Shakespeare's *Richard III*: "Now is the winter of our discontent/Made glorious summer by this sun of York." This marked the premiere performance of the Stratford Shakespearian Festival which was founded in the sleepy Ontario town of Stratford by the journalist Tom Patterson and the artistic director Tyrone Guthrie. The occasion was a milestone in the cultural life of Canada. Veteran drama critic Herbert Whittaker described it as "the most exciting night in the history of Canadian theatre."

903. *What was Tyrone Guthrie's innovation at Stratford?*

The Irish director Tyrone Guthrie agreed to act as founding artistic director of the Stratford Shakespearian Festival when it was but a gleam in the eye of civic booster Tom Patterson, because Guthrie had a dream of his own — to build in modern times a replica of the type of stage used in Shakespeare's day. Guthrie reintroduced the "thrust" stage, as distinguished from the proscenium arch stage with curtains. Guthrie's revival influenced the construction of subsequent stages and the mounting of productions around the world.

904. *What theatre company was founded by Brian Doherty?*

The Toronto actor, writer, and impresario Brian Doherty was the founder of the Shaw Festival at Niagara-on-the-Lake, Ont., in 1962. It is the only theatre in the world devoted to the production of plays by the Irish playwright George Bernard Shaw. The first productions were staged in the historic Court House, which was built in 1848. The modern Festival Theatre was erected in 1973. In its lobby are busts of Doherty and Shaw, the latter by Jacob Epstein.

905. *Which are Quebec's three leading theatrical companies?*

Quebec's oldest repertory theatre is Théâtre du Rideau Vert, founded in Montreal in 1948 by Yvette Brind'Amour. The province's leading repertory theatre is the Théâtre du Nouveau Monde, founded in 1951 by Jean Gascon, Jean-Louis Roux, and Guy Hoffman. Another leading repertory theatre is Théâtre de la Comédie-Canadienne, founded in 1958 by Gratien Gélinas.

906. *Is the National Theatre School a bilingual institution?*

The National Theatre School of Canada, founded in Montreal in 1960 to provide theatre personnel with professional training, is described as "co-lingual" rather than as "bilingual." There are separate but similar three-year programs of instruction in English and in French.

907. *Who are the Famous People Players?*

Famous People Players is a professional international theatre company founded in Toronto on July 1, 1974, by artistic director Diane Dupuy. The troupe employs the "black light" technique with life-sized fluorescent puppets and props manipulated under ultraviolet light. The puppets are modelled on famous people like Liberace, Liza Minnelli, and Anne Murray. Ten members of the troupe of thirteen are mentally handicapped. Dupuy, a native of Hamilton, Ont., founded the troupe to develop the capabilities of handicapped citizens and to prove that they may lead satisfying, productive lives given the right challenge and opportunity. Famous

People Players has performed across Canada, at Las Vegas and New York's Radio City Music Hall, and toured the People's Republic of China. In 1985, it opened its own headquarters, complete with workshops, studios, and a doll and toy hospital.

908. What are the names of ten of the most impressive Canadian plays?
No two people will ever list the same ten plays, but most critics will agree that the following stage plays are among the most impressive achievements of Canada's leading playwrights. Excluded from the list are musical productions like *Anne of Green Gables* and *Sunshine Town* as well as Broadway-style plays like *Same Time, Next Year* by expatriate authors.

1. Gratien Gélinas's *Tit-Coq* (1948)
2. Robertson Davies's *Fortune My Foe* (1949)
3. John Coulter's *Riel* (1950)
4. John Herbert's *Fortune and Men's Eyes* (1967)
5. Michel Tremblay's *Les Belles-Soeurs* (1968)
6. Herschel Hardin's *Esker Mike and His Wife Agiluk* (1971)
7. Beverley Simons's *Crabdance* (1972)
8. James Reaney's *The Donnelly Trilogy* (1973–75)
9. George Ryga's *The Ecstasy of Rita Joe* (1976)
10. David Fennario's *Balconville* (1980)

909. What was the first Canadian feature film?
The first feature film produced in Canada was *Evangeline*. Produced by Canadian Bioscope, a Halifax-based company of American expatriates, with the co-operation of the CPR, it was photographed in the Annapolis Valley. It was essentially a dramatization of Longfellow's narrative poem *Evangeline* about the star-crossed Acadian lovers. It was five reels long — about 60 minutes — and met with critical and commercial success upon its release in 1914. But as is the case with almost all very early films, no known prints or negatives have survived, only a few advertising stills.

910. *What is the name of the world's largest government film unit?*

The world's largest government film unit is the National Film Board of Canada. It was founded in 1939 to produce wartime propaganda films under its first commissioner, John Grierson, the distinguished documentary filmmaker. The Board is known by its initials — NFB — and in Quebec by its French initials — ONF (Office National du Film). In the postwar years it produced and distributed films in the national interest, especially those "designed to interpret Canada to Canadians and to other nations." Since its inception, the Board has produced over four thousand original films. In recent years, production has averaged more than a hundred new titles each year in both official languages. It has won more national and international awards than any other film production unit. The head office is in Ottawa, the main production studios in Montreal.

911. *What is the title of Norman McLaren's most famous short film?*

Although Norman McLaren has produced dozens of short films for the National Film Board, his most famous film is *Neighbours*. The eight-minute colour film, which treats live action as if it were animated, was released in 1952. It won an Academy Award and many other prestigious film awards and prizes. The film is the parable of two men who come to blows over the possession of a flower which shoots up between their houses. It shows the futility of war.

912. *Have any NFB films won Oscars?*

Indeed they have, not to mention two thousand or so national and international awards. Since its founding in 1939, until 1985, the Board earned eight Academy Awards. Winners are the following: Stuart Legg's *Churchill's Island*, 1941; Norman McLaren's *Neighbours*, 1953; Co Hoedeman's *The Sand Castle*, 1978; Beverley

Shaffer's *I'll Find a Way*, 1978; John Weldon and Eunice Macaulay's *Special Delivery*, 1979; Eugene Fedorenko's *Every Child*, 1980; Terri Nash and Edward Le Lorrain's *If You Love This Planet*, 1983; and Cynthia Scott and Adam Symansky's *Flamenco at 5:15*, 1983.

The NFB is not the only Canadian film producer to release Oscar-winning short and feature films. Private production houses and the Canadian Broadcasting Corporation have also released award-winning films.

913. *What is the Golden Sheaf?*
The Golden Sheaf is the name of the award that is given in various categories at the Yorkton Short Film and Video Festival. The festival, established in 1947 in Yorkton, Sask., is North America's oldest continuing film festival. It screens and judges the best Canadian and international short documentary films and videos.

914. *What are the titles of the ten best Canadian feature films?*
There will never be general agreement on "the top ten" in any area, especially film. Yet in 1984, the Toronto Festival of Festivals conducted a poll of one hundred film professionals — critics, teachers, industry personnel — and listed "the ten best" Canadian-made feature films of all time. Here are the titles of the films, generally in order of priority, with years of release and directors' names.

1. *Mon Oncle Antoine* (1971), Claude Jutra
2. *Goin' Down the Road* (1970), Don Shebib
3. *Les Bons Débarras* (1979), Francis Mankiewicz
4. *The Apprenticeship of Duddy Kravitz* (1974), Ted Kotcheff
5. *Les Ordres* (1974), Michel Brault
6. *The Grey Fox* (1982), Philip Borsos
7. *J. A. Martin, Photographe* (1976), Jean Beaudin
8. *Pour la Suite du Monde (Moontrap)* (1962), Pierre Perrault & Michel Brault

9. *La Vraie Nature de Bernadette* (1972), Gilles Carle
10. *Nobody Waved Good-Bye* (1964), Don Owen

915. *What is the importance of* Colas et Colinette?

Colas et Colinette is the title of the first operatic work with original music written in North America. The music and libretto were composed by Joseph Quesnel, a poet, composer, violinist, playwright, and actor in Montreal where the work was staged in 1790. The operatic work tells the story of a shepherdess who prefers love to security. It has been revived as a concert piece from time to time but is largely of historical interest.

916. *Who wrote the emotional song "Canadian Railroad Trilogy" and why was it written?*

Gordon Lightfoot, the composer and performer, wrote "Canadian Railroad Trilogy" in 1967, perhaps inspired by the Centennial of Confederation. He chose as his subject the saga of the construction of the Canadian Pacific Railway across the western half of the continent, and in the folk song he expressed the hopes and fears of the workers on the line. The opening lines go like this: "There was a time in this fair land when the railroad did not run, / When the wild majestic mountains stood alone against the sun . . ."

917. *What is Anne Murray's signature song?*

The song the public identifies with Anne Murray, the country singer from Springhill, N.S., is "Snowbird," which she introduced in 1970. It was composed by Gene MacLellan.

918. *Who is the pianist who abandoned the concert hall for the recording studio?*

The brilliant pianist Glenn Gould (1932–1982) announced, in 1962, "The concert is dead." He stopped performing at concerts, he even stopped attending concerts. He devoted himself to producing technically perfect recordings of the works of Bach and other classical composers. Born in Toronto, Gould made his New York début at Town Hall in 1955, the year he first recorded Bach's *Goldberg Variations*. The record sold phenomenally well and reinterpreted Bach's keyboard technique.

919. *A musician may add the initials A.R.C.T. to his or her name. What do the initials stand for and signify?*
The initials stand for "Associate, Royal Conservatory of Music, Toronto." They signify that the legitimate bearer has been awarded the Conservatory's diploma in performance, teaching, or composition. The Royal Conservatory of Music, founded in Toronto in 1886, acquired its royal status in 1947.

920. *Which is older, the Toronto Symphony Orchestra or the Montreal Symphony Orchestra?*
The Toronto Symphony Orchestra is older than the Montreal Symphony Orchestra. The TSO grew out of a group of musicians who began meeting informally in 1908, becoming the TSO in 1927. Its most famous directors were Sir Ernest MacMillan and Karel Ancerl. Its home is Roy Thomson Hall.

The Montreal Symphony Orchestra goes back to 1934; it acquired its present name in 1953. Zubin Mehta was its conductor in 1961–71. Its home is Place des Arts.

921. *What is the name of the country's principal opera company?*
The Canadian Opera Company is to this country what the Metropolitan Opera is to the United States. Whereas "the Met" was founded in New York as early as 1883, it was not until 1946 that the COC was established in Toronto. The founder was Dr. Arnold Walter. It acquired its present name in 1958 under Herman Geiger-Torel.

922. What are the country's three leading ballet companies?
The three leading ballet companies are the Royal Winnipeg Ballet, the National Ballet of Canada, and Les Grands Ballets Canadiens. The Royal, the oldest continuing ballet company in the country, was founded in the Manitoba capital by Gweneth Lloyd and Betty Hall Farrally in 1938. The National was founded in Toronto in 1951 with Celia Franca as artistic director and Betty Oliphant as ballet mistress. Les Grands Ballets Canadiens was so named by its founder, Ludmilla Chiriaeff, in Montreal in 1957.

923. Who are Canada's ten best jazz musicians of all time?
When asked this question for the *Canadian Book of Lists* (1978), the Toronto journalist and author Jack Batten ranged widely in the field of popular entertainment. He listed the following performing artists: Maynard Ferguson (trumpet), Oscar Peterson (piano), Moe Koffmann (alto saxophone and flute), Ed Bickert (guitar), Trump Davidson (trumpet), Rob McConnell (trombone), Don Thompson (bass), Phil Nimmons (clarinet), Sonny Greenwich (guitar), and Guido Basso (flugelhorn and trumpet).

924. Who are the greatest Canadian opera singers of all time?
When asked this question by Jeremy Brown and David Ondaatje for inclusion in the *Canadian Book of Lists* (1978), the music critic William Littler listed ten names. In alphabetical order, they are: Pierrette Alarie, Emma Albani, Maureen Forrester, Raoul Jobin, Edward Johnson, George London, Louis Quilico, Leopold Simoneau, Teresa Stratas, and Jon Vickers.

925. Many Canadians have "made it" on Broadway and in Hollywood. Who are the leading personalities?
No list of "Canada's own" who established reputations on New York's Broadway stage would be complete without the following names: Margaret Anglin, Len Cariou, John Colicos, Hume Cronyn,

Colleen Dewhurst, Marie Dressler, Robert Goulet, Lorne Greene, Ruth Harvey, Doug Henning, John Herbert, John Hirsch, Walter Huston, Lou Jacobi, Ruby Keeler, Beatrice Lillie, Raymond Massey, Kate Nelligan, Christopher Plummer, Kate Reid, Anna Russell, Bernard Slade, Eva Tanguay, Joseph Wiseman, George White, and Ira Withers.

At the same time the ''Canadian colony'' in Los Angeles has contributed mightily to the movies and television. Such names as the following must be mentioned: Dan Aykroyd, Lloyd Bochner, Geneviève Bujold, Rod Cameron, John Candy, John Colicos, Yvonne De Carlo, Katherine de Mille, Marie Dressler, Deanna Durbin, Allan Dwan, Glenn Ford, Michael J. Fox, Elinor Glyn, Lorne Greene, Monty Hall, Arthur Hill, Walter Huston, Norman Jewison, Victor Jory, Ruby Keeler, Margot Kidder, Ted Kotcheff, Rich Little, Gene Lockhart, Raymond Massey, Louis B. Mayer, Leslie Nielsen, Walter Pidgeon, Mary Pickford, Gordon Pinsent, Ivan Reitman, Anne Rutherford, Michael Sarrazin, Mack Sennett, William Shatner, Norma Shearer, Alexis Smith, Ned Sparks, Eva Tanguay, John Vernon, Jack L. Warner, Austin Willis, Fay Wray, Alan Young.

10. CANADIANISMS

926. *What is the meaning of the word "Canada"?*
The word "Canada" is most likely derived from the Iroquoian word *kanata*, which means "village" or "community." It first appeared in print in Jacques Cartier's account of his voyage of 1535. Originally the Iroquois used the word to designate a region along the St. Lawrence River between the Gulf of St. Lawrence and present-day Quebec City. Over the centuries its use broadened until, on July 1, 1867, it came to be applied to the Dominion of Canada.

927. *What is the official abbreviation of "Canada"?*
The official abbreviation of "Canada" is the letters CDN. First used by the Canadian Corps in World War I, they were subsequently registered with the League of Nations as the distinguishing sign for Canada. In Europe, any car operating outside the country of registration is required to carry an oval white plaque on the rear panel, near the licence plate, bearing in black letters the identification of the country of registration. Thus, CDN identifies Canada; F, France; GB, Great Britain; and USA, the United States of America.

928. *What is a "Dominion"?*
The word "dominion" means "sovereignty" or "territory subject to a king or a ruler." This is the title that Great Britain granted Canada by the BNA Act of 1867. The passage reads: "The

Provinces of Canada, of Nova Scotia, and New Brunswick shall form and be One Dominion under the name of Canada.''

It was Sir John A. Macdonald's idea to call the new country a "Kingdom" but it was felt that such a monarchical title would be resented in the United States. "Dominion" was chosen after Leonard Tilley found the word in Psalms 72:8: "He shall have dominion also from sea to sea, and from the river unto the ends of the earth."

At one time the word "dominion" was used in the sense of "national" as opposed to "provincial." Now the word used is "federal."

929. *Is it true that Tuponia was proposed as a name for the new Dominion of Canada?*
Yes indeed. Tuponia was one of a number of improbable names proposed in the 1860s for the new Dominion of Canada. (Tuponia is an acronym for The United Provinces of North America.) Here are some other unlikely yet proposed names: Albertsland, Albionora, Borealia, Britannia, Cabotia, Colonia, Efisga, Hochelaga, Norland, Superior, Transatlantia, and Victorialand. (The strange-looking and -sounding word Efisga is a combination of the first letters of England, France, Ireland, Scotland, Germany, and Aboriginal lands!) Luckily, the Fathers of Confederation chose Canada as the name for the new Dominion.

930. *Which heraldic devices appear on the Canadian coat of arms?*
Among the many elements that appear on the Canadian coat of arms, which was officially proclaimed by George V in 1921, are the following devices: St. Edward's Crown; a crowned lion raising a maple leaf; a lion supporting the Union Jack; a unicorn supporting the fleur-de-lis; a chaplet of roses, thistles, shamrocks, and lilies; a scroll inscribed with the Latin motto *A mari usque ad mare*; and a shield bearing emblems of the four coun-

tries from which the original settlers of Canada were chiefly drawn — the three lions of England, the lilies of France, the lion rampant of Scotland, the harp of Ireland — together with a branch carrying three maple leaves, the special emblem of Canada.

931. *How many heraldic lions appear on the coat of arms of Canada?*

Most observers will answer that one lion appears on the coat of arms of Canada, granted by King George V on November 21, 1921. But sharp-eyed observers will discover that there are six heraldic lions in all. One "lion rampant," along with the unicorn, supports the arms. On the arms appear "three lions passant guardant" and also "a lion rampant" and beneath the Imperial Crown "a lion passant guardant Or." The unicorn is the symbol of France, the lion the symbol of Britain.

932. *What are the official colours of Canada?*

Red and white are the official colours of Canada, declared and appointed by King George V on November 21, 1921, in a proclamation of Canada's coat of arms. The colours are notably displayed on the National Flag of Canada.

933. *What is the motto of the Dominion of Canada?*

The motto of the Dominion of Canada is *A mari usque ad mare*. The Latin phrase has two official translations. In English it reads: "From sea to sea." In French it reads: "*D'un océan à l'autre*." The phrase from Psalms 72:8, "He shall have dominion also from sea to sea, and from the river unto the ends of the earth," impressed the Fathers of Confederation, who adopted it for official use in 1867. It has been suggested that the motto should be amended to read "From sea to sea to sea," as Canada has three (not two) seas on its borders. In addition to the Atlantic and Pacific Oceans, there is the Arctic Ocean.

934. When did the beaver become the national emblem of Canada?

The Canadian beaver, *Castor canadensis*, was the early staple of the fur trade. The earliest heraldic use of the beaver occurred in 1633 on the device of a baronet of Nova Scotia. Frontenac suggested in 1673 that the beaver appear on the coat of arms of New France. When Sir Sandford Fleming designed the first Canadian postage stamp in 1851, the beaver appeared, busy building a dam. Since 1936, a plump beaver has appeared on the obverse of the five-cent piece. The semiaquatic mammal may not be a graceful or beautiful animal but it is an industrious one. Paleontologists maintain that in the distant past—at least 12,500 years ago—there were giant beavers. These forebears of today's beaver weighed at least 180 kg, or 400 pounds!

935. Have the maple leaf and the beaver been officially recognized as Canadian emblems?

Yes. The maple leaf was confirmed as an official national symbol with the proclamation of the National Flag of Canada on February 15, 1965. Its use as an emblem in Canada goes back to the mid-nineteenth century.

The beaver's use as an emblem dates back to the early seventeenth century. It attained official status as an emblem of Canada with an Act to Provide for the Recognition of the Beaver (*Castor canadensis*) as a Symbol of the Sovereignty of Canada, which received royal assent on March 24, 1975.

936. What is the name of the official flag of Canada?

The official flag is called the National Flag of Canada, and it was first flown on Parliament Hill, Ottawa, on February 15, 1965. Its adoption by Parliament followed much debate. It is officially described as "a red flag of the proportions two by length and one by width, containing in its centre a white square the width of the flag, bearing a single red maple leaf, or, in heraldic terms, described as Gules on a Canadian pale Argent a maple leaf of the first.'' For its stylized maple leaf, it is popularly called the maple leaf flag.

Innumerable banners and flags flew over early Canada, but since Confederation in 1867, there have been only three national flags. The Union Jack—the red, white, and blue flag of Great Britain—was recognized as the official flag until 1945, when it was replaced by the Canadian Red Ensign. This flag reproduces on a red ground the Union Jack in the upper left and the Canadian coat of arms on the fly. It was recognized as the national flag until 1965 when it was replaced by the maple leaf flag.

937. *How is it possible to see two quarrelling men in the National Flag of Canada?*

It is possible to see the images of two quarrelling men in the National Flag of Canada. Indeed, to give them some symbolic significance, in keeping with heraldic imagery, they have been dubbed Jack and Jacques. Perhaps they are having a quarrel about separatism.

How to see them? Examine a reproduction of the National Flag of Canada, the so-called maple leaf flag. Mentally quarter the flag, and clearly visible in the white panel above the maple leaf will be the profiles of two men, in silhouette form, their foreheads butted together as if in anger. If mentally doing it fails, with two pieces of paper section off the top left-hand quarter of the flag. The image appears in the white panel, looking down to the right. Similarly, if the top right-hand corner is sectioned off, the image appears looking down to the left.

Though the two men have been dubbed Jack and Jacques, they could equally be identified with Lester B. Pearson, proponent of the flag, and John G. Diefenbaker, its opponent.

938. *How many of the provinces have official mottoes?*

Eight of the ten provinces have official mottoes. The other two provinces, and the two territories, may lack official mottoes but they have unofficial ones. Here are the provinces with their official mottoes:

Alberta: "Fortis et Liber" (Strong and Free)

British Columbia: "Splendor Sine Occasu" (Splendour Undiminished)

New Brunswick: "Spem Reduxit" (She [England] Restored Hope)

Newfoundland: "Quaerite Prime Regnum Dei" (Seek Ye First the Kingdom of God)

Nova Scotia: "Munit Haec et Altera Vincit" (One Defends and the Other Conquers)

Ontario: "Ut Incepit Fidelis Sic Permanet" (Loyal She Began, Loyal She Remains [an allusion to the Loyalist settlers])

Prince Edward Island: "Parva sub Ingenti" (The Small Under the Protection of the Great)

Quebec: "Je me Souviens" (I Remember)

Here are the two provinces and two territories that lack official mottoes but have unofficial ones:

Manitoba: "Home of the [Hudson's] Bay" or "The Prairie Province"

Saskatchewan: "Wheat Province" or "Home of the RCMP"

Northwest Territories: "The New North"

Yukon Territory: "Home of the Klondike"

939. *All the provinces and territories have official floral emblems. What are they?*

What follows is a list of the provinces and territories with their respective floral emblems.

Alberta: wild rose
British Columbia: dogwood
Manitoba: prairie crocus
New Brunswick: purple violet
Newfoundland: pitcher plant
Nova Scotia: trailing arbutus
Ontario: white trillium

Prince Edward Island: lady's slipper
Quebec: white garden lily
Saskatchewan: prairie lily
Northwest Territories: mountain avens
Yukon Territory: purple fireweed

940. *The motto of the Province of Quebec is "Je me souviens." What is being recalled?*

The Quebec architect Eugène Taché chose the motto of Quebec, "*Je me souviens*," and inscribed it beneath the provincial coat of arms on February 9, 1883. The translation of the French phrase is "I remember." What are being recalled are the old values, French language and customs, Catholic religion, perhaps even the *Ancien Régime*, Quebec before the conquest of 1759. It was not until December 9, 1939, that the coat of arms was approved and authorized by a provincial Order-in-Council.

941. *What is the significance of the white garden lily and the fleur-de-lis?*

The white garden lily is the official floral emblem of Quebec. The *fleur-de-lis* (French for lily or lily flower) is the heraldic device based on the lily. The heraldic device was associated with the royal houses of France, as it is with Quebec today. The device appears on the provincial coat of arms and the flag of Quebec. Although long associated with Quebec, the emblem did not receive official recognition until March 13, 1963, when the Madonna lily (*Lilium candidum*) was declared the official floral emblem. The white lily is also known as the Annunciation lily, the Lent lily, the Bourbon lily, the St. Joseph's lily, and white garden lily. Its presence as a heraldic device signifies that Quebec remains French.

942. *What elements appear on the flag of Quebec?*

Adopted as the official flag of Quebec by an act given royal assent on March 9, 1950, the *fleur-de-lis* flag bears a white cross on a sky-blue background with a white *fleur-de-lis* positioned in the centre of each of the quarters formed by the cross.

943. *Which provinces use the Red Ensign as their flags?*

The flag of Ontario has been, since May 21, 1965, the Red Ensign with the shield of the arms of Ontario placed on the fly. The Royal Union Flag (commonly known as the Union Jack) occupies the upper quarter nearest the staff.

Since May 12, 1966, the Red Ensign with the shield of the arms of Manitoba has been the flag of Manitoba.

944. *What is the National Anthem of Canada?*
The history of the National Anthem, which is "O Canada," is a tribute to both the French and the English of this country. The patriotic song takes its origin from the thirty-two-line verse called "Chant national" written by Sir Adolphe-Basile Routhier, a Quebec jurist and poet, which was set to music by the Quebec composer Calixa Lavallée. Performed at a concert in Quebec City on June 24, 1880, it was an immediate success.

The English words, which have little in common with the French words, were written by the Montreal judge and poet R. Stanley Weir and first performed during the tercentenary of Quebec in 1908. Over the years changes have been made in Weir's words.

It was not until the passing of the National Anthem Act, 1980, that "O Canada" was given parliamentary recognition as the National Anthem of Canada.

945. *What are the words of the official version of "O Canada"?*
Here are the words of the official version of "O Canada." They appear in this form, in English and French, in the National Anthem Act, 1980, where they are identified as the "National Anthem — Hymne national."

O Canada! Our home and native land!
True patriot love in all thy sons command!
With glowing hearts we see thee rise,
The True North strong and free!
From far and wide, O Canada,
We stand on guard for thee.

God keep our land glorious and free!
O Canada, we stand on guard for thee.
O Canada, we stand on guard for thee.

O Canada! Terre de nos aïeux,
Ton front est ceint de fleurons glorieux!
Car ton bras sait porter l'épée,
Il sait porter la croix!
Ton histoire est une épopée
Des plus brillants exploits.
Et ta valeur, de foi trempée,
Protégera nos foyers et nos droits.
Protégera nos foyers et nos droits.

946. *Words of Tennyson are included in the English lyrics to "O Canada." What are the words?*

The words "True North" come directly from the Epilogue to *Idylls of the King* (1873) by Alfred Lord Tennyson. The Poet Laureate of Great Britain was referring to the loyalty of Canada, "that true North, whereof we lately heard." R. Stanley Weir, the author of the English lyrics to "O Canada," felt they were particularly appropriate.

947. *If "O Canada" is the National Anthem, what is "God Save the Queen"?*

"God Save the Queen" is the royal anthem. First published in 1744, the traditional English lyrics and melody constitute the National Anthem of Great Britain. In the United States, the tune has been known since 1831 as "America." Although "God Save the Queen" has been sung for centuries in Canada, it has fallen out of favour in recent years, at least on ceremonial occasions, where its place has been taken by "O Canada."

The status of "God Save the Queen" as the royal anthem of Canada rests on recent practice rather than on parliamentary approval. A bill introduced by the government in the House of

Commons in May, 1964, to recognize the words and music of
"God Save the Queen" as constituting the royal anthem was not
acted upon. A private member's bill introduced in May, 1980,
sought the same recognition but did not receive the necessary
unanimous consent. So the status of "God Save the Queen" as the
royal anthem owes more to precedent and sentiment than to politics and statute.

948. What are the words of "God Save the Queen"?
Here are the traditional words of "God Save the Queen," which
is often granted unofficial status as the royal anthem of Canada.

> God save our gracious Queen,
> Long live our noble Queen,
> God save the Queen;
> Send her victorious,
> Happy and glorious,
> Long to reign over us;
> God save the Queen.

949. What is the "royal salute"?
The "royal salute" is an abbreviated combination of "O Canada" and "God Save the Queen" that is played but not sung on
semi-official occasions.

**950. Why is "The Maple Leaf For Ever" so seldom heard these
days?**
"The Maple Leaf For Ever" is not sung much these days, but it
was once on the lips of every English-speaking Canadian. The
patriotic song, which almost became the country's anthem, was
written one fall evening in 1867 by Alexander Muir, a Toronto
school teacher, after a maple leaf fell on his sleeve and clung
there. The silver maple tree from which it fell is still standing and
producing leaves on Laing Street in Toronto's west end.

Muir wrote the words and music in two hours that evening. He paid thirty dollars to have the lyrics printed but sales were slow and he netted only four dollars for his efforts. The song's refrain is especially appealing — "The Maple Leaf, our emblem dear, / The Maple Leaf for ever! / God save our Queen, and Heaven bless / The Maple Leaf for ever!" But the pro-British sentiment and seemingly anti-French lines (such as the opening "In days of yore, from Britain's shore, / Wolfe the dauntless hero came") rendered it unsuitable for singing on public occasions.

Gordon V. Thompson, the patriotic music publisher, sponsored a contest in 1964 for new lyrics to fit the old tune. Over 1,280 entries were received. The winner was declared to be "Our Home, Our Land, Our Canada" by Victor Cowley. It has not been heard since then.

951. *Canadians enjoy singing "This Land Is Your Land," but is it really a Canadian song?*

"This Land Is Your Land" was composed in 1956 by the popular American folk singer Woody Guthrie to celebrate the beauty of the United States. The song was Canadianized by Martin Bochner, manager of the group known as The Travellers, and the bilingual, Canadian version was sung from coast to coast. The first verse runs: "This land is your land, / This land is my land, / From Bonavista / To the Vancouver Island, / From the Arctic Circle, / To the Great Lakes waters, / This land was made for you and me." There are also British, Australian, and Spanish versions.

952. *What is the best known of all Canadian songs?*

According to folk song collector Edith Fowke, the best known by far of all Canadian songs is "Alouette!" The popular folk song has long been used by both French and English Canadians for community singing. Although a traditional song of French origin, it is particularly close to the hearts of Quebeckers. In the song, an *alouette*, or skylark, is warned: "Alouette, gentle alouette, alouette, I will pluck your feathers yet."

953. *What event is recalled in the moving lament "Un Canadien Errant"?*

The fate of the French-Canadian rebels who fled or were exiled for their part in the Rebellion of 1837 inspired the sad song "Un Canadien Errant." The words were composed and set to an old tune shortly after the event itself by an eighteen-year-old lad, Antoine Gérin-Lajoie (1824–1882), who became a librarian with the Library of Parliament. In English translation, the first verse of "A Canadian Wanderer" runs: "A Canadian wanderer, / An exile far from home, / Wept as he made his way, / In a strange land, alone."

954. *What is the name of the first Canadian Christmas carol?*

The first carol written and sung in what is now Canada is known by its Huron title *Jesous Ahatonhia* which means "Jesus, He is Risen." It was written in the Huron language about 1641 by the missionary Jean de Brébeuf to be sung at Huronia. It was translated and published in French in 1899 and, since 1926, has been sung in the English version written by J. E. Middleton. The English version, cumbersome yet memorable, begins: " 'Twas in the moon of wintertime when all the birds had fled, / That Mighty Gitchie Manitou sent angel choirs instead . . ." The carol celebrates the birth of Jesus in native terms, and the tune is reminiscent of "God Rest You Merry, Gentlemen."

955. *Who wrote the rousing "Ode to Newfoundland"?*

The author of what has become accepted as "the national ode to Newfoundland" was Sir Cavendish Boyle (1849–1916), who served as governor of Newfoundland from 1901 to 1904. He was dubbed the "Poet Governor" for his ability to compose verse for public occasions. On assuming office he wrote the words of "Ode to Newfoundland," which begins: "When sun rays crown thy pine-clad hills, / And Summer spreads her hand, / When silvern voices tune thy rills, / We love thee, smiling land." Boyle's words were set to music by his friend the English composer Sir C. Hubert H. Parry, who is best known for his arrangement of Blake's "Jerusalem." "Ode to Newfoundland" was first publicly performed in St. John's, Nfld., on January 21, 1902. It has remained popular for more than eighty years. Even the phrase "pine-clad hills" caught on.

956. *Which song, more than any other, is likely to bring tears to the eyes of Nova Scotians everywhere?*
The song is "Farewell to Nova Scotia," a most moving folk song collected by folklorist Helen Creighton and popularized in the 1960s by the singer Catherine McKinnon. Its nostalgic refrain goes: "Farewell to Nova Scotia, the sea-bound coast! / Let your mountains dark and dreary be, / For when I am far away on the briny ocean tossed, / Will you ever heave a sigh and a wish for me?"

957. *Who wrote the moving song "Mon Pays" which is so popular in Quebec?*
"Mon Pays" has been called the unofficial anthem of Quebec. The song was written by the *chansonnier* Gilles Vigneault in 1964. The following year it was sung by Monique Leyrac at the International Festival of Song, in Sopot, Poland, where it was awarded first prize. It has been immensely popular ever since, for it speaks directly to the *Québécois* about the land. The refrain runs: "Mon pays ce n'est pas un pays c'est l'hiver / Mon jardin ce n'est pas un jardin c'est la plaine / Mon chemin ce n'est pas un chemin c'est la neige / Mon pays ce n'est pas un pays c'est l'hiver." The song is called "My Country" in English, and the refrain runs in translation: "My country it's not a country it's winter / My garden it's not a garden it's the plain / My road it's not a road it's the snow / My country it's not a country it's winter."

958. Why is Ontario sometimes referred to as "a place to stand"?
A Place to Stand is the name of the promotional film, directed by Christopher Chapman, that was shown at the Ontario pavilion at Expo 67. The film depicted the province's beauty and variety. The theme song, with words by Richard Morris and music by Dolores Claman, was particularly rousing. The first verse runs: "Give us a place to stand / And a place to grow / And call this land / On-ta-ri-o, / On-ta-ri-ari-ari-o." So in the song Ontario is not only "a place to stand" but "a place to grow."

959. Who is the author of the celebrated quip about Canada being nothing more than "a few acres of snow"?
The oft-quoted remark was made by the French author Voltaire in his novel *Candide* (1759). Referring to England and France, one character says: "You know that these two nations have been at war over a few acres of snow near Canada, and that they are spending on this fine struggle more than Canada itself is worth."

960. Who called Canada "Our Lady of the Snows"?
"Our Lady of the Snows" is the title of a poem written by the English poet Rudyard Kipling and published in 1897, the year Canada introduced the Imperial Preference policy — lower tariffs on goods imported from Britain. The poem begins: "A Nation spoke to a Nation, / A Throne sent word to a Throne: / 'Daughter am I in my mother's house, / But mistress in my own.' " Many resented the English poet's implication that Canada was a land of ice and snow. Kipling was familiar with the church of Notre-Dame des Neiges in the Montreal district of Côte-des-Neiges, and possibly with the verse by Thomas D'Arcy McGee titled "Our Layde of the Snow" about this church. In 1985, Morley Callaghan published a novel titled *Our Lady of the Snows* about a prostitute.

961. *What was the first Canadian postage stamp?*
The threepence Beaver was the first Canadian postage stamp. The red-orange stamp, designed by Sir Sandford Fleming, was issued on April 23, 1851. A prized addition to any philatelist's collection, a specimen in mint condition is worth about ten thousand dollars. Only 150,200 copies were issued.

962. *Which Canadian stamps are the most valuable?*
All stamps issued in the pre-Confederation period (before 1867) are valuable. Especially valuable are the threepence Beaver (the earliest stamp), the sixpence Prince Consort, and the twelvepence Queen Victoria, all 1851 issues. (The latter stamp sold in New York in 1980 for $126,500.) All the 1857 issues are scarce, especially the twelvepence Queen Victoria.

The scarcest of all Canadian stamps, and hence the most valuable, is the 1868 issue of the two-cent Queen Victoria. (Any green specimen in mint condition on laid rather than woven paper is worth more than the twelvepence Queen Victoria of 1851.)

Modern issues are scarce by default. Printers have to make errors and then quickly correct them for modern stamps to become especially valuable. Various printing errors (like the inversion of the blue portion, the doubling of the word ''Canada'') were detected in the five-cent 1959 St. Lawrence Seaway Issue. (Used or unused, one of these could command fifteen thousand dollars.) The six-cent 1969 Christmas Issue was printed with some sheets lacking the colour black. (An unused block of four is worth in excess of ten thousand dollars.)

963. *What is the ''Weeping Princess''?*
The ''Weeping Princess'' is a reference to a one-cent postage stamp of Princess Elizabeth printed in 1935 from a flawed engraving plate. The flaw created the illusion of a tear falling down the cheek of the young princess, the future Queen Elizabeth II. The flaw was corrected, creating something of a collector's item.

964. *What is the "monkey stamp"?*
This is an uncomplimentary reference to Canada Post's thirty-two-cent commemorative stamp of Montreal printer Trefflé Berthiaume, issued in November, 1984. When the stamp is inverted, the lower portion of Berthiaume's face resembles the profile of a monkey.

965. *What are your chances of having your portrait appear on a Canadian stamp?*
Your chances are nil, at least while you are alive. After you are dead, your chances increase, assuming that you have distinguished yourself by, say, becoming an outstanding public figure like a prime minister or a great artist. It is the policy of Canada Post to honour distinguished Canadians with commemorative issues only after they are deceased.

The only living person whose portrait may grace a Canadian stamp is the Queen of Canada. This practice was breached in pre-Confederation Canada when Charles Connell, the Postmaster General of New Brunswick, caused his likeness to appear on that province's five-cent stamp in 1860. It caused a scandal and half a million stamps were recalled. Connell claimed he never authorized the stamp.

966. *Which Canadian coins are the most valuable?*
There is no definitive list of the most valuable coins minted since Confederation in Canada. The list of coins that follows, based on the 1984 *Official Canadian Coin Guide*, includes those coins that are identified as being "Very Rare" (in very good condition) or possessed of a retail value in excess of eight hundred dollars.

Edward VII, gold sovereign, 1908, $1,000
George V, gold sovereign, 1916, Very Rare
George V, 5¢, silver, 1921, $800
George V, 50¢, 1921, $3,000

George V, 1¢ ("Dot Cent"), 1936, Very Rare
George V, 10¢ ("Dot Dime"), 1936, Very Rare
Elizabeth II, 10¢ ("Large Date"), 1969, Very Rare

967. *What are the so-called "Godless coins"?*

The "Godless coins" are currency minted by the Canadian government in 1911 honouring King George V but omitting the customary legend *Dei Gratia* ("By the Grace of God"). There was such a public outcry at this seeming irreligious break with tradition that the following year the legend on all coins — 1¢, 2¢, 5¢, 25¢, and 50¢ — was reworked to read *Georgius V Dei Gra: Rex et Ind: Imp* ("George the Fifth by the Grace of God King and Emperor of India").

968. *Of what metals are Canadian coins made?*

The 1¢ piece is made of bronze. All other coins — 5¢ piece, 10¢ piece, 25¢ piece, and 50¢ piece — are made entirely of nickel. Since August, 1968, there have been no silver coins. The rising cost of silver made such coins more valuable than their face value. At one point in 1968, the 25¢ piece was actually worth forty cents.

969. *What is meant by the "Devil in the Hair" bills?*

The Canadian government issued federal bank notes, or dollar bills, in 1954 with the unintentional image of the "Devil in the Hair" of Queen Elizabeth II. Certain unshaded portions of her coiffure created the illusion of an ugly face behind the ear. All denominations were printed from the "devil" plates but before too long new plates were prepared which eliminated the apparition.

970. *What are the colours of the Canadian bank notes?*

All Canadian bank notes, or bills, are coloured differently. The $1 bill is green, the $2 bill is dusty pink, the $5 bill is blue, the $10 bill is purple, the $20 bill is yellowish green, the $50 bill is orange, the $100 bill is brown, and the $1,000 bill is pink.

971. *Whose portrait appears on the $1,000 Canadian bill?*
The portrait of Queen Elizabeth II appears on the $1,000 Canadian bill. Her portrait also appears on three other bills — $1, $2, and $20. Portraits of Prime Ministers appear on the rest: Sir Wilfrid Laurier on the $5 bill; Sir John A. Macdonald on the $10; W. L. Mackenzie King on the $50; and Sir Robert Borden on the $100.

972. *What do the names Towers, Coyne, Rasminsky, and Bouey have in common?*
The signatures of these four gentlemen have appeared on Bank of Canada notes — paper currency — for they served successively as governors of the Bank of Canada from its creation in 1935 to the end of 1985. A Crown corporation, the Bank of Canada was created to regulate ''credit and currency in the best interests of the economic life of the nation.'' The bank has the sole right to issue paper money for circulation in Canada. It acts as fiscal agent for the federal government and sets the weekly bank rate. Management is handled by the governor, deputy governor, and twelve directors appointed by the minister of finance. The signatures of G.F. Towers, J.E. Coyne, Louis Rasminsky, and G.K. Bouey have appeared on bills illustrated with portraits of George V, George VI, and Queen Elizabeth II.

973. *What is the Royal Canadian Mint?*
The Royal Canadian Mint is a Crown corporation for producing coins, plaques, and other devices. It began in 1870 as a branch of the Royal Mint. It became a Crown corporation in 1969. It is headed by the Master of the Mint, who is the chairman of a five-man board. The Mint is in Ottawa with a branch in Winnipeg.

974. *Why would anyone erect an immense, 9-m, or 30-foot, replica of the Canadian five-cent piece outside Sudbury, Ont.?*
The world's largest known nickel deposits are in northern Ontario, near Sudbury. To mark two centuries of nickel mining, the Canadian Mint in 1951 issued a commemorative nickel with twelve sides. A Sudbury fireman, who thought it would be a good idea to draw attention to Sudbury's role in nickel production and also create a tourist attraction, promoted the erection of a giant nickel. The idea became a reality and since 1967 it has been the focal point of the Canadian Centennial Numismatic Park. The Big Nickel is 9 m, or 30 feet, high and .6 m, or 2 feet, thick. It towers over its neighbours, the Copper Penny, the Twenty-Dollar Gold Piece, the 1964 "Kennedy" Fifty-Cent Piece, and the U.S. Penny.

975. *Does Canada have a distinctive cuisine?*
In the sense that there is a French cuisine or a Chinese cuisine, there is no Canadian cuisine. However, if by distinctive cuisine is meant regional dishes and specialties, then there is a distinctive Canadian cuisine.

There are regional delicacies galore. The Inuit of the Far North introduced the world to arctic char or ilkalu. The Indians of the West relish venison, buffalo, bannock, pinchberries, saskatoon berries, and wild rice. The cuisine of the rest of the country owes much to Irish, Scottish, English, and other cooks and chefs.

The Atlantic provinces are fabled for their specialties. Newfoundland is envied for its Atlantic salmon and cod. Baked cods' tongues and flipper pie, not to mention fish and brewis (salt cod and biscuits), are specialty dishes. From the same province come partridge berries, marshberries, squashberries, and bakeapple. From Nova Scotia come Annapolis Valley cranberry apples, Solomon Gundy (a herring dish), and Acadian blueberry grunt. New Brunswickers eat Restigouche salmon, Buctouche and Caraquet oysters, Shediac clam chowder and lobsters, not to mention delicious fiddleheads. Prince Edward Island is the home of Malpeque oysters bisque and Rustico lobster thermidore.

More than any other region of the country, Quebec has its distinct cuisine, which extends from habitant pea soup, onion soup, *tourtière*, to maple syrup and Oka cheese. Ontario is respected for its cheddar cheese and fresh-water fish, as well as its orchard fruits, including McIntosh apples.

Manitobans delight in Winnipeg goldeye (a fish dish), Selkirk whitefish, and Lake Winnipegosis wild duck. Saskatchewan has whitefish, pickerel, lake trout, saskatoon berries, partridge, and prairie chickens. Albertans boast of their western beef steaks and chuck wagon stew as well as their sweetgrass buffalo and beer pie. British Columbia has five types of salmon, halibut, and king crab.

976. What is the difference between Winnipeg goldeye and Calgary red-eye?

Winnipeg goldeye is a dish; Calgary red-eye is a drink. The dish is a tasty fresh-water fish of the shad family, usually smoked. The drink is equal amounts of beer and tomato juice. Those who enjoy such things note that another favourite dish in Calgary is beef and red eye — roasted prime rib and baked red kidney beans.

977. Where on the West Coast is high tea still a custom?

The taking of high tea is still an honoured custom at the Empress Hotel, the stately hotel set in gardens overlooking the Inner Harbour of Victoria, B.C. It was built in 1904–08, the last of the CPR's chateau-style hotels. Murchie's blends the Empress afternoon tea. Rogers Chocolates are another Victorian tradition.

978. What are the country's leading brands of beer, wine, whisky, and cigarette?

The best-selling beer is Labatt's Blue. The leading wine has traditionally been Andrès' Baby Duck. The top-selling whisky is

Seagram's V.O. The most popular cigarette, manufactured by Macdonald Tobacco Inc. of Montreal, is Export A.

979. *Are beers brewed in Canada stronger than beers brewed in the United States?*

Let this question be answered by Michael Jackson, an authority on the world's beer styles and the author of *The Pocket Guide to Beer* (1982).

"It is widely believed in North America, and oft repeated with great confidence, that Canadian beers are substantially more potent than those in the U.S. This is a myth. They are, indeed, stronger, but only slightly. It is true that in the U.S. light beers, and most cheap brands, are pretty low in alcohol, but most of the better-known regular brands have been 3.5 percent and 4.0 percent by weight. All of the main Canadian brands have 4.0 percent. The exaggeration of this small distinction arises because the two countries use different systems for expressing the strength of their beers. A brew of 4.0 percent *by weight* (the system used in the U.S.) has 5.0 percent *by volume* (the scale employed in Canada). Hence the notion that Canada has five percent beers. Four and five percent can mean the same thing depending on which side of the border you stand."

So Canadian beers are only slightly stronger than American brew.

980. *What is the country's largest winery?*

The largest winery is Andrès Wines. Founded by Andrew Peller in 1961, the company has plants in six provinces and the greatest volume of sales. Peller, born in Hungary, was a brewer in Hamilton, Ont., before becoming a vintner. The name of his winery recalls the baptismal spelling of his first name. The company launched its phenomenally successful sweet wine, Baby Duck, in 1973, which has only lately been eclipsed in popularity by Château-Gai's Alpenweiss.

Canada's six leading wineries are (with year of incorporation);
Andrès Wines (1961), Bright's (1874), Calona (1832), Casabello
(1966), Château-Gai (1928), and Jordan & Ste-Michelle (1920).

The first of the small "estate wineries," Inniskillin, appeared
in 1975.

981. Do Canadian wines taste "foxy"?

All of them did; now only some of them do. "Foxy" describes the
taste and smell of Canadian wines produced from the Concord and
Niagara grapes of the wild Labrusca vines native to North America. (The word itself seems to derive from the unpleasantly sharp
smell of a fox's wet pelt.) Domesticated Vinifera vines were
imported from France as early as 1946, but not until the 1960s did
the principal wineries in the Niagara Peninsula and the Okanagan
Valley begin to replace the Labrusca with the Vinifera vines, with
a consequent improvement in flavour and bouquet.

982. What are the world's two leading brands of whisky?

The two leading brands of whisky are Seagram's V.O. and Hiram
Walker-Gooderham and Worts Ltd.'s Canadian Club Whiskey.

The "V.O." on the Seagram's product stands for "Very Old."
(The Latin inscription on the bottle label reads "Ne Plus Ultra"
which means, roughly, "None Better.") Canadian Club Whiskey
is advertised as "the world's lightest whiskey" and "the best in
the house." (It has been identified with a brilliant advertising
campaign, launched in leading publications in 1946, which presents the spirit as the choice of hearty and hardy adventurers who
are members of "the Canadian Club.")

Canadian whiskies are made with rye, so in Canada they are
known as rye whiskies. In the United States, they are known as
Canadian whiskeys. The Canadian product, which has been aged
an average of five years, is light of body and tastes more like
Scotch than the American or the British product.

As for the spelling of the word, in Canada, Scotland, and England it is "whisky," but in Ireland and the United States it is "whiskey."

983. *Do any Canadian hotels meet the standards of the international organization* Relais et Châteaux?

There are five hostelries in Canada among the three hundred or so in twenty countries included in the *Relais et Châteaux* organization. To qualify, establishments may have no more than one hundred rooms; they must display exceptional character, courtesy, comfort, cuisine, and calm. They emphasize luxury and haute cuisine. Member hostelries in Canada are Hotel Spanière, Val Dor, Que.; Le Manoir des Erables, Montmagny, Que.; L'Hostellerie les Trois Tilleuls, St. Marc-sur-Richelieu, Que.; The Windsor Arms, Toronto, Ont.; The Millcroft Inn, Alton, Ont.

984. *What architectural style came to be considered Canada's national style?*

The so-called château style of architecture came to be considered particularly Canadian in the first half of the twentieth century. The French medieval style with high roofs and gables was evolved by the architect Bruce Price in the 1880s and adopted by CN, CP, and the federal government for their public buildings. Notable buildings in the château style are the Château Frontenac in Quebec City, the Château Laurier in Ottawa, Banff Springs Hotel in Alberta, and the Empress Hotel in Victoria, B.C.

985. *Is it proper to refer to a Canadian as a "Canuck"?*

Propriety depends on the person. There is much disagreement about the connotation of the term "Canuck." It denotes a Canadian, but to many it has negative connotations, to others positive connotations. It seems to have a facetious, sarcastic, or derogatory edge; then again, it may have an offhand, endearing quality. "Canuck" goes back to 1849 when it referred to an English

Canadian. Six years later it was used for a French Canadian. Today the term refers to a Canadian of either French or English ancestry. It is more frequently heard outside the country than within.

If references to "Canuck" are rare, references to Johnny Canuck are even rarer. Editorial cartoonists as early as 1869 depicted Canada as a clean-cut young man, wearing the outfit of a habitant, logger, farmer, or rancher, named Johnny Canuck. The youth and innocence of the personification contrasted powerfully with the age and experience of Uncle Sam (for the United States) and John Bull (for Great Britain). During World War II, Johnny Canuck was the name of a comic book hero who almost single-handedly defeated the Axis.

986 . What are the meanings of the words "Anglophone," "Francophone," and "Allophone"?
Simply put, an "Anglophone" is an English speaker, a "Francophone" is a French speaker, and an "Allophone" is someone who speaks a language other than these two, such as an immigrant with no English or French. The suffix *phone* is the Greek word for "voice."

Among Francophones in Quebec in the 1970s, a professional translator or interpreter was jokingly called a "telephone."

987. What is meant by "a mid-Atlantic accent"?
From time to time Anglo-Canadians are said to speak English with "a mid-Atlantic accent." Presumably the description of speech characteristics has nothing to do with Bermuda, an island in the Atlantic, but with the Canadian propensity to merge British and American characteristics in their speech. Now and then the description is applied to the slightly affected speech of radio and stage performers.

988. *What is Alpha Flight?*
Alpha Flight is the name for a team of Canadian superheroes introduced by Marvel Comics. The team made its first appearance in Issue No. 120 of *X-Men*, but proved so popular it acquired its own *Alpha Flight* comic book in 1983. Recruited by Department H of the Ministry of Defence, it makes its headquarters beneath Parliament Hill. When the Ministry disbands the group, the leader, Vindicator, assumes the name Guardian and revives the team to fight evil wherever it may lurk in whatever form it may take.

Alpha Flight has seven regular members. Aurora is a split personality, a prissy teacher with the power of flight. Northstar is a champion skier. Marinna is a yellow-skinned amphibian. Puck, an exbouncer, is noted for his spunk and compassion. Shaman is both a physician and a Sarcee medicine man. Snowbird, who works for the RCMP in the Northwest Territories, is a transmorph, or shape-changer. Sasquatch, a former Green Bay Packers footballer, teaches physics at McGill. The Guardian, who dies shortly after reforming the group, worked as a petrochemical engineer with the Ameri-Can Company. Not part of Alpha Flight, but responsible for its formation, was Wolverine, a Canadian secret agent whose undercover work led to the creation of Alpha Flight and its training Beta Flight and recruiting Gamma Flight.

All these characters are mutants in the sense that their human or humanoid bodies have been modified or mutated by some external force. They have secret identities. Shaman, for instance, is Michael Twoyoungmen, and combines the latest of medical science with the most ancient Indian native wisdom. The seven characters have dedicated their lives to save Canada from its enemies.

989. *What is the most characteristic Canadian expression?*
Students of Canadian English maintain that "eh?" is the most characteristic Canadian expression. The colloquial expression sometimes means "What do you say?" but is more often simply a verbal question mark. It rhymes with hay. Its use has been satirized by Bob and Doug McKenzie, who in their television skits

are always saying to each other, "G' day!" and "How's it goin', eh?"

990. *What is the Canadian pronunciation of the letter z?*
Anglo-Canadians pronounce the last letter of the alphabet "zed," unlike Americans, who pronounce it "zee."

991. *What is the native Canadian toast?*
The English say, "Cheers!" The French say, "Salud!" The Swedes say, "Skol!" The Germans say, "Prosit!"

The native and national toast is "Chimo!" The word is both Indian and Inuit and literally means "greetings." When used in a toast it means "cheers." It is pronounced either "chee-mo" or "chy-mo."

992. *Is a Bluenose a person or a thing?*
A Bluenose, or Bluenoser, is a popular description of someone from Nova Scotia. The description dates from the nineteenth century. According to the author Thomas Chandler Haliburton, writing in 1849, Nova Scotians were called after "a superior potato of that name." So a Bluenose is a person.

The *Bluenose* is the most famous sailing ship of the century. The 40-m, or 130-foot, sailing schooner, launched in 1921 at Lunenburg, N.S., was the last and greatest of the Nova Scotian clippers. Under Captain Angus J. Walters it won many important trophies before it was lost on a reef off Haiti in 1946. In 1963, Oland's Brewery built a replica, *Bluenose II*, which was donated to the province. The likeness of the original vessel has appeared on the obverse of the Canadian ten-cent piece since 1936.

993. *Who were "cheechakos" and who were "sourdoughs"?*
Both were prospectors in the Yukon during the Gold Rush of

1896. "Cheechakos" were inexperienced gold seekers, green-horns. The word is Chinook jargon for "newcomer." "Sour-doughs" were experienced gold seekers, old hands. The word refers to fermented bread dough, popular in the Klondike, which was saved from the previous baking to avoid the need for yeast.

994. *What are the French names of the provinces and territories?*
There are distinct French forms for the names of the provinces and territories. The forms that appear below reflect current Quebec usage. Here they are from east to west and north.

Terre-Neuve. La Nouvelle-Écosse. Le Nouveau-Brunswick. L'Île-du-Prince-Edouard. Le Québec. L'Ontario. Le Manitoba. Le Saskatchewan. L'Alberta. La Colombie-Britannique. Le Territoire du Yukon. Les Territoires du Nord-Ouest.

British Columbia is sometimes referred to as La Colombie-Canadienne. The Dominion of Canada is, simply, Le Canada.

995. *What is the difference between a Quebecker and a Québécois?*
In contemporary usage, a Quebecker is likely to be an English-speaking native or resident of Quebec; a *Québécois* (the feminine form is *Québécoise*) is usually a French-speaking native of Quebec. The term French Canadian, for a French-speaking native of Quebec, fell out of use at the time of the Quiet Revolution of 1960.

996. *Which words do Newfoundlanders use for full-time and part-time residents?*
A full-time resident of Newfoundland or Labrador is called a "liveyere," a contraction of "live here" or a form of the local English word "livier" (one who holds a lease). A part-time resident is called a "come-from-away," a reference to a mainlander

or other who does not spend much time in Newfoundland or
Labrador.

997. What is meant by the term "Cajun"?
The term "Cajun" is a corruption of Acadian, a person who lived
in Acadia. In Louisiana, where many Acadians settled, a Cajun
is anyone who claims Acadian ancestry. The Acadians were the
original French settlers who lived in the Maritimes, particularly
Nova Scotia.

998. Do Newfoundlanders object to Newfie jokes?
As anyone who has ever visited St. John's, Nfld., will attest, the
funniest and sharpest Newfie jokes are told by the Newfoundlanders themselves. There is naturally some resentment when mainlanders tell the stories against Newfoundlanders, especially when
the jokes are racist. There is, of course, no such being as a
"Newfie"; there are only Newfoundlanders.

**999. The U.S. Declaration of Independence, 1779, promises
"Life, Liberty, and the Pursuit of Happiness." What does the
BNA Act, 1867, guarantee?**
The BNA Act, 1867, which brought into being the Dominion of
Canada, guarantees "Laws for the Peace, Order, and Good Government of Canada." The historian W. L. Morton enjoyed pointing out to his students and readers the differences in expectations
between Americans and Canadians. The comparison may be
extended to the Constitution Act, 1981, which ensures that "everyone has the right to life, liberty and security of the person and the
right not to be deprived thereof."

**1000. If the United States is regarded as a "melting pot," what
is the image that applies to Canada?**
The United States was first described as a "melting pot" of peo-

ple in 1908. The notion that Canada was a "mosaic" of people dates from 1922. The difference between the two countries is that Canada, unlike the United States, encourages rather than discourages the expression of ethnic and other differences. The image of the "mosaic" was given wide currency by John Porter, who called his sociological study of social class and power in Canada *The Vertical Mosaic* (1965). The perception of Canada as a multicultural collage rather than a unicultural melting pot had particular appeal to the *Québécois* and immigrants in the post-Centennial period. At the same time, ethnic differences began to attract considerable attention in the United States, and the phrase "the unmeltable ethnics" was coined to describe their persistence in the supposed melting pot.

1001. *What is multiculturalism?*

One of the key recommendations of the Royal Commission on Bilingualism and Biculturalism, appointed in 1963, was the recognition of the bilingual and multicultural nature of the country and its people. The commissioners noted that while Canada has two official languages, Canadians derive from a great many ethnic groups. This multicultural heritage should be preserved and enhanced, they argued. In response, Prime Minister Trudeau, in the House of Commons on October 8, 1971, committed his administration to "a policy of multiculturalism within a bilingual framework . . . as the most suitable means of assuring the cultural freedom of Canadians." In practice, this has meant federal grants to ethnic groups for heritage projects and greater visibility for leaders of ethnic communities. The result has been an enlarged and enriched sense of Canadianism.

INDEX

Included in this Index are key words and principal personal and place names. The numbers refer to question numbers, not page numbers. The Preface offers the reader a schematic analysis of the book's contents.